HOTEL BELMAR

THE GHOST HAS THE KEY

S.K. CARNES

Published in the United States by:
Susan Carnes
www.susancarnes.com
Editor: Maureen Dietrich
History Collaborator: Joaquín López Hernández
Cover and photo image design: Siniša Poznanovic
Interior design: Mark Cameron

ISBN 978-0-692-13982-0

This book is dedicated to heroism, hope and honor:

Heroes that walk the razor's edge of adventure, and selflessly dare to enter the belly of the whale. May they strike fire and bring back light.

Story tellers that sprinkle heroic deeds with stardust.

The Mexican lady who gathers the pieces from the vandalized graveyard so they can be used for restoration.

*The **Virgin de la Esperanza**, Our Lady of Hope.*

OTHER BOOKS BY S.K. CARNES:

My Champion

The Way Back: A Soldier's Journey

Epiphany: Starting Over in Oregon

TABLE OF CONTENTS

The Hotel Named "Beautiful Sea"

Touch legends written on these walls,
whispered along these storied halls.
Phantom fingers spinning webs,
lacing lore with silky threads.

IT IS HAPPENING AGAIN, AND IT'S JUST NOT FAIR! WHERE'S THE FUN AND games, the rest and relaxation in this paradise I've found? It's Mazatlán, México for goodness sake! No, not yet? Sure enough. Just as I paste the last picture into my scrapbook of "Lori growing up in Wisconsin," and sit back to check "organize old photos" off my bucket list, I hear a nagging voice saying something is unfinished, incomplete, lacking. I flip the pages to review early life. Did it start here? Me and my best friend Cynthia skating on a frozen pond in the woods; us riding my pony, gathered with family at a smelting party on the South Shore of Lake Superior. Such fun it was, so why do I feel a pang of guilt? Like something is unfinished. I smack the book shut with the decision it's time to move on. At least, after 50 years, I have filled the scrapbook and don't need the excuse of when I retire I'll have time. Maybe that is the problem, too much time.

I set it on the shelf with the other collections that depict my days at school, college, universities, my family life, moving West, careers teaching and counseling and finally retirement in México. Mentally, I congratulate myself on my achievements. The walls of this busy house are covered with my paintings. My partner Bill is complaining he can't find space to put up another one! And look next to the scrapbooks! See, right on the same shelf are three books I have written and published. It's high time to shop for cruises, go see the grandkids and go out with the girls! But there is another notion surfacing to drown out my celebration of getting done. I can almost see it like a shape in the water. Oh no, is another project manifesting, something else to finish? It's just not fair!

"Enough thinking," I scold, taking charge of the rebellious child I am. Time for a walk on the Malecón boardwalk along Olas Altas beach. First, I have to see myself in the mirror to be sure I don't look like the rag tag country girl I know I am inside. But who is this woman past midlife looking back at me? She looks like my mother once did. I undo my hair barrettes and brush waist length fine angel hair, white with a touch of gold, up and up some more, fasten and make a braid of it to twist and turn under and clip high on my head so I look all together. If not young, at least neat. There, that's better, I tell myself. Capturing all that hair is like taming my thoughts.

But still the restless feeling persists, like something is calling me. And as the sun sinks, the magic time of day comes when shadows lengthen and the sky becomes a caldron of colors.

"Lori, that's what retirement should be like, a grand finale of fireworks!" I declare. Who am I kidding? I know it isn't finished. I consider the saying I used in my counseling career, "a tree that stops growing begins to die." I feel it coming on. What? Another scrapbook? Is that my unfinished business?

So out the door and out to the Malecón alongside the Pacific Ocean. Off to my right are timeless waves cresting and rolling over and sucking back, with the sun sinking below the horizon. I look but don't see the green flash as the sun sets on the horizon and mentally whip myself for not being ready or worthy, but I do enjoy the gathering pink and orange reflecting on the clouds. Lovely. To my left, in the last light of another gorgeous day I see the Hotel Belmar, its straight lines determined to be modern. And I stop to circle my thoughts like a wagon master.

When I first saw the Hotel Belmar, I immediately knew she was a remarkable grand dame just a little down on her luck. Yes, and eclectic, for her vintage wardrobes sprung from all corners of the world as did the characters who came to stay with her, as did the stories that they left with her. Now that I have grown old enough to be in my second childhood, I realize I wanted to hear such stories. Would she tease or tell, I wondered. Or were they lost to memory? Had the stories of queens, stars, crooks and derelicts, like a bouquet of long stemmed roses, been shelved so long that the petals were askew, dried, or flaked away leaving naked stocks and dry dust to blow away in the wind? I wondered about these questions every day as I passed the hotel on my daily walk along the ocean.

It's twilight. I have just revisited memories of my long ago youth and feel in the mood to pause and consider the faded elegance of the hotel. I think: it's time. I read "**Bienvenidos to the Hotel Belmar in Mazatlán, Sinaloa**" in letters, bold and plain, on a sign at the entrance. The lettering has no grace, but the ancient doors framing the entrance are castle strong and opened wide. The Belmar parlor is unlit; dark compared to the last rays of day sparkling on the sea behind me. The mirror framed in dark carved wood has lost its silvering but I see my image there, a little old perhaps, but I still have the look of an adventurer I think. I like

the sound of that! Yes, and in the shadows behind me, I spy a gigantic desk fit for Father Time. Is this him sitting at it? Father Time I mean? I turn, a little startled, to face him.

"Come in," says the silver haired man, beckoning with hands both withered and elegant, like maybe he is timeless. That's the look I wanted when I combed my hair up. Not old, timeless! So I walk

Hand Painted Spanish Tiles in the Belmar

around taking note of the shelves and antique furniture of what was once a great library, and catch a whiff of a heady fragrance called 'Grandeur.' Maybe it's not too late, I think. He smiles, like he has been waiting for me and approves of my curiosity. So I thank him and follow the creamy mismatched marble passageway into the hotel, feeling like I am entering a museum that is still alive and kicking. The heart of the Belmar still beats!

Come in? I wonder, how far is 'in'? Along this jumble of corridors are tiles like a coat of many colors, but more. More, because of the motifs. The patterns dance together like Ginger Rogers and Fred Astaire doing the funky chicken. Jarring, but rich. It is like when I paint and put my oils out on the palette and then they get mixed up and new colors happen. The paint on the walls is transparent like the skin of an ancient matriarch, layered and pockmarked by the years. Yes, just like that.

And the music. Is that an organ playing out above the swimming pool I see off to the right? Salsa music from room 32, next door someone plays a recording of Joni Mitchell and Enrico Caruso sings up on level five.

Several wandering souls pass me by, quiet as ghosts. They look sort of lost in a good way. Lost in their own stories? They smile at me. Smiles that say "come in," and no one cautions me to proceed to the front desk, so I'll just look around. On the wall at the base of a ramp I see a little shrine preserving under glass a banner ad from an English speaking newspaper. It reads: **"The Belmar Hotel: Destination of the Stars."** Destination of the stars. Living among the stars. I turn the phrase around in my mind as I climb the ramp wondering how long ago that was true.

I stop to look at an entire mural on the ground floor. A determined faced grandmother is pulling a child with wild black hair up a rough cobblestone path. They are holding hands as they climb out of their Mexican village. This picture tells a story, I think. Turning off, my ascent is on rounded polished golden steps. Once magnificent, they are now patched and in places worn through by wayfarers. So many stories! Landing after landing, like the grandmother, I climb round and up, round and up, until almost at star level the staircase ends in a solid wall.

This architecture of dead ends is disappointing, but I descend to try another way up. Like the grandmother in the fresco I am determined to ascend the rise, and the Belmar has an elevator. Of sorts. It takes a leap of faith to get into it when the cage finally lurches its way just short of the fourth floor landing. Above me I think I hear chanting. I must be mistaken. Yet there it is, repetitious and hauntingly simple, reminding me of the Latin Mass of my youth. I listen, cross myself without holy water, and step down onto the elevator platform to be beamed up by fits and starts to a shaky stop on level six. Strange how the tones echo along a tunnel of solid floor-to-ceiling dark wood, leading me into the bowels of the wing. I touch the walls that close me in, a whole forest preserved in varnish, warm and rough and shiny and dark and then spy the metal of the padlock on the last door. Hiding what? Secrets. It is stifling here. Musty air. Almost dead. Another place of endings.

The foreboding leans toward panic, so I rush back to where the light floods the landing through open windows. I breathe, deeply flushing my lungs of dismals, dreads and dead ends. From here I can view the city and beyond it the shining light of the El Faro lighthouse. Listen. The 'from somewhere' chanting is closer now. It floats out across the Mexican village in the mural below me. I like it. And now, I can begin to hear the words telling me to *touch legends written on these walls, whispered along these storied halls. Phantom fingers spinning webs, lacing lore in silky threads.*

The long corridor now is like an entrance. And I think of the words "come in" like an invitation to explore the past, present and future of this hotel, maybe all at once like ghosts can do. As I glance around on the second level, I notice mattresses in empty rooms reminding me of a dormitory or maybe even an infirmary. Sadness is heavy here, but up on the balcony I can hear laughter as joyful as a fiesta. And on the uppermost level, the Diva sings to the lighthouse, an eternal melody. I bet the stories are tuning up in the wings. Getting ready to burst forth like firecrackers to light up the dark night of our fears. How far will these stories of the Belmar take us? All the way to the Milky Way where the stars live?

I leave the Belmar, taking note of the mural, wondering if I am the grandmother or maybe the child. I don't like the idea of dead ends with guilt as my companion. Instead, I am inspired to write a whole book about this hotel! Maybe this is the shape in the water that I felt was forming. The new project. And that feeling I had earlier, the guilt that teased at me like Pacific Ocean waves against the seawall, seems to be sucking back like the waves. Somehow, I think this place is the labyrinth that will bring me home.

How would it start? I wonder. Ah yes...Once upon a time a very rich man decided to build a grand hotel on the beach of Mazatlán, Sinaloa, México and to name her after the beautiful sea—*Belmar*...

Original Sign for the Belmar Hotel

2

THE LETTER

I AM AT HOME IN THE KITCHEN MAKING COFFEE AND DROP WHAT I AM doing when I hear the whistle blast "You've got mail." The postman is insistent; his whistle loud and clear above the background drone of the buses and street vendors of El Centro, Mazatlán. I meet him at the front door where he waves a letter instead of slipping it into the mailbox. *"De Estados Unidos,"* he explains as he hands it to me with a triumphant smile. I press a coin into his hand to acknowledge his special delivery, then he is off on his bike melting into the already hot October morning. The letter is postmarked in mid July. Ah yes. The Mexican mail. Faster then a speeding bullet, I laugh. Able to leap across borders in a single bound.

Such a surprise! It's from Cynthia Jarvinen, my chum in almost forgotten Snowbound Elementary School. How long has it been? Decades? And the postmark is from our hometown Oulu, Wisconsin. No wonder it took almost three months to arrive. Time stands still in Oulu. I carefully unseal the envelope, remembering. "Those were the days my friend," I hum, "we thought they'd never end." I stop and catch my breath. Along  with a letter the envelope holds a clipping from the *Pine River Times*, Bayfield, Wisconsin's newspaper. Oh no.

I sit down to read an obituary for Cynthia's mother. It is a short summary of the life of Helga Lahti Jarvinen, a faithful member of the Finnish Oulu Evangelical Church. Of Finnish descent, she graduated from dance school, married a Wisconsin lumberman, Lars Jarvinen, now deceased, and will be interred at Ever Rest Cemetery.

For an instant I am back in Wisconsin. Cynthia and I are daring each other to pump swings higher then ever before. Golden hair flying, she calls out that she has made it to see Lake Superior on the horizon! We munch on crunchy *rosetti,* so delicate and delicious, deep fried golden by Cynthia's mum.

But the best treat of all was to sit by the fire at night as Lars, Cynthia's lumberjack father, spun his tales of Finnish gnomes, gods that thundered, and spirits of New Finland's great north woods. He told stories of Wisconsin's waterways, its heroes the voyageurs, of brave sailors paddling the rivers daring rocky shoals, deadly undertows and towering waves. His low rumbling voice and great callused hands made everything true, rugged and rich.

He crafted a cedar strip canoe for us to drift the Brule River. Cynthia would paddle in the bow and call the way forward. Approaching the rapids, excitement rising, she would flash a knowing smile back at me, blue eyes wild as the river. Our hearts beat in time with the slap of the waves. Fast and faster as we shot on through. Growing-up years in Oulu were colored by magic. Evenings soft as the music of the loon crying at night and days filled with the excitement of discovery on the big lake's South Shore.

Friendships like ours should never end. Now, with the envelope open before me, the smell of the pine forest wafts up from the card inside. I envision the driftwood on the beach. But the pleasant memory dissolves like mist before the sun replaced with a jab of guilt over what I did. We did. And for an instant I think of him, the man I'd love to blame. Regret takes hold, displacing the memory before I can build my defense. But I think it anyway, telling myself that it wasn't my fault, Cynthia just moved on. Hadn't she always loved to dance?

Through a lifetime of saving pennies and dimes, Cynthia's mum made it possible for Cynthia to study at the Colorado School of Dance and Cynthia set her course, dancing right out of my life. Long after I also left Wisconsin, I heard a rumor that something dreadful had happened in Colorado. Something so terrible and life changing that it brought Cynthia down, sent her home to Oulu to live with her parents, caring for them, sharing her mother's broken dreams and trying to heal her own life.

So now, as I unfold the letter inside, I feel a foreboding like I am releasing sighs. The letterhead is a drawing of a tree with a swing hanging from a hefty limb. My attention goes immediately to the red heart on the swing board. Cynthia writes in a graceful script, elegant in its simplicity.

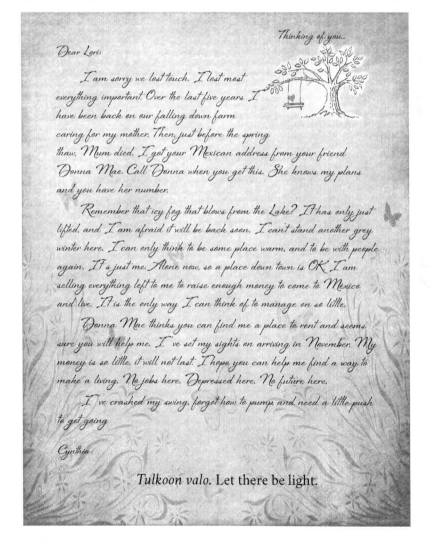

Thinking of you...

Dear Lori:

I am sorry we lost touch. I lost most everything important. Over the last five years I have been back on our falling down farm caring for my mother. Then, just before the spring thaw, Mum died. I got your Mexican address from your friend Donna Mae. Call Donna when you get this. She knows my plans and you have her number.

Remember that icy fog that blows from the Lake? It has only just lifted, and I am afraid it will be back soon. I can't stand another grey winter here. I can only think to be some place warm, and to be with people again. It's just me. Alone now, so a place down town is OK. I am selling everything left to me to raise enough money to come to Mexico and live. It is the only way I can think of to manage on so little.

Donna Mae thinks you can find me a place to rent and seems sure you will help me. I've set my sights on arriving in November. My money is so little, it will not last. I hope you can help me find a way to make a living. No jobs here. Depressed here. No future here.

I've crashed my swing, forgot how to pump, and need a little push to get going

Cynthia

Tulkoon valo. Let there be light.

Right out of the blue, I hear Lars whisper across time the seaman's rule: "A whistle marks a change of course to starboard."

The term jogs something inside of me. Like maybe the answer is trying to come to starboard? The letter asks that I find a place for Cynthia to live, some place central and cheap and near me, and.... *Starboard.*

"The Belmar Hotel: Destination of the Stars." The boast from the banner ad flashes before my mind's eye. I have just visited the hotel and noted its reputation. It has a star-studded history across a hundred years. And only a three block walk away. Everyone in the Historical Downtown of Mazatlán knows that the Belmar offers the best deal in town. Where else can a person get a room with a view, room service, WiFi, a bar, right in the center of everything? And the Belmar hosts a community of fascinating people with stories to tell. Maybe a few ghosts haunt some boarded-up rooms, but that would be a plus for Cynthia who believes in the slightly fantastical—the paranormal.

Starboard. I love the idea. And the Belmar, the destination of stars, would be the perfect place for Cynthia whose star had fallen. Like the hotel, she might be a little down on her luck but she grew up spellbound by legends. A new banner for the Belmar flies colors across my mind. "The Belmar Hotel: Star Catcher."

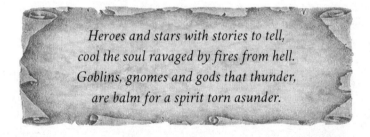

Heroes and stars with stories to tell,
cool the soul ravaged by fires from hell.
Goblins, gnomes and gods that thunder,
are balm for a spirit torn asunder.

Boys Growing Up
Next to the Belmar

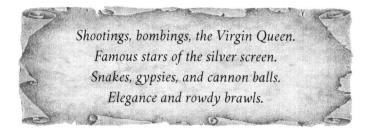

Shootings, bombings, the Virgin Queen.
Famous stars of the silver screen.
Snakes, gypsies, and cannon balls.
Elegance and rowdy brawls.

RAISED UP ON LEGENDS. THAT WOULD BE CYNTHIA AND ME. I THINK ABOUT the people who have lived at the Belmar or visited there, even some who have died there, all with stories to tell. They say that 'no one dies if you remember them.' Now with Cynthia coming to live in the hotel, I have another reason to write their stories down in a book as she loves stories as much as I do! Unfortunately, I have a chorus of excuses discouraging me: my Spanish is not good enough to interview Mexicans, and anyway, I don't know the right people: it's too late, all is lost, and why should anyone talk to me anyhow? My mind sums it up with the image of the dead ends along the corridors I explored in the Belmar. But that mural on the ground floor of the hotel remains my inspiration. The grandmother pulling the child up the rough cobblestone path won't let me go. Grandmother Belmar. And the chant at the top of the stairs has caught my fancy saying "Tell my stories. Make them into a book." It is like the Hotel Belmar has a soul. How crazy is that?

Since I don't know where to start, I've decided to just begin, especially with Cynthia arriving soon. 'Once upon a time' is today. I am on my way to visit Jorge Puente who is the best story-teller I know in Mazatlán. He promises to share little known facts about the Belmar. This will be fun and I won't tell people what I have in mind. That way, if I fail it will be between me and the mural. I hum "over the mountain and through the woods to Jorge's house I go" as I ramble from my street to his.

Limestone caves riddle the rocks of the hill where we both have our homes. These caves were used to store ammunition for Mexican forts. Over a 17-year span in the mid-1800s cannons poking out of the forts exchanged blasts with American, then British, then French ships block-ading the harbor. The streets are steep in this part of town and the rocks make a niche for our local Our Lady of Guadalupe statue, all flowered up for Christmas. Ah sweet reverence!

But across from the statue is a violent mural of the bombing of Mazat-lán from a biplane in 1914. That site memorializes an historical event in the Mexican Revolution, a stupefying attack targeting a fort dug into the hill, with the explosion of nails, coal and dynamite from a pigskin bag thrown from the wings of a crude flying machine. The pilot overflew the fort, hitting a shoe factory instead. As a reward for the better-aimed second attempt that pilot became head of the Mexican Air Force. Above it all stream bright traditional paper flags used at Mexican funer-als. These images combine much of what I know of México: at any moment, you could fall through the street, wash out to sea, or death and retribution can fall out of the sky.

Jorge's house is easy to find, covered in seafoam green tiles. His entrance

Mural of the Bombing of Mazatlán,
mural by Rafael (2012)

door is waist high above the street in case leaky pipes burst or torrential rains cascade off the hill causing a flood. I find a way up, admiring a half dozen papier mache clowns parachuting off the roof, a wreath of snowmen, and twinkling lights all round.

"I see you are all decorated for Christmas, Jorge," I say.

"Come in. Come in. It's Christmas all year round at my house. Red and green like the Mexican flag."

For sure. Jorge has even painted the traditional Mexican *equipale* leather and wood slat chairs red and green. I sit and admire a bevy of *piñatas* that hang from the ceiling and notice that the hall is covered with pictures of old Mazatlán. He has snapped photos of beloved friends to cover a kitchen wall but I can't find my picture in his collection.

Jorge looks like an overgrown Christmas elf dressed in a bright red and green T-shirt and jogging pants, suntanned and handsome, wiry and agile in his late 60s. His grey, carefully trimmed beard frames a face shaped to grin and he wears a baseball hat pulled low over laughing eyes. With all the energy of the energizer bunny, he speaks of his mother and father while bringing a picture to show me. Mom has a long suffering, sweet and gentle countenance and Dad looks like a businessman, intense, and straightforward. Jorge has this same honest look but the deep dimples around his mouth suggest a bit of a rogue, as do his mischievous grin and twinkling eyes.

My story-teller friend settles into a reflective mood in a comfortable living room chair as he describes the Belmar in the 1950s, the decade he was old enough to belong to *La Pandilla*, the gang in his neighborhood.

"Dad ran a shipping company that supplied produce to La Paz over on the Baja. My parents would go to the Belmar to socialize and dance. To me, growing up in the 1940s and 1950s, the musicians who played at those dances looked like they were dead already. You know stogy and old.

"But to Mexicans and foreigners with pesos in their pockets, the Belmar was *the* entertainment hotel. Expensive big band Mamba and Banda bands played in the two ballrooms. Patios and gardens were filled with music. The present day jewelry store next door to the Belmar entrance was once a glassed-in salon where people dined and socialized. On one side the ocean, on the other the kitchens and the grand Las Palmas Ballroom. Look in and see that there are no pillars in that space, and then visualize twice the size, because half of the grand ballroom is walled off now. Above are some of the best rooms in the hotel including the one called the John Wayne room. To the right of the entrance and the front desk, there was another dance floor near the pool where the hotel built another wing of rooms in the 1960s. Today foodie bars open out to Olas Altas, but once it was the Belmar game room set up with tables to drink, eat and play dominoes and cards. So now, a little history of the Belmar and then I will get to how me and the gang worked it over."

I am borderline alarmed that at the mere mention of the gang of his youth Jorge's face brightens, his gestures widen and his speech becomes animated. Having made and lost fortunes over the many years he lived in California, Jorge easily wields the language and idioms of both México and the USA while understanding the politics of both countries. He explains that México has always been eager and constantly ready to accommodate the wishes of those to the north, "for a price." I bet he wants to tell me how México has the last laugh, and he proceeds to do just that.

"Lewis Bradbury, the main shareholder of the Tajo Mining Company, married his maid from Rosario, Sinaloa and together they had six children in the late 1800s. He mined silver and gold in Rosario and to shelter it, left it to his Mexican wife. Lewis Jr., heir to that fortune at the turn of the century, decided he should locate a new warehouse for his fortunes in the very center of Olas Atlas beach in the old town center where the treasure trade was making Mazatlán rich and famous. And here's where we Mexicanos show up to help out, you know, 'fill the bill' as you Gringos say."

Now Jorge is looking slyly out of the corner of his eyes and speaking in a more confidential tone, like any great spinner of tales telling secrets.

"It's 1919 you see, and from Washington, DC, 2000 miles away, comes this news. The dry crusaders have gotten through ratification of the 18th amendment to the US Constitution! Well, Lewis changed his plans right there and then. By the time Prohibition was in place in 1920, his warehouse opened for business as a luxury hotel, the first in México on the water. The Belmar became the playground of the likes of John Barrymore, Rudolph Valentino and Mae West and later on John Wayne, Betty Grable, Rock Hudson, Jimmy Stewart, Ava Gardner and Hollywood's bad boy, Errol Flynn.

"The greater Belmar was a warehouse to store precious gold. But there in the dark below, slithered imported boa constrictors to guard the treasure and rid the hotel of mice and rats."

Jorge pauses to let that sink in. Before I can interrupt, he answers my unspoken question, pretending as he speaks to be fancied-up with finery and manners.

"Yep, Rudolph, Rock, Jimmy, Mae and the gang checking into the opulent rooms of the Belmar, taking a stroll around the hotel's plush, gilt-lined hallways and exotic gardens, probably donning tuxedos while the ladies slipped into crushed velvet and satin for a gala night of dinner and dancing in the elegant Belmar ballroom. Well, they were all none the wiser that snakes were on patrol beneath them."

Another pause for effect.

"Except Mae's beloved Schnauzer disappeared.

"And about those snakes," Jorge grinned. "Once a week, they would wash the snakes in the swimming pool."

Tame Python Hunting Snake

I look incredulously at him.

"I saw them do it," he nods vigorously. "What a sight it was. Of course, since they handled the snakes all the time, they were tame and would go right in and soak. These were big old snakes and hunters that took live prey."

As I try to digest the idea of big old snakes eating Mae's Schnauzer

Winged Warrior Storyteller Jorge Puente

and swimming in the guest pool, Jorge's story telling shifts gears. It is as if the ghost of the Artful Dodger created by Charles Dickens in his "Oliver Twist" story takes a seat at our table. With a dimpled grin, Jorge proceeds to debunk and add color to the old and grey stories commonly told, like any good story-teller does.

"Ice Box Hill, where we both live, which we call *Cerro de Neveria* in Spanish, was not so named. That is an Americanism. The *real* name is Ice Cream Hill. It was named that way because the ladies used to sell ice cream on the side of the hill, so the locals used to say 'Let's go to the *Neveria* to get ice cream at the hill.'

"And yes, Ice Cream Hill had many cannons. Everyone wanted to control Mazatlán it seemed. The pirates, the Germans, the French, the Spanish. Mexican generals marched into it and out of it, the Americans occupied Mazatlán, and of course the gangs were always fighting for control. Gunfire, yes. But in my time, the cannons never fired a shot from Ice Cream Hill, we never defended anything, it's all a tale."

Having debunked two well-known legends of Mazatlán history, Jorge takes aim at another.

"You know the famous Devil's Cave on the side of our hill that tourists like to peek into? Sure enough it was an escape route for soldiers at the forts and later ammunition was stored there. And we both know that is where the ice from San Francisco was kept cold. But now the rest of the story. You see the ice got stolen all the time. The church taught that stealing was a sin, so the ice company went to the Catholic Monsignor about it. Knowing that we Mazatlecos are superstitious, he came up with the tale that the Devil lived there, cooling his heels on the ice. One brim-fire sermon later, and no one dared to go steal ice from the devil."

Next, he embellishes upon what I have long thought represented the hospitality of the Belmar, the chairs at the entrance...

"You know the big, brown leather rocking chairs all along the entrance passage into the Belmar hotel? Well, picture beautiful women sitting in all of them watching guys cruise the main in their fast muscle cars. Our Mexican women loved the look of bad boys in bad machines."

Jorge got badder.

"In 1944 at the Carnival Queen's Coronation Ball, the Governor was killed. Shot to death in the ballroom of the Belmar. The police were desperate to pin it on someone. It had to be the work of The Gypsy, the one we called *El Gitano*. His kin were rootin' tootin' tough and his dad and uncle grew up chopping sugar cane. They thought it was in his blood to protect the new crops. As a kid, he used a sling shot to break pottery jars the women carried on their heads, breaking them when they were full of water 'cus I guess he liked the look of women wet and wild with anger. You know, he was like a wild stallion. Passionate."

I look sharply at Jorge and realize he approves of that notion.

"In time, he grew up to be a *pistolero* guarding a drug lord. He was famous in Mazatlán as a sharp shooter. He shot daisies out of the hair of the women who were in his company."

"He was that good?" I ask doubtfully.

"Well, except that one time when the girl moved and... he missed. Too bad. He became the last of the *pistoleros* for his boss. Finally, he was wounded in a gun fight and holed up in a cave where he got captured. When I was eight years old, the government put The Gypsy in the worst most awful jail in all of Mazatlán up on *Cerro Del Vigia*, Lookout Hill. They made a special cell for him and the army guarded him.

"My gang, La Padilla, held that hill so I can tell you that he was the handsomest man I had ever seen, so handsome we all were in love with that face, those eyes. The women thought that The Gypsy had the blackest eyes they had ever seen—so black they could fall right over just looking into them. Mystery. Treachery. Death. All of that talent rotting in jail, but he didn't stay there."

"He didn't?"

"No. They said that he escaped, but we knew different. He had the tongue of a gypsy and he talked them into letting him out at night. Travelers say that our women are the most beautiful in the world, don't you know. And it is the gypsy blood in them that makes them dangerous. You can see it when they dance the Flamenco, or the Tango or the Salsa, and you can hear it in the songs we sing in Mazatlán. Yes, The Gypsy was out at night. And he had many children with many women. He became a legend. We all wanted to be like him."

"Is that why you wanted to be in a gang?"

"Everyone was in a gang, we thought. But it was not easy to join La Padilla. We would take little kids who wanted to join and first tie them up and dress them in girly ruffles and make fun of them. Then, we stuffed jalapeño peppers up their noses and made them slaves. Oh, but you should have seen us. I dressed up like Hopalong Cassidy all in black and me and my sidekick came out with our guns blazing like in the OK Corral. We had caps, but those caps just made noise. We needed something better, something that messed up fancy holiday folks, and the high-falutin' Belmar too, and we found it at the Cathedral."

"Another devil story hatched with the Bishop maybe?"

"Yes, a devil story. Every year there was a student's day, the kids were out on the streets on that day, and that's when the Belmar staff would get afraid and shut and bar their big doors on the side entrance by the pool to be safe. You know those doors are fourteen feet high and six inches thick and have those special pointy brass bolts like castles have to break up battering rams."

"Battering rams," I echo, and glance at the picture of Jorge's mother, now fully appreciating the long-suffering look on her face. But Jorge is in his glory remembering the gang so influenced by the heroes of his day, Hopalong Cassidy and The Gypsy, and ready to describe the events of Student Day and The Belmar.

"What a day we had! All the city gangs met in the big square between the Municipal Palace and the Cathedral, the Plaza De La República, and made mud out of the soil they had dug for the gardens and the renovation of City Hall. We fought a war using cannonballs formed of that mud. What a mess. And the police? Well, after we ambushed passers by, they remembered that they had been young once and what harm was it anyhow, just getting dirty.

"I didn't know there were so many grumpy people in Mazatlán," says Jorge shaking his head, gritting his teeth in disapproval. "We thought we would take our act over to the Belmar where we might be able to impress the stars. Besides, we had muddied each other and everyone passing by, until we were tired and thought we should clean up before we went home. What better place to do it than in the big swimming pool of the Belmar? There were so many of us that we succeeded in storming the doors, and we did jump into the pool. What a grand day we had!"

Because I had raised three boys of my own, I thought it best not to egg Jorge on or even give this story much attention. One never knew how earthy things could get. So, to change the subject I quiz him on the stars he had just mentioned who frequented the Belmar. Who else came? Did he know stories about them and the Belmar?

"Well let's see. Because they could drink and party without end, they came here to hang out far from the media. John Wayne and Errol Flynn sailed in fabulous yachts and anchored them off shore. I think it was Flynn or maybe Tyrone Power who wanted to make a casino out on the middle island of the three off our coast. The city fathers put thumbs down on that one though. It was okay to take American money but they didn't want to support American enterprise that might lose their coastline in the doing even though Flynn wanted to fund a drawbridge out to the island.

"The stars came to make movies. John Wayne went up to Durango and founded a movie company there that is still important. But he kept a room at the Belmar just for himself. They did not rent it to anyone else for ten years.

"Walt Disney, his wife Lilian and his troupe of celebrities on the way back from making a movie in México City were put up in the Belmar when their plane was forced down in bad weather. They raved about the accommodations, and made arrangements to return.

"Who else? Let's see. Oh, yes. Desi Arnaz, Lucille Ball, David Niven, Tyrone Power and his wife Linda Christian graced the Belmar with return visits. Gregory Peck used to relax and play cards with the locals.

"Some of the stars," explains Jorge, "came for the deep sea fishing. Wayne fished with my uncle's Unifleet charter boats. One afternoon Burt Lancaster and Lee Marvin motored in drunk and empty handed, but John Wayne didn't return for hours, causing some concern. It seemed that Wayne hooked and landed a 1500 lb. black marlin, a record back then.

"Other Hollywood stars included Betty Grable, Jimmy Stewart, and Ava Gardner who came regularly just to get away, and stayed at the Belmar and later at the Playa Mazatlán Hotel."

Jorge remembers two movies filmed in Mazatlán during this time: "The Sea Bat" with Boris Karloff and "Kings of the Sun" starring Yul Brenner.

"Brenner," he says, "was always mad about the way Mexicans pronounced his name."

Jorge knows that fact because he was 10 years old and worked as an extra along with hordes of others on the movie.

"You must remember that Mazatlán was the first great Mexican resort," Jorge continues. "So, the stars also came here for the events. The Carnival. And the contests. Some world level, some silly, some almost forgotten. For instance, I watched the Strongest Man in the World Contest where men trotted to the top of *Cerro del Creston* where the El Faro lighthouse is. Each wannabe Strongest Man had to carry a huge boulder on his back up and down to the finish line. Now that is something to remember!"

"I can't imagine it," I say, vividly recalling my own hot and sweaty half-mile slog up the 325 steps of Cerro del Creston to the highest lighthouse in the Americas at 515 feet straight down to the surf. Hidden in the boulders above sheer cliffs were bands of feral cats, menacing faces of hate, spitting doom to my dog should she dare to stray. Even a water bottle was too heavy to carry. A rock? Why the amethyst on my finger ring was too much for me!

Jorge stands to stretch his legs and suggests names of people to talk to about the Belmar. He wants me to look up issues of *Correo de la Tarde*, the old newspaper most likely to have pictures of the news and events in the Belmar in its hay-day. And he points me in the direction of the Municipal Archives which I had walked by for years, never going in.

This writing about the Belmar is turning from a task into an adventure. A mystery. A journey. I will have so much to share with Cynthia. And with her living there, on the inside, maybe she will want to help me write my book. Certainly, I will meet some people and hear their stories all interwoven with the Belmar. From what Jorge tells me, the hotel has a rich past. I can talk to people who live there now, and maybe figure out what the future holds. With a shiver, I remind myself there are stories of ghosts seen in that old hotel No, I won't broadcast my ambition just in case I, well, just in case I run into a dead end and have to retreat back down the staircase. Or run into a ghost! Ha. I'll have some stories to tell at parties. Yes, I'll keep this book idea between myself and Cynthia.

True enough, my idea of the Belmar as a crumbling curious old hotel is taking shape. Expanding right before my eyes. It is like a line drawing done with a hard pencil. With every story the drawing deepens as shadows and highlights are added. The picture is coming to life like Pinocchio. Once a notion, it becomes real.

Just when I had wrapped myself in my private inner vision, I am jarred - no flabbergasted - out of my safe place.

"Hi Sue." A friend standing at a bus stop on Angel Flores, my street, calls her greeting to me. She is from Cerritos, a part of Mazatlán miles away to the north. "I hear you are writing a book about the Belmar."

"How did you find that out?" I ask in astonishment and dismay.

"Oh, it gets around. Good for you. We all want to know about that place. Hurry up."

ORIGINS OF THE CARNIVAL

SINCE JORGE PUENTE HAS GIVEN ME A MAP TO TREASURED INFORMATION, I am in a hurry to follow and research for my book about the Belmar. Certainly, Cynthia will want to know some history about her new home in the hotel, and she might be able to contribute insider information. How lucky is that! I let her imminent arrival be my incentive.

I scan the windows and doors of buildings on Calle Constitución for the first stop, the Archives of Mazatlán. I know I have seen it in this block just before Avenue Benito Juárez but never paid much attention before—never needed it before. Ah, there it is, but my hopes dim for I can see it is not open. After questioning the local Blue Shirt volunteers who give advice to tourists throughout the city, I learn that it is never open. Much like the white rabbit in "Alice in Wonderland," I am in a hurry with nowhere to go. Certainly Mazatlán is a wonderland. And like Alice, I am clueless. The difference is, I have the internet.

So, I go home, fire up my computer and contact Mazatlán's famous Cultural Detective Dianne Hofner Saphiere who is multilingual and creates links between our Spanish and English speaking communities. We become friends on Facebook, and she sets up a meeting for me with the Archives staff in their new digs over a mile away. To get there, I walk along Belisario Dominguez crossing streets with named plaques on the side of buildings. Estrada, Zaragoza, Hidalgo. I turn toward the harbor along Morelos, across Cinco de Mayo, Aquiles Serdán, Azueta, Carvajal, almost to Rosales. The streets of Mazatlán are named after the heroes and events of the Mexican Revolution. I imagine that a side benefit of writing about the grand Belmar Hotel will be that the names, just names now, will take on meaning and personality. Indeed the hotel is a kind of Facebook and I am about to be friended by celebrities.

My search for facts begins with Encarnación. Encarnación Garate Osuna to be exact. Three great names all wrapped up in the personage of a distinguished, kind, knowledgeable gentleman who heads the staff at the Archives. He speaks English flawlessly. I am now convinced that fate has a sense of humor for the word 'incarnation' means embodiment and his job is all about making history live on.

Words cannot describe the charm of this man. At our first meeting, he is dressed in an immaculate shell pink shirt and crisply pressed pants, but the warmth of his personality creates rapport beyond professionalism. His staff seems genuinely pleased that an American has located this best kept secret to unlock the door to the past.

The Mazatlán Archives: (l-r) Dianne Hofner Saphiere, Encarnación Garate Osuna, Sue Carnes and Lorena Ferral

The Archives are presently housed in a bodega of industrial proportions. Its giant face is plain and drab. Inside, giant store rooms are filled with labeled crates stacked in rows and columns where Encarnación and his workers find pictures and articles about the Belmar which I photograph for translation. I thank him profusely, we exchange e-mail addresses, and by the time I trudge back to my home on Angel Flores dozens of files on the history of the Carnival have arrived via e-mail. Like magic, they all involve the Hotel Belmar as the center of the happenings.

It is all becoming clear to me now that the Belmar is a portal of sorts—a channel to a time of glory, violence, sex, booze and passion. I can hardly wait to tell Cynthia. Being a dancer, she will appreciate the glamour and grace of the great minds evolving the Mazatlán Carnival. In a flash, I see it like an opera; no, a ballet, and the Overture is beginning. Encarnación is the maestro and Cynthia will dance the story. Hoping this vision is prophetic, I quote a favorite passage I use at times of change. "Of magic doors there is this: You do not see them even as you are passing through."

History unfolds as I read about Mazatlán's Carnival transforming for decades in the offices and ballrooms of the Belmar Hotel. But its roots go far deeper than the hotel and the city, indeed they are embedded into México's culture and civilization itself. I wonder how far back to go as I learn that symbols and elements of the festivities unfolded over thousands of years.

Stories of ancient times contain the word 'Carnival.' *Carnous navilus* was the Latin name of the naval vessel that bore the Teutonic god of the North south to join in the annual pagan winter festivities. Then Christianity came along, and the Vatican interpreted scriptures that recorded the fasting of Christ before his crucifixion. In 325 AD, the Nicene Council declared the 40 days and 40 nights before the passion, death and Resurrection of Christ as a time of purification, and called it Lent. Catholics kept austere decrees: Lent was to be a time of self-examination and penitence, demonstrated by self-denial, in preparation for Easter. To me, growing up Catholic, it was a time of no meat. Hence, the Latin term *carne vale*, "farewell meat," fits the last debauch prior to the fasting of Lent, the Carnival. The big Carnival in New Orleans is named *Mardi Gras* which is French for "Fat Tuesday," reflecting the practice of the last night of eating richer, fatty foods before Ash Wednesday beginning the fasting of Lent.

To sum it up, Carnival became the name for a religious practice, born of pagan religion, adopted by the church or Rome, and modified by local native culture. Whew! In modern terms, it is the last hurrah.

THE CARNIVAL MAZATLÁN STYLE

I READ THE ARTICLES ENCARNACIÓN HAS GIVEN ME, MANY OF WHICH HAD been written up as news in a turn of the century newspaper Jorge had referred to: *El Correo de la Tarde*, "The Evening Mail." A "debauch" is how Carnival was described. And it was definitely shaped by the local citizenry. Enrique Vega Ayala, the Official Chronicler of Mazatlán, wrote in color-ful lively expression how the locals of Mazatlán modified the idea of Carnival. Carnival provided the earliest settlers a chance to practice excesses forbidden the rest of the year and this respite from guilt and sin became very popular with the masses and hard to control.

Celebrating the Official Beginning
of Carnival Mazatlan

It seems Mazatlecos cel-ebrated Carnival as soon as they arrived by setting an island in time to practice forbidden fun. Sinful? Perhaps, but then they could wallow in religious guilt and penance during Lent so why not have something to repent, right?

So as early as 1827 there is a record of the soldiers guarding the port protesting lack of payment. The protest turned wildly strange when 40 or 50 masked intruders dressed like animals or costumed in long robes and pointy wizard hats invaded the neighborhoods and homes of the settlers, improvising rude songs, marking the landscape with dyes and flour. Messy yes, but all in the spirit of gay abandon.

The masquerades gained in gusto with the passing years and in the last decades of the 19th century no authority, not even mounted police, taxes, and the black plague could dim by much the madness of "The Flour Games" as they were called. Afraid of rape and pillage, families barricaded themselves in their homes, traps were set, blocks were mined, shells were lobbed across battle lines, children were injured, and some even died.

At first, festivities had included drum rolls celebrating México's victories in battle. But into the 1890s, combat won the day when the city split into two gangs to act out violence during Carnival. On one side were the *Abasto* fighter/entertainers representing the market workers with home territory from the 21 de Marzo street, then called the Street of the Lighthouse, to Calle Tiradores now named Zaragoza. On the other side were wharf workers who lived in the land of the *Muey* (*muelles* is docks in Spanish) that stretched from the Faro to South Beach.

The Carnival had descended from innocent merriment into rock throwing battles of charging carts and carriages streaming battle flags. In short, it was a time to fly in the face of the advancing civilization of English speaking society with bad behavior hinting at that shown by the Huns sacking Rome. Threats of dynamiting the opposition brought the city fathers together to find a solution to the war called Carnival. In a rush of insight, Jorge Puente's description of his gang attack on the Belmar and its highbrow foreign guests suddenly made some sense to me. It was just another way México, so battered by other nations, had the last laugh.

Desperate to save the defacement of public places and gain control, local authorities decreed that Carnival festivities "be celebrated in private homes; where refined ladies could toss *cascarones* (hollow eggshells) filled with glitter while the men hurled ashes, flour and dyes, at their own peril." But this control did not accommodate the idea of a monstrous bash. Ah yes, Carnival required expanded vision.

In 1898, the locals along with an Irishman, a German, a Spaniard and an Italian formed a committee of civic leaders headed by Dr. Martiniano

Carvajal charged with the task of civilizing Carnival Mazatleco style. It was well known that visitors to the city for Carnival were appalled by the savagery displayed by warring neighborhoods, calling it "the behavior of barbarians." Mazatlán had been a smuggler's den. Was it still? Mazatlán could do better than to throw projectiles and blow up barracks. The city had its poets and dancers and artists. Why not show off culture that created rather than destroyed? And they would keep the competition, only it would be the best of the best and not the worst of the worst!

Somehow, the committee sold the idea to the city. They organized a procession of carriages and bicycles to eradicate the immoral flour games and replace it with the pure and more restrained confetti and streamers. They set the costume as *Domino* which meant the masquerader wore or carried (in the case of women) a mask just to cover the eyes, and a cloak to envelope the body and sometimes a hood called a *bahoo* (think Zorro). Thus attired, they were to revel in good-humored mischief and euphoria (no more rock throwing, no dynamite) and for a few days, they would experience a healthy therapy, a world to escape the reality of death and destruction México was experiencing.

To do this, they borrowed elements from the Venetians and ancient civilizations to enhance the drama but keep body and soul together. In 1898 and 1899, Carnival crowned Ugly (*feo*) Kings or Buffoons to preside. Instead of storming the Bastille as the French did to dismantle the monarchy, the tradition of poking fun at heavy-handed rule fit the mood. Queens were incidental. The first king was

1900, Winnifred Farmer is the
First Carnival Queen.
1831, Sinaloa is declared a State

ridiculed, but the next won the position with oratory. A step up, but there still was lacking the beauty and grace choosing a queen could bring. After all, this was the country that revered the Virgin Queen. And didn't the most beautiful women in México reside in Mazatlán? To inspire the revelers, and substitute romance for brutality, it was decided that a beautiful queen should preside over Carnival with her male escorts playing second fiddle to her.

The first queen was the beloved American Winnifred Farmer who had grown up in Mazatlán. She made her triumphant entry on a streetcar pulled by mules, accompanied by the Minister of Joy (her king) and other characters right out of the tradition of light opera. On the Tuesday before Ash Wednesday, Queen Winnie paraded on a stunning black horse looking every inch a magnificent Amazon. The first grand costume ball was held in the Circulo Benito Juárez facing on the Plazuela Machado. The famed poet Don Esteban Flores, editor of *El Correo de la Tarde*, described the spectacle, christening Mazatlán's Carnival at the beginning of a new century with glowing words.

As I read and note the history of the Carnival, my e-mail inbox is flooded with pictures Encarnación sends me of the queens. Clearly the city of Mazatlán was proud of the Carnival shaped by the locals. Its celebration put a cultural face on the revelry celebrating the joy of life and passion for the arts: music, dance, literature, poetry and painting. The neighborhoods of Mazatlán stopped competing and joined into a city. On the way to the Archives, I had traveled the street named for the leader of the first Carnival Board, Dr. Carvajal. I was pleased to know of the honor behind the name. It was just the beginning however. So many streets, so many Spanish names, a rich history!

In one of the many articles Encarnación sent me, I read that:

> though there were lean years, when the city was blockaded, starving, and out of funds, not even the bubonic plague of 1903, the siege of 1914, the assassination of President Madero and Pino Suarez, the bombardment of the city, the extreme financial straits of the

Constitutionalists or the agricultural disputes in Southern Sinaloa, were enough to call it off.

All of this? I was amazed at this description of the turbulent times that came before the Belmar Hotel, and I vowed to learn more about them. That history intrigued me, and I wished someone could tell me about it first hand. Ha. Only the ghosts knew the real story. They held the key to the answers to my questions.

As I continued searching I found a description of the present day Carnival on the internet. Something I could give Cynthia so she would have an idea of the culture of Mazatlán, her new home.

Carnival has been perfecting itself for over a hundred years and is now an International extravaganza, this brainchild Carnival in Mazatlán—the first to be governed by a committee, and the largest in México. It is unique for its variety of music, its showcasing of commerce and culture in its competitions, and its beer. The events listed in last year's publicity were: the official presentation of the candidates for King of Joy, Queen of the Floral Games, Queen of the Carnival, and Infant Queen; Crowning of the King and the Queens; 'allegorical vehicles' (carriage floats) parade; the symbolic ritual of the 'Bad Mood Burning,' the Naval Battle; the Evening of the Arts; the 'Anything Goes' Ball; the 'Children's Ball,' the International Pacific Queen Contest and the recognition of local artists and poets through the 'Clemencia Isaura Award' for Poetry, 'Mazatlán Award' for literature and the 'Antonio López Sáenz Award' for painting.

Now I had bragging points to relate to Cynthia about where she was to live. And I had pictures. A parade of queens that were crowned within the Belmar. I was sure much of the planning for Carnival was inspired by the luxury and cosmopolitan decor within the Belmar. Early on, at least. Perhaps that would be of interest to Ms. Cynthia Jarvinen whose very name was a blend of cultures. She would be arriving in a week.

There was a time when I thought I knew all about her. So much time had passed with no communication. Again guilt surfaced but I pushed it away with hope that time had been gentler to her than it had been to the once grand hotel she would call home. I was worried.

6

THE LADY REMEMBERS

THE NEXT DAY ON A WARM MAZATLÁN MORNING I AM WALKING KARMA, my rambunctious German Shepard, down to the beach for a run when I spot a familiar face.

"Clayna, we should have breakfast together sometime," I call over to the attractive lady seated among friends at a table overlooking the Malecón in front of the Belmar. Her looks belie her age. She has elegance and grace and a mischievous smile framed by a very full head of curly grey hair.

"You have been saying that for seven years," she raises one eyebrow, and looks down at the table pretending to grieve for herself.

"Seven is magic," I say, ignoring the veiled accusation. "I heard that you grew up at the Belmar."

Clayna blushes and bats her eyelashes. "I know you are writing about our hotel here, and I can inform you of many things. Some things, of course, must never be told," she said wetting her lips and my curiosity. We settle on *mañana*, and just as I reach toward her to touch her hand in agreement Lucky, Clayna's fierce little dog, launches himself into my dog's startled face.

Clyna Robertson in front of the fountain in the foyer of Las Palmas Ballroom

33

Keep yer distance from my Clayna, Lucky snarls. I yank my German Shepard out of the tussle with the terrier and struggle to stay on the sidewalk, while the big dog insists that we cross over the street to the entrance to Olas Altas beach where the throwing stick lays hidden under the staircase. I think how obsessed the dog is with rescuing that stick. Me hurling it as far as I can into the cresting waves, my dog charging after it as the breakers roll over her. And I think back over the years I have watched Clayna swim alone out into the deep ocean in all kinds of weather, her dog Lucky keeping an on-shore vigil.

She was the first woman to wear a bikini on Olas Altas beach, the place of high waves in old town Mazatlán. I bet she caused a scandal! I imagine curvaceous Clayna striding into the ocean, the picture of temptation, wearing almost nothing while the women hid the eyes of their men. I had been tempted to do the same when my partner Bill described this woman he met on one of his first sojourns along the Malecón. He claimed that it was her regal carriage that impressed him. How refined she was. How cultured. She spoke several languages and she certainly spoke to him. I guessed her to be lovely for sure, smart, and courageous and flamboyant. Should I be jealous? I had to know this woman. Now, seven years later, I would learn about the Belmar, the gathering place for the rich and famous as it existed in its hay-day in the memories of the lady, my friend Clayna.

I arrive on time the next day, my notebook in hand, and she is there ahead of me. She introduces me to her friend Marta who she claims "speaks perfect English," and I apologize for my pidgin Spanish.

"Marta and I met while attending Evergreen College in Washington State. Of course we wanted to study in the United States. It was the thing to do. I will tell you about the Belmar of my time, a golden time for this hotel. Marta has come along to translate what I cannot say properly."

The two women nudge each other like they have a private joke. I ponder the word 'properly.' Clearly, they both have command of the nuances of English and I wonder what else.

"Along here," Clayna gestures toward the jewelry store beneath the upper rooms of the Belmar, "were the balconies. Women of high society sat on rocking chairs, lined up so that they could look out across the street and sidewalks to the ocean beyond the beach from this..."

"Vantage point," interjects Marta.

"And it was possible to be included in this ...ahhh"

"Prestigious?" offers Marta.

"Yes, this prestigious group, but one must never wear the same dress twice and to belong, one must be rich, educated or ...ah... good looking."

"Possible to be included," I repeat, and make a note to look up the Spanish caste system, while Clayna flashes and averts her eyes, then tosses her silk scarf exposing her shoulder. I did not ask her which of these terms fit her, thinking to myself that all of them may have described the young and glamorous Clayna.

"So, you called this a golden time?"

Marta responds. "Well, they had shrimp coming out of their ears, the bill fish were jumping out of the sea, the movie stars walked among us, and we had the Belmar, the place of unforgettable celebrations. Like on New Year's Eve!

"Special tables were set up just behind the balconies so that the old families had a front row seat to socialize and to be seen. The women were preening in their finest gowns, never the same dress twice of course, a-glitter with jewels and smelling of gardenias and roses."

Before it's Clayna's turn to reminisce, she sticks her nose high in the air, then lists some of the illustrious family names.

"Starting at the front, we were all served champagne to sip as the clock ticked to midnight."

FELICE AÑO NUEVO

HOTEL BELMAR

CENA

CREMA DE TOMATE

CABRILLA AL HORNO

POLLO C PAVO ASADO CON CHICHAROS

VERDURAS GUISADAS

FILETE MECHACADO CON CHAMPIÑONES

FRIJOLES

POSTRE

FLAN DE VAINILLA

CAFE O TE

Mazatlán, Sin. enero 1 de 1934.

Marta explains that her home country of Argentina shared a special ritual known to the Latin world. She becomes animated and speaks passionately like the experience is unfolding in the present.

"We call it *Nochevieja*, or the 'old night' of the past year. In just moments it would be possible to secure good fortune for all twelve months of the new year."

"Don't forget Marta, the gold ring in the glass of champagne," Clyna exclaims with enthusiasm. In my mind I imagine a crystal goblet containing a ring that shifts and shimmers golden in the sparkly. I wish I could have been rich, educated and good looking enough to enjoy New Year's Eve in the Belmar.

"Yes, the champagne must be sipped so as not to drink the ring down, for, as you can imagine, that would be a harbinger of bad luck. Everyone gets instructions, there comes a warning, then to the chiming of the cathedral bells—twelve times— each person gobbles one of the *las doce uvas de la suerte*, the twelve lucky grapes each time the bell sounds. Anyone who had been sipping bubbly from Catalunya could find themselves a-giggling and loosing concentration just like those since ancient times at the clock tower of the eighteenth century Real Casa de Correos in Madrid's Puerta del Sol back in Spain, where it is said, it all began."

"And then the red underwear," Clayna reminds Marta with a confidential wink.

"True enough, convention says you must swallow the grapes while wearing red *ropa interior*, or underwear, a bra, a sock, a garter, whatever. And stranger yet, the undergarment should be given to you by someone else."

Clayna thinks that the Basques brought the custom with them along with their music and food when they fled to México to escape Spain's civil war. I share that I had eaten in Basque restaurants where sumptuous banquets were served home style.

But Clayna is already far away lost in the music in her head. She has turned sideways in her chair, her hands raised like she is dancing. She murmurs, her words low and enticing "I dream I again dance in Belmar's Andalusian Salon." She snaps her fingers, and looks down her nose over her shoulder in a cold and haughty manner, flaring her scarf to show its color.

Marta says "Flamenco," and winks at me. It seemed that this gypsy dance also came from the Basques, and that the Flamenco was performed in one of the ballrooms in the Belmar named after the region of Spain called Andalucía. The name carries images of mystery: the smell of exotic spices, the intricate patterns all over walls. Temples. Markets. Passionate music. I remember the sitting nook by the main desk of the Belmar tiled with the image of a beautiful woman—perhaps the Queen of Seville. And the tile that still decorates the walls, the arches, the stairways. These *azulojos* tiles are intricate and even a touch mystical.

Even though half a century has passed since México sent her French occupiers packing, when Bradbury traveled Europe to find decor for his great hotel, Europe's ruling class still harbored bitter thoughts of México. Maximillian I, a member of the Royal Family of Austria had declared himself Emperor of México and refused to leave with the French. Benito Juárez showed him no mercy. He was executed. But Bradbury boldly came advertising México rising. And brought his money.

I glance up along the street façade of the Belmar and note the twisted pillars that give it a Moorish look. My eyes settle on the column with no middle part, remembering that the broken column was a symbol the Masons used to suggest that beauty as the central column to eternal life might be a dead end. As if reading my mind, Clayna mentions that with the French came the Free Masons. They challenged México's churchly beliefs. Most of México's soldier statesmen became closet Masons. Society was more and more liberal in the Catholic México of Clayna's youth. Just in time for her. After the bloody Revolution came the separation of church and state she calls the "Golden Years," and it was then that the Belmar was christened, a monument to enlightenment and pleasure.

I see a look cross Clayna's face as she speaks the words "bloody revolution." Words that hint at the horrors Mazatlán endured in the time when executioners ruled the streets of the Pearl of the Pacific, and those streets ran red with the blood of her citizens.

In a change of subject, Clayna mentions the Belmar swimming pool, her favorite place.

"In the old days, it was a diving pool. Very deep."

Perhaps because I am still thinking about terrible times, I fish for her response.

"I heard that two little girls drowned in that pool. Rumor has it that they were drowned by their mother."

Clayna dismisses that flatly.

"It was simple neglect. You know, you get busy talking." She frowns over my remark like she doesn't want her memories of the pool spoiled.

Since I appear satisfied with her pronouncement, she resumes her memory of golden times, a far away look in her eyes.

"Five pesos would buy me Coca Cola from the Belmar Cantina and I would spend the day swimming in the pool. The hotel served delicious cold *botanas* at the pool and I would eat *tapas* of fried baby squid and dream in front of the huge Italian oil paintings in the lounge. I could pretend I was a princess or a goddess and then go splash around swimming and diving like I was a flying fish. There was the smell of cigars, the men bent over their tables in the game room by the pool, and I still remember the slap, slap sounds of dominos falling against one another."

"Pure ivory domino tiles in those days" coaches Marta.

"Golden Days," I add.

"And then came my special day. My *Quinceanera*. The invite said July 31, 1955 with a celebration and dance in the grand Las Palmas ballroom."

"Oh yes," I interject. "That would be your coming of age party. I read that in olden times, girls were completely prepared for marriage by the elders of the community so that they could cook, weave, run a household, bear and care for children by the time they were fifteen. All that because after that time, if they were not married, they would have to become nuns." I let that sink in. Noting the blank look on Clayna's face, I quickly ask, "Did you get pictures?"

"Yes, I suppose, but they are all lost," she says with eyes downcast. "It was so long ago."

"So many moves, so few photographs," sighs Marta.

But I think about the Archivist Encarnación and the boxes of records stacking the bodega where the *Correo de la Tarde* newspaper could be stored. I tell them that it might not be too late to find what had been lost.

And with Cynthia coming soon, I hope that is true for me too. I want so much to find what I have lost.

7

AN AWKWARD REUNION

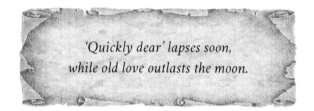

'Quickly dear' lapses soon,
while old love outlasts the moon.

THE AIRPORT READER BOARD DECLARES THAT THE FLIGHT FROM MINNEAP-olis to Mazatlán has landed. Finally, the first person is deplaning, and now a couple is coming through the door into the waiting room searching for loved ones. Slow at first. Customs must not have been too bad though, for a whole slew of people are arriving now. Drivers hold signs so people can find their rides. The large room is filled with family and friends laughing, hugging, grabbing up bags and then leaving. No Cynthia. Not yet. I wonder how she has changed. Is she still graceful and slim? Will I even recognize her? I had considered my own image in the bathroom mirror that morning wondering if she would know me. Of course. I hadn't changed. I put some concealer on my wrinkles and fluffed my hair to soften my facial angles.

My thoughts wander back to childhood memories of Cynthia and me in Oulu, Wisconsin where most everyone held hard work as dear. Ancestors of lumberjacks and dairy farmers, the Finnish community was as rugged and shy as the bobcats and deer, as quiet and deep as the Great North Woods. I have to smile remembering the extreme modesty and self-deprecating humor of my neighbors growing up. Daddy used to say, "A Finnish introvert will talk to you while looking down at his own shoes, but a Finnish extrovert will talk to you while looking down at *your* shoes."

In contrast, the tales spun around the home fire hearth of a Finn were mystical and fantastical stories starring mythical beings with superhuman qualities. Finland is a study in opposites: the hottest of saunas and the coldest of waters.

Sisu. The term for white knuckled courage, surfaces on the reader board of my mind. It's what gets them through hard times. I hear my father's words explaining the term. "Intestinal fortitude. Guts." Cynthia's father Lars had it. He was stoic and determined against all odds. Other folks might scream and holler obscenities over running their foot through with a picaroon, but lumberjacks like Lars would display *sisu* and hardly say "ouch."

But wait, now a woman is coming through alone, spinning round like a compass searching for North, glancing back like someone is following her. Could that be Cynthia? My father would say that "the lady is so thin the grass would not know of her walking over it." She is that frail! And she seems to be limping. She lugs a battered bag. No modern luggage on wheels for this lady. I realize with a start that I would know her if I could see her eyes but she wears dark glasses. We approach each other hesitantly.

"Cynthia?" The question begs an answer.

"Here I am sure enough. Oh Lori. Thanks for coming."

She drops her bag and opens her arms to me and we hug, but I am careful not to crush her with my enthusiasm. Hoping to smell the countryside where we grew up, I take a long breath of her. Her long hair is more silver then gold and smells musty without a trace of northern pines. Ah well, I don't tell her how wonderful she looks either. We both know she doesn't.

"You must be exhausted from your trip," I say as I reach for her bag.

"Oh no, I'll carry my own weight," she says, pulling herself up straight and proud. "Please Lori, show me the way, and I'll be right on your heels. You climb a tree from the base you know. That's the way of it. Let's be off then. The trip went well enough."

I can feel her need to hurry away from whatever is dogging her.

"Not used to crowds?" I ask.

"No. I just want to get outside and be warm. I'm so happy to have my feet on the ground and I want to feel the sun. It's been so dark, so cold, so long."

Her words are shadowed with gloom, like heavy fog blotting out light, like doubt covering certainty, but I shrug off the weight of such thoughts.

We enter the brightness of Mazatlán daytime, and drive past neighborhood signs written in Spanish, through jumbled up traffic, taking all the turns to the *Playas* and the old city. Cynthia has her nose against the window asking about the smog, the thermoelectric plant and the prison we pass on the highway. I can sense her disapproval of garbage along the road, the cloud of engine exhaust and the in-your-face graffiti marking territories along the way. We make the turn onto Zaragoza Street, and then left onto Paseo Claussen where the beach is a symphony of movement like life itself. The breaking waves march in rows of azure and white as people wearing smiles and brilliant colors stroll the Malecón above.

The Monument to the Women of Mazatlán

Cynthia stares as we pass the monument to Mazatlán women, *La Mujer Mazatleca.* I say a little prayer that the statue's wide flung arms of bronze will embrace the new arrival. Maybe. If Cynthia lets it happen. She is hard to read as she has her face turned away from me, looking at the Monument of Life with its joyous dolphins, and the buildings that dazzle high on the cliffs. If I could only see her eyes. We pull to a stop in a parking spot on Olas Altas near the outdoor ocean swimming pool and the golden domed restaurant on Angel Flores Street.

"Cynthia, are you in a hurry to get to the hotel? You can see it from here, but what do you say we stop for lunch before you check in?"

She turns her face toward me and I think her cheek is wet, but she brushes her hand across her face to hide tears that might betray her.

"Okay by me. My treat."

"Not on your life. We'll chalk it up to old times and a house warming gift. Come on. Be my guest. You can return the favor later when I visit you in your new digs."

After a long climb up the winding flights of steps in the patterns and colors of traditional México, we are seated high above the panorama of Olas Altas Bay. I think what a contrast this place, named for the high waves, is to the somber November grey skies and naked trees of Wisconsin in early winter. The icy ground would be strewn with birch and maple leaves that crunch brittle and broken underfoot, their once bright colors now shades of brown. Barren.

"If the snow does not come soon, the water pipes could freeze and break," she says. I remember this dismal time and then, with a pang, how lovely the winter landscape can be drifted in pure white. Covered over. Again I look at Cynthia's face trying to see her eyes through those dark glasses.

We order wine and I watch my friend relax. We are on the highest of the three levels of the restaurant under the golden dome and all alone. Remembering that she loves stories, I explain that Mexicans believe domes shelter and protect their owners from harm. I don't tell her that this dome was built by a drug dealer who met a violent death, as many of them do, in spite of his magical dome. I want her to feel safe enough to tell me a story—*her* story.

"So Cynthia, it's warm in the shade here under this dome, huh? Are you thawed out enough to tell me what's gone on?" I hope my voice is soft and soothing and not prying. Her face is white and implacable. I have a vision of shoveling snow, exposing pipes that have broken.

Cynthia takes a purposeful gulp of her white wine emptying the glass.

I order another for her. She takes off her dark glasses and wipes them with her napkin.

"These glasses are so dirty. But even the shade is bright here. Too bright for me? I wonder. So long in the dark. See, my eyes are as dried out as last summer's leaves. I have to put lubricant into them. Sometimes I use optical ointment. Just one of the many maladies I now have because of what happened."

She puts her glasses back on, beams a smile up at the waiter who is filling her goblet, takes a little sip of the newly poured wine and faces me. I have seen her poor eyes through blinking lashes glued together with tears. Now, even though covered by dark lenses, I can imagine them shining bright blue as the cloudless sky. The eyes I remember. Unchanged.

She begins, speaking wistfully like she is sad thinking back to earlier days. She looks just like her mother did all those years ago.

"You knew my intentions. I had high hopes when I went off to be a star, a dancing star. No, a shooting star aimed at being the best of the best. Queen of the Universe. And I had the nerve to do it. We say, that 'the brave eat the soup, while the timid die of hunger.' And then of course, my mother told me I should do it."

I have degrees in psychology and have learned that the child is often impelled to fulfill the dreams of the parent who lives vicariously through the child. Sometimes. I could have given Cynthia examples from my work in the schools of parents coaching from the sidelines, pushing their children to reach levels that they themselves had never reached. Actually, I guess it was the same for me, only I just never fit the mold. Cynthia did.

And so I say, "Yes, you were great at dancing! My parents showed me the articles your mom put into our hometown paper. And we were all excited you were so successful. I always meant to come to Colorado to see you in a show. You actually were making it big. Making your mom proud."

"I did, sort of." Cynthia puts her fingers to her lips thoughtfully. "But I didn't do it just for my mom, I did it because I loved it. Maybe I was just one of those rare ones who inherited the talent and wanted so much to use it. Nothing weird. Just the love of dancing. And back then I believed in what I grew up with. Courage is the father of success, my father said. Now, I am not so sure. Not sure of anything."

A red flag? I saw how Cynthia looked away from me. Like she was withdrawing. Instantly I recalled sound advice I learned in counseling classes: if you are a hammer you look for a nail to pound. And so I agree with her.

"Okay, Cynthia. What happened to me didn't happen to you. You were doing what you wanted to do pure and simple, and you were good at it. So, what was the view from the top like?"

"Oh Lori, I don't know how good I was, just what the reviewers said. Maybe I got too proud, but I loved dancing, getting better, scoring jobs, people cheering and then ..."

"Then what?"

"It is a horror story that hasn't ended yet. I could tell you sure enough right now, but... Oh it's not that I'm tired. Not me. But the time is not right. You were my friend from the time we were children. The story I will tell, well, it is about a different person than you know. A cold hearted person that you might not like. Forgive me. Let me go to this hotel and find a place for myself to live. You know. My own turf. I'm sorry. I just don't know how to lean on anyone. Maybe I'm too scared."

In my mind I have a chilling vision of the shooting star crashing to earth. I realize Cynthia wants to catch her breath and be stronger before she continues. It may be too big a story to tell after such a long day of travel. And why not give her the time? We have the rest of our lives ahead of us. Also, her journey has not ended. She must secure a place to live. It is my idea that she will like the Belmar.

"You scared? Such foolishness. But of course let's wait 'til you want to tell me more. All in your own good time. The Belmar is just over at the center of the bend of Olas Altas. Two friends have volunteered to help you with useful advice. They are guys you can trust to look out for you. Most of the Belmar staff only speak a few words of English and I speak Spanish poorly. I'd just be in the way. But Nicholas Osuna is the bellboy in the Belmar and he knows what the rooms are like. Wesley Holady knows all about the hotel and says he even knows the ghosts in the place, some before they became ghosts. They will give you the best advice. Besides, I always admired your ease with men."

"And you always ended up with them, didn't you Lori?"

There is a silence a second too long as I take in what she said. A compliment? Or...but I pretend it is, smile and swallow the defense I've got simmering should I need it. I shift the conversation to something safe.

"I know you want some alone time and don't need a boss, so you should go ahead with your plans, get your room, and then I will come see what you have picked. For now. I hope you like the Belmar and it's not a Hotel California 'Programmed only to receive, so that you ...can never leave.'"

Cynthia and I croon the words of the 1970s classic song, our voices joined to make light of the desperation of being captured, overpowered, or stuck in an intolerable situation. Songs can do that. Songs ease fear by moving through it, letting the melody carry you like floating on a river. I think dancing is like that too because you move with the energy like in martial arts. I don't bother telling Cynthia all this because we don't need the words to explain what we already know. That's how it is between old friends. Between the old friends we used to be to each other, before....

What good will regret do? I speak to the task at hand."Before we head out to the hotel, I'd like to call Nicholas to meet us at the reception desk. We might run into Wesley reading outside the Belmar bar. I've told him you are coming, and he is gearing up to tell you stories about the hotel. When you have chosen a room, settled in, rested and ready, you can call me and I'll walk over and you can surprise me. I'll loan you my cell phone and my house phone number is in it. Okay by you?"

Cynthia nods agreement. "Yes Lori, thanks, that is more than fine. But I can do without your phone. You gave me your card, and I will call for sure, but I don't need to put you out any more than I already have. I appreciate your help but being a taker is like running the well dry. I want to be a fountain not a drain. My father used to have a Finnish saying that explains how we are, you and me: It goes something like 'quickly dear lapses soon, while old love outlasts the moon.' And, I will feel best when I can hold up my end of things."

I can see her relief that I have not imposed my will on her or rushed to rescue her. I feel like she has her guard up. Maybe she's not so comfortable with me as I thought she would be. It's not in her upbringing, her Finnish heritage, to spill her secrets at a first meeting. She has the pride of a Finn, and something else, like a kind of anger. At me? Or is she mad at herself for having to ask for help. Well, dependency would destroy her. She is like a drowning person and instead of saving her I only need to remind her that she knows how to swim.

·8·

WITH CYNTHIA IN ROOM SIX

CYNTHIA IS DAZED AND BEWILDERED BUT WOULD NEVER ADMIT THAT TO Lori. And should Lori try to help too much, she would say just what her father told anyone who came too close or tried too hard to help "you may as well keep your breath to cool your porridge."

As they head toward the hotel, Lori introduces her to Wesley who sits out front of the Belmar most any day and this day too, reading. Wesley tells her that he knows most of the people who stayed at the Belmar long term, even some of their ghosts, and would be happy to advise her. She sees him as a fatherly figure. Older, wiser, warm and very Irish. Immediately she trusts him.

Cynthia removes her dark glasses to look into the long passage at the entrance of the Belmar. She glances over at the dark library and knows she is taking up residence in an unquiet place. But she doesn't say anything to Lori. Maybe later.

Nicholas, the hotel's bellboy, is at the reception desk waiting for them. He has a smile and a presence that is calming, and he offers his hand. Cynthia looks up into golden brown eyes that sparkle with fun but widen to show concern. She knows he loves women when he touches her, for he is gentle but commanding, his big hands look work worn and capable. He attempts to carry her bag, but she declines saying she can do it herself.

Clearly Lori has spoken with him about room accommodations, but Nicholas checks it with Cynthia. His Spanish words are simple enough for her to understand. She hears *por mucho tiempo, una habitación económica,* and *una cocina completa.* But he speaks some English too. "I help you *siempre.*"

She likes him, the look of him. He might have been six feet tall in his prime. She guesses him to be in his late 60s. His black hair is grey at the temples and he is lean, neat and handsome. One more thing. She reads in the way he stands near her that he is willing to take charge, to help her make the best decisions. No wonder he has been at the hotel so long.

Lori is at the desk talking with Alicia, getting keys, discussing details. They call Cynthia over to be sure she knows what she is getting. Alicia speaks English well enough that Cynthia understands the room is almost empty but will be furnished with appliances and every effort will be made to make it comfortable. Many people have taken rooms like it and finished them to their liking. It is a do-it-yourself kind of room and cheap because of that. Other long term guests have made these rooms very comfortable.

"If you cannot stay in this room, you can come back and we will try to find you another," Alicia says, and biting her lip she hands the keys to Nicholas. Did Cynthia imagine that Nicholas looked heavenward? For in a flash his arm comes round her like he is herding chickens, and he winks kindly. "*No problema Señorita.* No worries, okay?"

"We'll take it from here Lori," Cynthia says, dismissing her. "I've already imposed enough. I can tell Nicholas won't steer me wrong. He's your friend and like you said, he has already made me feel safe. Enough is as good as a feast. So go on home. I have all the help I need to get settled in."

"I feel happy and sad at the same time," Lori answers, "but I know you're in good hands. Get some rest. Call me when you're ready."

They stand for a moment frozen in time in this place where time has torn away what once was. Cynthia knows she has been cold and aloof but it is the best she can muster. She cannot let her guard down. Lori is disappointed, mouth closed hard like what she thinks might tumble out if she lets it, so she turns away, leaving Cynthia her warmest smile, a "thank you" to Alicia and a nod to Nicholas.

Nicholas points out things as they walk through the hotel: *es la bella Reina de Sevilla*, the shrine of the Queen of Seville. Cynthia touches the exquisite tiles he says are *a mano*, hand painted. The picture with a bench built into a niche is so near the desk to suggest that the Queen could be

The Queen of Seville

the patroness of the Belmar. The Lady wears a glorious golden crown, five emerald brooches and a richly adorned robe, but it is her expression that fascinates Cynthia; the tears on her face show profound sadness, and yet she looks kind and caring as if the dominion of this queen is heaven and earth. For a second, the dread gripping Cynthia's heart, cold as the ice on Lake Superior, melts before the miracle of compassion a woman can have for another. Breathless with wonder, Cynthia recognizes the Queen. She has seen her face before somehow. Where? She searches her memory. Clearly the image has power, but there is not time to linger at the shrine, as Nicholas calls her attention to two huge framed posters hanging in an alcove, once a doorway into the bar.

"*Mira,*" he says.

Cynthia regretfully pulls herself away from the Queen of Seville to see the bullfighter and flamenco dancer posters Nicholas is so proud of. They are quintessentially Mexican, portrayed in the style of art deco with all its elegance, the male tempting death, the female seducing, teasing, gracefully provocative. Cynthia remembers how she once could dance with such passion.

They walk through what once was a grand ballroom, *un gran salón.* The columns at the entrance are completely covered with tile of a different but equally intricate pattern. Nicholas runs his finger over a hole in the tile like he wants to explain, but smiles instead and they go on. Past the swimming pool, down stairs and alongside an old fashioned well that he says still *functiona.* Across a cemented flat area that he describes as the old garden and up the steps to find the cheapest room in the hotel. He says, "*Espero,* I hope you like."

Cynthia notices the large trees on the edge of the garden and the exquisite black ebony balusters on the stair. A million footsteps have etched the golden tiles and she is silent like she might be entering hallowed ground, or if not sacrosanct, at least a space that has endured. But when Nicholas opens the door to the empty room, she bites her tongue and says "Oh."

Bleak. Cynthia thinks the word to sum up her new tiny living quarters. You've come down to this, she nags at herself. You who wanted to be a dancer. You who can just barely walk. She steps stiffly to the window to see the view and hide her disappointment. Out on the street, a pulmonia is passing, blaring music. A strange sound yet familiar, and very loud.

"*Es Banda,*" Nicholas informs her with pride, but as he watches her grimace over the sound he turns away, crestfallen.

She tells him that it reminds her of Whoopy John and the Six Fat Dutchmen. Yes. Transplanted from Minnesota to México, louder and brassier then ever. This was not her favorite music when she lived in the land of Lake Superior and here it is again following her. Is this a harbinger of the way things will be? She is familiar with the concept of the geographic cure which is no cure at all, because no matter where you go, there you are!

Nicholas edges himself out the door, shaking his head, frowning, like he doesn't understand or maybe understands too well. Cynthia is clueless, disappointment is heavy in her voice, and she doesn't hear his goodbye, softly said, *"Hasta luego, adiós."*

"Blarin' 'n brassy, a blinkin' blur" she says aloud.

Now that Nicholas has left her alone, she is free to limp, and limp she does over to the window to see the view of the street, clearing off a spot in the dust coating the window. Below is a Mexican family strolling toward the beach. The mother moves forward with long strides, the child jumps with joy and Dad carries a basket for their picnic. Just like my family was, she thinks. Touching her bag with her shoe, she wonders what would she bring to this room, this hotel, this city, this life? She takes a deep breath of musty air that reeks of better times and thinks the room suits her. It *is* her —stark—a flavorless leftover of a life in shambles. Sucked dry. "Shambles" she says aloud, and turns the word over in her mind, the stale flavor heavy on her tongue. And she thinks the state of the room will help her explain to Lori what events have brought her to this bare and broken place.

She turns away from the window, feeling like a little dance to celebrate her new Spartan existence. Like a Ms. Bojangles she thinks bitterly. Dance. And the lameness falls away as she dances a lick of the old soft shoe remembering that Bojangles jumped so high he might not likely touch down. The song, like rain pelting parched earth, settles in her memory. And suddenly, in the corner spun white with spider webs, she sees Bojangles. He dances in worn out shoes to the song of life, sad and sweet, and then he is gone back to his prison cell in New Orleans and the music with him. She touches down onto her one sturdy chair collapsing in tears and laughter. Mixed. She knows then, with that vision of the Hobo dancer, what she now brings with her wherever she goes. The gift to see spirit. And she thanks Bojangles for his visit and being her first guest.

Cynthia studies the cobwebs. The gossamer threads shine silver, coating the corner in a translucent unbroken shroud. It is like death, she thinks. The living cannot see through to the other dimension. But since her terrible fall out of the speeding car that shattered her face and broke her skull, the web opens to her at times not of her choosing. She fears her gift for its unruly blessing. There is joy, understanding, connection, and knowing that the "beyond" exists. But also there is confusion, craving and the coldness of the in-between that emanates from ghostly visitors. And there is Roy.

She begins to unpack her belongings, so pitifully few that it takes little time, and she comes at once to the Bible. Her mother's Bible. She puts it to her cheek drawing a breath of roses her mother pressed and left inside the pages. I'll read it tonight Mum. I promise. She sets it carefully on the bed where her pillow should be, and finds her notebook under folded clothes. It contains her research on ghosts. She knows that if she is to tame her fear she must study it, turn a spotlight on to dispel the shadows. And her research had turned up classifications for the other worldly. She likes that. Putting ghosts in little boxes makes them less terrifying.

She begins to read her findings. There are specters, demons, and psychotics, and also monsters, heavenly visitors, humans, and aliens. There are wild and wooly visitors like a senate of griffins. She has listed a clangor of robots in the mechanical class. Someone had long ago christened bunches of ghosts in descriptive terms: a pleasure of pixies, a cackle of mad scientists, a depravity of revenants or a rustle of reapers. All the names bespeak mystery, wisdom, humor or threat like "The Borg" in Star Trek literature.

Cynthia wonders why some ghosts hang around a special place or person and decides they have unfinished business. They might be caught in a loop replaying their demise, trying to understand it. Some did not realize they had crossed over and continued on living as usual after their bodies were buried. To them, the living are intruding on their territory.

They seem capable of mischief and mayhem, like running the water tap, opening doors, and breaking things. Some come as guides, working to benefit the haunted. Some have an unrealized dream and work vicariously through a living person. Then there are ghosts like Roy whose unfinished business is revenge.

When Nicholas had opened the door to her room it was clear that no one had lived in it for a long time. No one living, that is. Cynthia thinks of the stories her father told her as a child. For a brief moment, she entertains the idea that she has come to the Belmar to collect the stories of those who lived and now haunt this place, but then her mind questions: who would that benefit, and why would it matter? Deep down, she knows she has come to escape. She shivers although it is hot in the hotel, remembering how Roy's ghost had followed her to Wisconsin, feeding on her agony over the slow death of her parents. Cynthia takes a deep breath to calm herself. Even though she hates to ask for help, she had been forced to call upon the kindness of her old friend. But how can she forgive Lori? For a moment she feels herself slipping back into that place of panic where darkness sucks her down.

Cynthia fumbles to the bottom of her bag to find the little packet of letters from her mother, and that something...important to her now. What could it be—she is not sure until —there it is; a holy card picturing la Esperanza de La Macarena, the Queen of Hope. Because Cynthia was a dancer, her mother sent this card to her. And now Cynthia is receiving it again, for she understands it in a new way, recognizing the Queen of Seville in the shrine by the front desk as the Queen of Hope.

Virgin de La Macarena, Our Lady of Hope, Patron Saint of Bullfighters and Flamenco

The card says that she is "The Patron Saint of Bullfighters and Flamenco." Cynthia had danced with passion, with joy and delight. Hers was a dance of life and death that soared to Heavens Gate and was her downfall. Now, it is as if her mother is soothing her, as if the Queen of Hope knows her heart. Tears of thankfulness overflow, spilling down her cheeks like the tears of the caring Queen in the picture as Cynthia accepts the blessing of the card.

And just then comes a knock on her door.

9.

THE LOOKING GLASS LOCKET

A KNOCK ON THE DOOR. CYNTHIA WISHES IT HAD A PEEP HOLE TO SEE WHO is calling. Maybe Lori. Maybe Nicholas. Maybe the government ready to deport her or... maybe the hotel staff who have learned she is not flush with money enough to rent this room for long. But when she edges the door open, she sees no one. The hall is empty. She looks down the expanse wondering how anyone could vanish so quickly, and there on a hook alongside her door, shining silver bright, she spies a gleaming silver pendant on a chain. As she unhooks the chain to examine the locket she wonders why she hadn't noticed it before. Unless... The outside is a

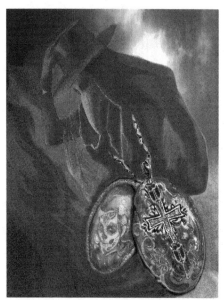

The Looking Glass Locket

flaming cross with a golden birdlike image on the front of it. She sees a clasp and tiny hinges so fingers it open to look inside, all the while reasoning out the mystery. I should bring it to the front desk. Whoever found it, knocked on the door and hung it up thinking it belonged to the occupant of this room. Inside the locket is a mirror—no—a skeleton image of the face of a woman. Cynthia snaps the locket shut recoiling from the image that evoked the horror of her own face after her skid across the highway. She gin-

57

gerly opens the locket to peer inside again and sees only a small mirror. How strange, she thinks.

Alicia is not at the front desk, but Nicholas is leaning against it as Cynthia approaches. Nicholas has worked at the Belmar for 50 years, beginning as a bellboy and now serving as a jack-of-all-trades who knows most everything about the old hotel. His eyes are downcast and his smile is a little sad as if he is all too aware of the room she has chosen. Perhaps she wants a different room. The knowledge that other guests have come to the desk rejecting the accommodation comes to her in a flash.

Cynthia holds the locket out for him to see, explaining that someone must have lost it. He regards the pendant, keeping his distance from it as if it holds some sort of spell, and as his smile melts, his brow furrows.

"*No Señorita, no está perdido. Es* not lost and *lo he visto antes*. I see it before. You rent room six *en* C. No?"

"Yes, Nicholas. But it looks like no one has lived in that room for years."

"*Si Señorita.* Take *el medallón* with you. *Es el medallón de la muerte negra que visitó Mazatlán. La enfermera de las calles lo lleva.*"

Seeing Cynthia does not understand, Nicholas struggles to put his explanation in English. "*La muerte negra es* black death. *Y enfermera de las calles*—street nurse—*es famosa* en Mazatlán. *Ella*, she live in *su* room en old time."

"What does that mean?"

"*No se, Señorita*. I go to work now."

Beyond Nicholas is the sunlit entrance of the Belmar. Lori lives out there only blocks away. Cynthia wonders if the locket is a sign that she should tell Lori the rest of her story and ask her for help. Not now, she thinks.

She wearily limps back to C block where she can be alone in her room to try to fathom her choices, the mystery of her life, her desperate journey now further complicated by the Spanish language. All too much. She picks up the Bible hugging it against her heart for a moment, taking in the protection it affords her. Putting it with her notebook on a broken chair, Cynthia stretches wearily on her bed, the locket at her fingertips, and soon falls into a fitful sleep haunted by a vision of a little girl running through empty streets.

Is she lost? The alleys are strewn with figures in black. She cannot find her way through the labyrinth. As she dreams, Cynthia is wondering if the child is running to escape or could she be racing toward something? She is wearing a silver pendant around her neck. Bits of information infuse the dream, coloring it like dancing fireworks. The locket belongs to the nurse of the streets. *Es famosa en Mazatlán, en* old time, the famous healer that once lived in this room. At last the child stops running. She opens the locket and the mirror inside reflects Cynthia Javenin's face, so beautiful and tranquil it could be the face of an angel.

The dream ends. Cynthia is flooded with compassion for the child and consolation for herself. She gazes at the locket on the bed beside her feeling power to bridge to *"en* old time" and deep peaceful sleep sweeps her away to a place where "alone" is but an illusion.

10

CYNTHIA'S STORY

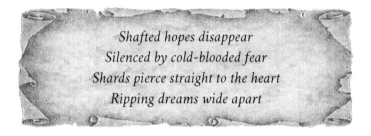

Shafted hopes disappear
Silenced by cold-blooded fear
Shards pierce straight to the heart
Ripping dreams wide apart

SOMEBODY FIGURED IT OUT WHEN THEY SAID THE MORE THINGS CHANGE the more they stay the same. I thought about that with Cynthia and me. I had always envied her the ability to embody feelings while I studied them. I could write up a label but she was the elixir inside. I was the fan, she the celebrity who lived the world I only read about. It was like I lived dry and wordy in my head, and she was the hope that juiced my life. Funny how, jealous or not, I didn't know how much I had missed her until now. I had labored to live in straight lines while she lived in circles, swinging higher and higher.

I waited for her to call me like I always did when I was a kid. When Cynthia finally phoned me and said "Come on over" I was ready for another shot of free spirit that I could sit on my duff and admire. I wanted her right up there performing on the pedestal I'd put her on.

Alicia at the Belmar front desk points me in the direction of the swimming pool beyond which is the garden, Section C, and Cynthia's room number six. But I want to revisit the mural at the base of the stairs knowing I can go along the corridor, then cut through the garage that was once a ballroom. It is full of oddities and markings like a cave and opens into the full length of the garden that once flourished there.

Every time I look at the mural I notice something else. This time, the grandmother with the little girl in tow looks wiser than I remembered. Like she is bringing the child to a higher place, sort of like Cynthia's mother did with her. Maybe the little huts down at the base of the hill they are climbing are like Oulu where Cynthia and I grew up. Yes, Cynthia was destined for greater things than life on level ground.

The Mural of Early Mazatlan

Past the mural is an open space, a kind of lobby. I can see the huge cement vault to the left across the wide passageway that leads to Constitución Street and the entrance to the German company Melchers Sucesores next door. The Casa Melcher (the house of Melcher) was the center of an international trading district before the First World War. An endless flow of goods from America and Europe flowed through the Port of Mazatlán into the German warehouses to be shipped inland, and Company profits brought expansion into the world of banking. Once horse drawn wagons clanked and clopped into the Belmar, bristling with armed guards. In time, armored trucks rumbled and reverberated through the massive Belmar northern gates as they delivered gold and silver to secure coffers in the vault.

Above me are balconies tiled in the intricate blue and white patterns of Seville, Spain, bordered with black banisters and railings of precious ebony. I walk past a cement fountain without water. Although antiquated and dusty, the foyer hints at elegance and I can imagine the sounds and smells of glamour as crowds of people in colorful and bejeweled attire laugh and converse outside the famous Las Palmas ballroom. And now, only the sound of my own footsteps as I wander down the ramp, through the 12 foot doors fit for a castle into a ballroom turned into a garage. I look up, up, and higher still, imagining ageless Doric capitals on the columns. Once simple and elegant against the ceiling, they were far too fancy for a warehouse and had to be squared off. I can imagine the work order: "Change classic to crude."

There are great piles of furniture stacked against the vault wall in the vast room of concrete. Broken legs and arms of a style at once utilitarian and common protrude from the mishmash. I think this lot was brought in after the Belmar had fallen from favor. Certainly they are not original furnishings. Did those still exist somewhere?

On I walk, noting faded indistinct murals on the drab once gleaming walls, more piled furniture, some parked cars, and then to the right, a wide pavement continues down and across the garden expanse. At the far end, 14 foot doors accented in pointed brass mark the southern Belmar entrance to Sixto Osuna Street, the old road of gold. Again I think of castles I have seen and the feudal system of Europe. Over the years, the Belmar must have housed the leaders of many civilizations, nobles, freemen, servants, peasants, villains and slaves, representatives of the entire Medieval to Modern order. This hotel no longer stores silver and gold but instead it is a treasury of history I hope to mine for my book. I realize that Cynthia might help me. If only she likes living within the subject matter while I do the describing.

The cemented garden I cross over erupts now in random islands of green where trees, trying to escape a jail of rough concrete, grow tall into each other, and common untrimmed bushes compete for the meager space expediency sets. I have read that this was once an artfully arranged garden of exotic plants bearing rare flowers and fruit. Nothing short of romance in bloom, it was a beguiling cornucopia of color and scent laced with light and shadow. To my left, a motor home is parked on a concrete field for tennis courts. The courts exist only in my imagination or the pages of history, but I stop as if to listen to the sounds of this place, the smack of the racquet, the shouts of the players. My mind serves me up the lyrics of a song about paving paradise "to put up a parking lot.'"

At my feet, there are grids above a network of chambers. Could they empty into the fabled tunnel where precious metals were hidden? Where snakes slithered in pursuit of rats? Where pirates, troops or refugees made their escape to the sea? I take a deep breath of the secrets haunting this place and hurry on to the stairs of C, the oldest section of the Belmar where once were housed the offices and living quarters of the builder Bradbury, his clients and friends, and now the neighborhood Cynthia has chosen.

The Belmar Inner Courtyard Gardens of long ago

Many of the ruins in Mazatlán's Centro Historical follow the Spanish concept of an inner courtyard away from the bustle of business. The hall at the top of the stairs looks back at the main hotel across such a place. I am high enough here to look through the branches of an old mango tree screening the garden, and behind it the old well alongside the staircase to the swimming pool. When we were kids, Cynthia and I made a tree house in the back forty of the Great North Woods we occupied. A private little refuge, just her, me, and the birds. I revisit my notion that Cynthia would not choose to live at ground level.

All the doors into the apartments are closed except one, the entrance to Cynthia's room.

I try not to notice how narrow, how empty, how dusty, how colorless apartment six is. Across the hall overlooking the garden below, blank spaces house a kitchen area and end with a bedroom. In between there is room for a table, a bathroom with a shower, a desk for an office or study and on the far side of the bedroom, doors open onto a balcony. I am determined to seize upon something positive. There is a view to the street and the garden, the window glass is intact and already a sprig of greenery is set to sprout in a beer bottle filled with water.

Cynthia is all smiles like she has checked into her palatial dream.

"Hi Lori. Lots of potential right? Nicholas snipped off some leaves to spruce up the place. He offered me a cactus, but no table to put it on yet. Clumsy as I am, I'd probably step on it and get blood poisoning. It's a little short of furniture, but they tell me I can go shopping right here in the Belmar."

"Yep, I know where the mall is, right in the garage," I say, "and I bet the price is right."

"They seem to have stripped this room. I think they have not rented it for a long time." Cynthia looks away, a hint of a frown clouds her face, and the pause says more then the positive tune she sings.

"But if I stay here, they will bring me a stove, sink and refrigerator and like you say, I can find all the things I need in other rooms or the garage. I can think of it like searching for treasure."

I follow Cynthia's glance to a bit of jewelry lying on the bed. A beam of light pregnant with dust glints off the silver pendant. She turns a slow circle in the emptiness, stirring up ancient smells I can't place and then continues in a voice that is not quite convincing.

"I don't need much anymore."

"Oh well," I say, ignoring her tragic tone, "you still like 'pretty.' Such an interesting locket. A flaming cross? But this other, ah, gold image across the front looks like the skeleton of a bird? A raven?"

"It's not mine. It came with a knock on the door. I thought someone lost it, so brought it down to the front desk but Nicholas freaked and wouldn't touch it. Said he'd seen it before, said it was from a bad time and that it belonged to a nurse who lived in this very room. I think maybe someone dropped it off back here since no one wants it once they know what that flaming cross and long nosed bird's head stands for. Want to know?"

"Sure," I say in a worried, unconvincing tone.

"The bubonic plague. The black death. That's what. Isn't that an interesting house warming gift though? Maybe right from the nurse that lived in this room?"

I say nothing and she continues as if she hopes I will share her experience.

"Lori, look inside and tell me what you see."

"Okay." I open the locket and see a mirror and my own silly face looking back at me. "Perfect. A selfie. Are you going to wear it?"

"No, let's leave it right there with the nurse where it belongs!"

Cynthia whirls in a pirouette with no allowance for being lame. And her eyes flash with a kind of anger that is not directed outward. It is like lightening exploding within a thunderhead.

"I think it's time you know what has brought me to show up on your doorstep. Passed time. But really, there is not even a good place to sit in this room. I don't want to bother you. I'm not asking for anything like money or things, but just your good analytical mind. You know me, sort of dreamy, and now much, much worse. I've gone beyond loving stories to getting lost in dreams, to being flakey, to...well now, I may be just plain nuts. Lori, I think I am losing my mind. And you have studied! Courses and courses in psychology. You even have degrees. Me? I'm just a washed up dancer."

Cynthia reaches for her dark glasses and then puts them back down. But she keeps her face turned a little away from me. Her hair looks uncombed.

"Cynthia. Stop such talk. You told me there was a side of you I wouldn't like. I hope I am bigger than that and besides, I remember who you are not just a side of you. That's what I can do, remind you. Interesting play on words don't you think? Re-mind? Don't all heroes go through terrible trials? What's the saying today when someone great stumbles? They've fallen on bad times?

"Come on. Let's go get some coffee and I'll be happy to listen. But don't expect me to agree you're all washed up. People with *sisu* don't think that way and anyway, I need you to look up to. You had the courage to leave and have a life while I stayed home."

I am already half out the door, happy the locket is staying put. Cynthia is right behind me, and she turns to consider security. She scowls in displeasure but sets the lock.

Once out on the street, we have choices left and right and decide to get a coffee at Looney Beans coffee shop because Cynthia likes the name, saying it suits her. We find privacy at a booth in the back. The hustle bustle of the street is barely visible here behind the little water feature that soothes. I make small talk, we order, and Cynthia is quiet waiting for interruptions to cease. Coffee is delivered in big warm mugs of blackness, its rich toasty aroma rising to the ceiling. We are alone and it is quiet. Cynthia takes a deep breath to calm herself knowing the time has arrived. I look at her expectantly.

"What do you think of my face Lori?"

"What do you mean? You are too thin but gorgeous as ever. Looking for compliments are you?"

"Yes as a matter of fact, and now I'll tell you why. I'm in the mood to tell you the whole thing, though I wasn't going to. But maybe you and all your schooling can, well you'll see."

There follows a moment of silence, the kind of quiet before you parachute jump while you gather your wits and get ready to throw your life to the winds. I stop sipping coffee, put my cup down and wait, forgetting to breathe, remembering her words, "I wasn't going to."

Cynthia inhales deeply and words spill out of her like a great sigh.

"I didn't see it coming. But, I had been getting ready for it all my life. Studying like you. Yes, funny you mentioned it, but I think it began with my father telling us all those stories of heroes and heroines. Maybe he felt guilty that mum gave up dancing for a life with him in Oulu. When I danced, it was as if I had the wings to fly away and he saw that. I was his dancing girl. He knew I had my mother's talent and was determined to give me the chance to use it like she never had.

"Early on, he took me aside and warned me that I looked too innocent, too small and weak, too blond and pretty. A trophy girl, he said. So for him, I lifted weights to get stronger. He even bought me a gun and at least I learned how to load and fire it. One of my boyfriends taught me how to fall in case we crashed on his motorcycle. Once I got to Colorado, I thought I had learned enough to be safe. Dancing was so exciting, especially with the new moves I was mastering. Moves that had men watching me. I sort of enjoyed the way they looked at me."

I bite my lip at her words, noticing her voice cracking a little, sounding an alarm as she describes seductive dance and the lust it engenders.

"People came to watch the rehearsals. They sat in the dark, sometimes clapped or cheered and this guy came often. Then one night after a rehearsal as I left the hall and walked the road to my cabin he came up alongside me in his car. I sort of knew him. He said he was a big fan and had watched me dance over and over. That was my undoing. I didn't run, but came closer. So happy he had enjoyed my dancing. So flattered that I forgot everything my father told me. He introduced himself as Roy Cassidy and reached his hand out the window. I was close to the open window and he grabbed my arm hard. I froze when I realized he was not going to let go, then screamed and fought him but he threw me into the car like I was a sack of groceries and took off up Big Thomson Canyon."

There is a note of desperation in her voice. I lean forward as if to be of help.

"He was talking to me now. Telling me what he was going to do. Creepy sexual things. Laughing at me. *Laughing.* Not a night goes by that I don't still hear that damn laugh. He said that he would kill me afterwards and throw my body into this place he knew. And no one would find me. He laughed some more and I looked for something to hit him with but there wasn't anything big and heavy enough. Nothing.

"I didn't think it through, just got as far away as I could, scrunched up against the door, my hand on the latch, waiting until he slowed for a curve. Now or never, I opened the door and jumped, rolling, rolling on that country road. I thought it would never end. And then it did, and I was all bloody but still alive. I tried to get to the side of the road in case a car came ...and then one did.

"I saw the lights and the driver saw me and stopped, got out, ran over and crouched down looking at me. He didn't have a phone to call an ambulance. I told him he had to take me to a hospital. He said he didn't want to get his car bloody. I told him again. I begged him. I threatened him. He couldn't leave me there. The guy who grabbed me would come back and kill me, him too. He had to take me in. That did it.

"He had a blanket in the car and wrapped me up and we went to the hospital. I don't know who he was. I must have looked so bloody bad, and the way I talked to him, screamed at him, well, he never wanted to see me again. And I never tried to find him either, I was so humiliated, asking like that.

"But Roy followed up. I think he turned his car around and drove behind us to see what hospital I was taken to. Then he came visiting. Can you believe that? I was all in bandages but could see him in a blurry sort of way and he told me to never talk. Never say a word or he'd kill me. But I had his name, Roy Cassidy, and I made a plan. It would be a long time before I could do much about it but I knew what I would do to that man that took away my dream. I would make him pay."

Cynthia stops talking and takes a sip of coffee now grown cold. She picks up her dark glasses, puts them on and looks toward the ocean at the waves marching in, steady as a clock ticking, time passing. I don't interrupt, sit on the edge of my seat holding my breath, fists clenched in my lap, waiting. When she is ready, she continues.

"The doc who did plastic surgery on my face wanted a picture of me before I got hurt. I'll never forget what he said and how he said it. So regretfully. 'You were beautiful, just beautiful. I can never make you look the same.' And I told him then, like I told the man who brought me to the hospital, protesting all the way. 'Yes you will.' But that night I cried and cried over his words."

Another sip of coffee. I say nothing. What could I ever say? Cynthia slowly takes off her dark glasses and looks straight at me, her eyes sparked with what her father would have called *sisu*. I feel like I am looking at the goddess heroine in a Finnish tale.

"The doc tried over and over, operation after operation, while I learned what it was like to be a freak. The sight of me was so sickening that when I tried to eat out other diners left their food. Even full plates got left behind when they spied me trying to eat through a straw. Finally, after more than a year and twenty-three operations, the Doc and I both agreed that I had healed miraculously well and looked very much as I once did. Oh, if you look close you can see hairline scars between the skin grafts, but I had my face back and my arms and legs had healed over, though my knees and hip would never be the same. Now it was time for me to put my plan to work.

"I got a lawyer. I hired a detective. This man, Roy Cassidy, had hurt other women but none would testify against him. Charges were not filed. The women didn't have pictures to show what he did to them. But I did. And I learned to use my gun and bought a better one. I got a coach and went to the shooting range until I was an expert shot and could picture myself hunting him! I alerted my friends, my family, the sheriff, and then, under the full protection of the law and feeling like I could defend myself, I filed charges to go after him. When he threatened me, I told him to 'bring it on, I will kill you for your trouble.' Imagine that!

"I think he became afraid of me. He was arrested, tried, and sent to jail. Once he got there, other women came forward and Mr. Roy was sentenced to prison where he got into a fight and was killed. He was dead. Good and dead, and I thought I could breathe easy. Finally justice was done. Only, not the doctor or the plastic surgeon, not justice, not even Roy's death could put me back the way I was. I was sort of back together physically but I would never dance professionally again. When I returned to Wisconsin I put miles between me and what happened. True, my battle with Mr. Roy Cassidy who wanted to rape and kill me was won. He went to his grave by his own conniving. But the war. Will it ever be over?"

I sit back and try to take it all in. No words of consolation come to me but I reach to touch her hand, only she pulls it away. So much has happened to my best childhood friend. My pretty, graceful dancer friend. I remind her of her big hearted courage, tell her that she soared higher and higher on her swing as a girl, higher then I had dared to go. "I was too afraid. Never got high enough to see Lake Superior," I tell her. "But you did."

"Yes, I saw the Great Lake. And now, I see the other side," she replies.

I don't know what she means. I give Cynthia a questioning look, but she turns her face away. It is as if she slams a door shut between us. She finishes her coffee and stands ready to go.

"Later," she says. "That's enough telling for now. At least you know why I ended my career. And I told you in my letter about my parents dying. I want to try to make this room in this old hotel my home. One I might be able to afford. I will have to find some way to make money, you know. Put your mind to what that might be. I hope with this rush to a new life in México I have gone far enough to put it all behind me. Maybe here I can be safe."

Safe. For the first time I hear fear in her voice, like dreams and talent have failed to protect her or put her back together. And how can she hope to feel safe living in this empty room in a haunted hotel? She won't let me pay for the coffee, but I notice her hand trembles as she fumbles for coins for the waiter. My heart hurts. She had just put 2700 miles between her old home in Oulu and the Belmar in Mazatlán, México. How far is far enough when fear gets inside you?

THE WOMAN IN WHITE

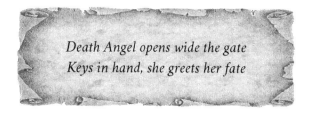

Death Angel opens wide the gate
Keys in hand, she greets her fate

My misgiving about Cynthia's mental state persists. Two days after she has revealed her horrific story of kidnapping and defacement, she calls me with news of another encounter—this time with a ghost, the Belmar's fabled Woman in White. Cynthia's helpless anxiety leaves me breathless, lost in the listening until she runs out of words. Although I am at first deep in doubt, she paints the scene with such intensity I am there, right alongside her in my imagination.

It was just at twilight when Cynthia saw her in the Belmar passageway. At that time of day when night shadows obscure reality. Stunning as the green flash that blazes from the dying sun, the lady slipped from the old Belmar bar, room keys in her hand, and skimmed soundlessly by. The woman stopped to linger at the shrine of the Queen of Seville. A woman in white, on the brink of tragedy. Cynthia knew how that felt, and she elaborates on her feelings.

"I wanted to console her, to catch her hand and somehow keep her from moving on, but when the woman looked at me—no, through me, I lost my balance and fell back clutching one of the tiled columns in the passageway. Lori, I just clung there helpless, while the lady turned oh so slowly away, gazed up the golden stairs, and ascended."

I can picture the scene: perfume smelling of sadness drifting down over

Cynthia who shivered as if she stood in a cold draft while tears glistened on her cheeks like dew turning to ice. But a part of me recoils from the story. She is seeing ghosts for goodness sake! That locket might have pushed her over the edge. It sure gives me the willies. She had already shared that she was worried about her sanity! And that comment that now she was "seeing the other side." I am beginning to understand what she meant. She had prepared me for this but still it catches me off guard. I wonder if I should go along with her. After all, she has had a terrible time. It was all just too much, I think, and make my decision. When I speak, I speak slowly and in a matter of fact manner so as to calm Cynthia down. She is taking this far too personally, like this apparition appeared just to her. Really!

"She was a ghost, Cynthia. Many have seen her. Dressed all in white and carrying her room keys, they say that she walks from the bar up the stairs to her room. And from what I've heard, guests have reported seeing her since the hotel was newly built. What mysterious disaster took the life of this lady? I have loads of information about the Belmar Hotel in the early 1920s. Surely it would have made the news, leave it to me."

"Yes, yes, oh I must know Lori," Cynthia continues, eyes wide, her voice hinting at hysteria. "It was as if she wanted me to know her secret. She looked at me and I froze like Lot's wife looking back at the sins of Sodom and Gomorrah. Looking back at her life. You know the Bible story where she turned to a pillar of salt? That was me, looking at that woman. Just for a moment, I was her. Oh. That must sound so stupid. But, Lori, I need to know about her. Find out for me. It is very important for me and for the book you are writing. I'm sure of it."

And so, I begin to unravel the story goaded on by a rhyme that strangely enough, is haunting my mind: "Death Angel opens wide the gate. Keys in hand, she meets her fate." Appalled at the imagery, I search the internet for news stories about the Belmar Hotel. Reports are so similar that the same person could have written most of them and I already had copied the commonly known information. But after a whole morning of reading, I think of a new word. Scandal. Ah! This handle gives me new internet screens to peruse. After lunch, I begin again—on and on—while all the things I am supposed to do today sit undone. It has to be there somewhere. I just know it, the rhyme gives me no peace, and anyway I can't disappoint Cynthia.

Then, late in the afternoon, I find something no one in this Catholic country wants to admit.

In a side column of El Democrata, Mazatlán, September 26, 1922, the headline reads "The wife of Gral. Abelardo L. Rodríguez committed suicide with a revolver." The sub heading announces that "La Bella Dama left no explanation for the lamentable event." And in the small print of the article I learn that General Rodríguez's beautiful wife was American, and that she killed herself in the Hotel Belmar. I read on, translating the Spanish words:

> "In the wee hours of the morning, the blast of the Smith and Wesson 32-20 caliber military/police issue echoed along polished corridors waking Colonel Camilo Gastelum, in a nearby room. He alone heard the sound. A familiar sound to a man who fought in the Revolution, but he dismissed it as the back fire of a car cruising main street Olas Altas."

The newly opened hotel was billing itself as a playground for the wealthy and influential, advertising glamour, gaiety, and celebration. It was no wonder something so horrendous was swept under the rug. It was decidedly bad for business. But, I found the reporting of the event provocative. Why was the only person who heard the report of the gun a General? And why didn't he know the sound to be what it was? Strange and stranger.

My curiosity aroused, I search for information about this lady. She is called La Bella Dama Eathyl Vera Meier, but news of her comes only through searching the internet about her husband. She had married Gral. Abelardo L. Rodríguez in 1921, a year before she took her life. Abelardo spent little time with her because he was very busy fulfilling his military duties. One sentence, buried in Abelardo's obituary, explained that Eathyl suffered from depression over the loss of their daughter in miscarriage, and "surely" that was the reason she killed herself. The word "surely" sticks crosswise in my mind. The very finality of it is like a door slamming in my face leaving me wondering what was on the other side.

It seemed the violent death of his wife did not derail Abelardo's rise to fame and fortune. He went on to become the President of México leaving behind a legacy of accomplishments that led him to say of himself, "I occupy the highest positions that a man can hope for in the military, political, and civil arenas." True enough. There was no shortage of information about México's picture perfect rising star.

> Already employed at fourteen, he loved sports, organized and captained baseball teams. He was gregarious and popular in the Northern District making friends on both sides of the border. He became Commander of the Nogales Police Force, and in 1913 he was a Lieutenant in the 2nd battalion of Sonora, became Brigadier General and soon Governor of the Northern district. In 1930, he was appointed to head the offices of the army and navy; that same year he became President of the Republic. Later, he was Governor of Sonora, his home state, and for six years he used his salary to promote sports and the education of México's youth. Money flowed into México under his guidance.

But what is this?

> The History Channel made a documentary entitled: "Abelardo: The Ambassador of the Mafia." From the dark underbelly of betrayal, lust, drugs, games, power, and romance came a picture of Abelardo as an artist in crime. His Mexican title was Baron de la Frontera, a man whose desire for power opened the way for the expansion of organized crime in México for Lucky Luciano, Bugsy Siegel, Al Capone, the beautiful Queen of the Mafia Virginia Hill, and Kingpin Meyer Lansky. Abelardo Rodríguez

was enriched, his secret hidden beneath his generosity.

The Cosa Nostra opened for business. The drug triangle of the States of Durango, Sinaloa, Chihuahua and the border of Tamaulipas welcomed the brutal, daring and young mafiosi eager for money and adventure while Mazatlán drew fanciers of opium, the finest in the world.

The Face of the Belmar 1935

But the Baron discreetly dropped out of politics after his brief presidency and became a world traveler and property manager. His repudiation of communism as slavery and his opinion that Fidel Castro was careless and irresponsible earned him titles: Freedom's Champion, the Legion of Merit from the United States, an honorary PhD from USC Berkeley, the Theodore Brent Award as Latin America's outstanding leader. Through it all, he invested and won for himself the title of the most entrepreneurial of all business-minded generals spawned by the Revolution. The author Paul Vanderwood wrote in his book Satan's Playground that "looting, confiscation, forced loans, filching, kidnapping, rustling and wanton lawlessness seems to energize the entrepreneurial spirit" and gave Abelardo the title of the "Richest Baron."

And the Belmar? The suicide of Abelardo's wife was downplayed in the media, but to those who have seen the Woman in White on her silent, sorrowful journey from the bar to her room, people like Cynthia who understand the pain of loneliness and loss, well, it would be natural that they would want to know her name and her story. Yes, Cynthia had indeed been curious, but so much more than that. Anxious? Yes, but more than that. This sorrowful woman was communicating something Cynthia had also experienced.

A chilling vision comes over me. I see the loveliest moonscape. Illuminated clouds dance whispy white in the velvety blackness, and then comes a shadow.

"The sound of the backfire of a car" extinguishing the light of the moon.

THE WOMAN IN WHITE

12

ABIMIEL AND THE CAPTAIN

"Locked and boarded up" is how Cynthia refers to rooms in the Belmar that are never rented. She believes that some of these rooms were rendered sacrosanct by Belmar guests who thought they were haunted.

We are walking up to her room when she points out a padlocked room known as the Captain's Quarters, explaining that our Navy friend Wesley knew the man who had lived in this room. She goes on, her voice low and confidential.

"Wesley says a carpenter by the name of Abimiel was the only one who ever lived here." She gestures at the heavy black door chained shut, stout boards nailed across the window.

"I'm on the lookout for Wesley in the hope he'll tell me more. I've just got to know. Abi, he calls him, because he says even though it was years and years ago when he heard them, he still remembers Abi's stories. Wesley says that's the way of it, he only remembers things from long ago. So far he's told me that Mazatlán was under siege during the Revolution. Abimiel served on a gunboat commanded by a Captain Malpica from Veracruz. Abi loved the Captain so much he finished the inside of his room to look just like his Captain's quarters. That's why the name."

Cynthia urges me to help shed some light on what happened. I can tell it was important to her. She talks about this Abimiel like she knows him herself, and finally she steers me to see the room—like maybe he'll come out and invite us for tea. The room is not up front with a view but is located back in a dead-end corner of the Belmar that is poorly lit, the staircase rising above it. Dust coats the black boards. The wall, perhaps once decorated with Spanish tiles, is stripped bare and blackened by mildew. To me it is derelict, dank smelling and dreary. But Cynthia is like a prospector following a vein of gold, so I ask her why she wants to know about the carpenter Abimiel?

"Yes, I meant to tell you, but have been postponing until I was sure you would take me seriously. Oh, I don't blame you for being skeptical. But since you helped me find out some details about the Woman in White, I am going to chance you won't send me to the looney bin.

"Okay, here it is, honest to goodness and best I can tell. One night, I smelled something burning in the hotel. It seemed to be coming from this room, but no one enters this room, or so I thought. When I tried to look between the boards at what was burning inside, a sailor came out through the door, never mind the padlock and boards. They parted for him to come through just like the Red Sea opened for the Israelites to flee Egypt. He was looking out toward the Pacific. That's why, Lori. Because the ghost of Abimiel appeared to me. I know I will see him again because..."

"Yes?"

"Because he called me a beautiful name, one I recognized but also seem to have forgotten. He knelt to kiss my hand but I pulled back. He called me Lady Maria Elena and said when I was ready to hear it he had a message for me from his Captain. Then, he just dissolved back into that room, that Captain's Quarters room of his. And before I could even catch my breath to call after him, I heard a volley of gunfire echoing all around in this niche under the stairs. Like in a circle with me in the middle. So, you bet I asked around. But no one else smelled fire, no one else heard the guns.

"Please, I'm asking you Lori, let's search this out. Together. I'll talk to Wesley about Abi and please look for records of Captain Malpica. I want to know the story so if I see Abimiel again, I'll be ready for what he might tell me."

So now I had a mission. And she is right. Clearly what we learned about the Woman in White shook up my convictions about the Spirit World. She used the word "together." Yes, I hope working with Cynthia will bring back the closeness we once shared.

I soon learn the research was easy enough and terribly hard at the same time. The internet and the Archives contain volumes of information. México was divided in over forty factions fighting each other while many foreign nations coveted its riches. The search took weeks of reading and during that time Cynthia had long talks with our Navy friend Wesley. It became a fun endeavor to join oral with written history. Exciting for her. Drudgery for me.

Beginning in Veracruz, my research told a bloody tale of conflict that swept all across México into what was known as the City of the Deer, Mazatlán. It is a story of heroism, revenge, and mutiny in the service of leaders who were assassinated by other leaders. All of them passionate, some killing for power, some fighting for the rights of the people. The Mexican Revolution seemed incomprehensible to me, a foreigner. The research I had done hinted that General Abelardo who, along with his star-crossed bride had checked into the Belmar soon after construction, was the last man standing, or were the ghosts in this hotel still fighting for justice? Were they somehow connected around that question? Perhaps the Belmar itself was the connection. The story Cynthia wanted me to follow felt unfinished, and led me further. I felt lost and overwhelmed in all of it, buried in books and facts, while my friends celebrated feast days, enjoyed the beach and socialized.

I began to order books about the Revolution, German interests and the First World War and what the seafarers of Mazatlán had to do with it. Finally, glimpsing perspective, I was able to piece together the tale of the dashing young hero from Veracruz—Abimiel's beloved Captain. But although I put a period to the last sentence of the story, it still felt unfinished. It is one thing to put a frame around a bit of history, to write it down. I found myself haunted by the idea of the ghost of Abimiel who passed right through boards, who lived in the mysterious in-between of life and death beneath the stairs, who was ungoverned by time. And what would his message mean for Cynthia?

The story of Hilario Rodríguez Malpica begins in 1889 when he was born into a famous seafaring Veracruz family. He was to become one of the unsung heroes of the Revolution, his part in it little known and yet pivotal.

As was tradition in his family the boy, just 15 yrs. of age, enrolled at the Heroic Naval Military Academy, the crucible that prepared classmates like Lieutenant José Azueta and Cadet Virgilio Uribe to fight with valor in the Revolution. The sea romanced young Malpica, and the drama of war became his passion. He graduated in 1909, a seaman seeking mastery of his world. To hone his skills, he attained degrees in artillery and navigation and served on all of Mexico's gunboats, winning the hearts and respect of captains and crews.

He was promoted to Lieutenant in 1913, to serve in the Navy under the brutal dictator Victoriano Huerta aboard the gunboat that bore the name of the prosperous city made rich from México's oil, the Tampico. This ship along with the Morelos and the gunboat General Guerrero were charged with protecting the Federalist harbors of Guaymas and Mazatlán, and to capture the prized Port of Topolobampo that was under Constitutionalist rule.

The charismatic young man was the ideal Mexican hero. Swash buckling and brave, he was a legend in the making who glowed with the charm of Old Veracruz, and caught the esteem of men and the eyes of women. They say that he lost himself in love for the stunning Maria Elena of the familia de Pino Suárez whose father, like Malpica's own, served alongside Madero, President of México. They say that her revolutionary ideas captured his mind while her brown-eyed beauty enslaved his heart.

Although serving in Huerta's Federalist Navy, the loyalty of Malpica was shaken by stories of Huerta's savagery to his own family and Maria Elena's. The dictator was dubbed El Usurpador, "The Usurper," a name that is still used to describe him today for his assassination of President Madero and Maria Elena's father, Vice President Pino Suárez, both pro–democracy leaders. México called this tragic time La Decena Tragica, México City's "Ten Tragic Days." When a courageous senator from the state of Chiapas, Belisario Domínguez, gave a public speech denouncing Huerta as a tyrant, Domínguez was brutally murdered, his bullet-ridden body found weeks later in a ditch. The Congress was enraged so Huerta dissolved it. Malpica's heroism would not be long contained with vengeance on his mind. Secretly, he had become a rebel and his plan was to pull off a mutiny, and join the ranks of the Constitutionalists.

Alvaro Obregón, a chick pea farmer and elementary school teacher from Sonora, distinguished himself for common sense strategy. He had been impressed by President Madero, who dreamt of democracy, and attained advanced educational degrees in the United States. Most intriguing to Obregón were Madero's experiences flying in airplanes.

Obregón was a natural leader and when Huerta killed his way to power, Obregón took his own skills to war, joining the ranks fighting against the Federalists. Obregón knew how to win. He shrewdly vowed allegiance to Venistiano Carranza and his Constitutionalists. And he made arrangements to purchase airplanes hoping to use them in battle. The farmer turned soldier marched down from the north accompanied by a determined army who wanted to take down El Chacal, "The Jackal," another title the dictator Huerta had earned.

General Obregón had no navy to take the harbors of Guaymas and Mazatlán. The undercover rebel, Lieutenant Malpica, stepped up with a plan to take or disable Huerta's navy. He had served, afterall, on all three Huerta gunboats that guarded the ports of Western México. He famously promised Obregón that the gunboat "Morales would be his," and led a mutiny of the crew of the Tampico while half her crew was ashore in Guaymas celebrating the Carnival before Lent. To increase his manpower, Malpica recruited sailors from the docks.

With his motley crew installed, Malpica attacked the unsuspecting gunship General Guerrero, attempting to ram her. The four battles that followed were documented aboard the American ships sent to rescue citizens from the savage battles for the port cities. What they saw was beyond words. It was difficult for them to remain neutral while watching the Tampico under Captain Malpica in her brave but impossible mission.

Beyond words. Yet, if I am going to help Cynthia learn about Captain Malpica, I need to find the words. I decide to talk with Wesley.

I find him sitting out in front of the Belmar reading, sporting a dark blue cap that makes him look like an officer of our Navy. Cynthia had asked him about the Captain's Quarters in the Belmar and found out he actually knew old Abimiel. Wesley said it took a Navy man to tell such a story and Abi wanted a Navy man to hear it. He wished he had seen it himself. I wish he had too, but I found it amazing that the Navy of the United States had sent gunboats and were alongside watching this spectacle play out.

The Tampico attempted to ram the Guerrero before her Marines were aware the ship was under new command. But in a twist of fate, the steerage of the Tampico failed and she had to limp into Topolobampo harbor for repairs where she was hunted down by the two bigger Huerta war ships with superior guns and range. The Morelos and the Guerrero fired often from the distance of nine or ten thousand yards while the Tampico attacked them both. In two battles, the Americans noted the better accuracy of Tampico and marveled at the bravery and skill of her captain.

On March 30, the Morelos left the Guerrero alone to blockade Topolobampo harbor while she took on coal and supplies. The Huerta battleship chose to move far out to sea beyond the range of the Tampico which had won the first two battles. General Obregón, the future president of México, was impressed and promoted Hilario Malpica to be Captain de Frigate.

Cannon fire aboard Gunship Tampico

On March 31, with the odds improved by the absence of the Morelos, Malpica steamed the Tampico out of the harbor and attacked the General Guerrero which fired back hitting the Tampico seven times, one shot damaging the ship beneath the water line. They fired at each other all day, but with dark falling, the Tampico charged the Guerrero again hitting her four times continuing "forward under wild fire" as reported by the watching

Americans. The Tampico only returned to harbor when the Guerrero spun and ran. Once out of sight, beyond the bar of the rebel harbor, the Tampico sank.

When the Morelos returned she was sent to find the enemy, and seeing the boat had sunk in the south side of the waterway, the Morelos fired eleven shots at the sunken gunboat and was smartly answered by eight shots back. Still, the two Federal gunboats conferred and decided the Tampico was not a threat anymore, stripped of armament, and like a dead duck, was unable to move. They left to resupply.

General Obregón ordered Gustavo Salinas Camiña to do something to even the odds. On April 14, accompanied by his mechanic Teodoro Madariaga, Salinas flew Sonora, his Glenn Martin pusher biplane, overhead and began bombing the Guerrero which fired back with small arms. The Huerta warships then put out to sea, and two months passed.

In the meantime, the fact that his command was now underwater did not weaken Malpica's resolve to defeat the enemy gunboats. He found dive teams to plug the holes in the gunboat's armored hull and improvised a compressor to pump air and refloat the Tampico for the fourth and final battle.

On her quest to resupply, the Morelos steamed past El Faro lighthouse hill into Mazatlán's harbor and ran fast onto a rocky shoal easily within rifle range from the top of Manzanillo Point, the peak of the towering mass of rocks of Isla de las Piedras, "Stone Island."

It was May of 1914. Mazatlán city had been under siege by the

Constitutionalists for a full nine months. Every citizen who could had abandoned the city. The water supply had been cut early so that troops and remaining citizens alike had to rely on water from cisterns and wells to survive. The gunboats had kept a supply line from the sea open enough so that the Federalists holding Mazatlán could hold off the rebels. A fierce gun battle between the sailors on the stranded Morelos and the Rebel riflemen raged until the cannons fell silent. What sailors left alive on the Morelos floated little boats and escaped leaving their dead behind.

Obregón's plane, the Sonora, that had bombed the Guerrero now flew down on the helpless Morelos dropping bombs. Federalist gunfire hit the plane and it crashed down on Stone Island. But the Rebels set the gunboat on fire and the bridge and foremast became a pillar of flames that set off the ammunition leaving the Morelos, once the pride of the Mexican navy, a blackened hulk on the shining waters of Mazatlán harbor.

Distraught but ever hopeful, the beautiful Maria Elena Suárez who had inspired Malpica watched and listened to the boom of cannons, the words of the rebels and the beating of her own heart. Her handsome lover had promised that with the help of his rebel crew, he could sail the Tampico to triumph over the General Guerrero and sink the Morelos. She believed and believed and refused to accept Malpica's probable failure. They had promised one another that they would meet in Mazatlán after the city was liberated from federal control. She would keep her promise.

Although Abimiel and the rest of the crew of the Tampico was comprised of mutinous sailors and workmen snatched off the docks to serve aboard the Tampico, they all worked feverishly, for they had come to love their Captain who now served the great General Obregón and the cause of the Constitutionalists. The Rebels shored up the hull, using chunks of wood from chair rungs to plug hundreds of holes in the boiler plumbing. The generator had been ruined by saltwater while the ship sat submerged and no electric power existed on board. The guns were now more dangerous to the crew than the enemy, and the boat's main engines were rusty and coated with grime.

Malpica decided to chance a desperate run to Altata north up the Sinaloa coast for an extensive overhaul. Thirty miles from the safety of Topolobampo the boiler burned out. With no way to fix the ship, it was at the mercy of the sea.

Fight or die. Captain Hilario Rodríguez Malpica

The destroyer USS Preble, an American warship came alongside. Malpica begged the Admiral in charge to tow his ship to port. Officers came on board and viewed the deplorable conditions of the Tampico. They were horrified. Three cows wandered aimlessly on board the Tampico, trampling over hay and spent ammunition. Captain Malpica presided over a crew fighting for their lives as well as freedom for México. The Americans reported what they saw. They reasoned, requested and begged American Headquarters to aid the stricken vessel but were forbidden to intercede.

"What will you do," asked the American Admiral, "if the Guerrero finds you adrift and helpless?"

Captain Malpica, bandaged from being shot, drew himself up tall and proud and said, "I'll fight her and sink her if she will only come within range of my guns." At his insistence, the two commanders shared a drink and agreed to meet again for a cocktail Malpica promised to make. As the American ship steamed away, her Admiral feared it would never happen. In a vision, he saw Malpica drinking the cocktail prepared by the angel of death.

The next day the General Guerrero steamed into sight and Tampico hoisted a huge ensign of the National Navy to the gaff. The two boats would be fighting each other under the same colors. The Tampico fought bravely, her ammunition damaged by sea water, her guns loosely secured by broken bolts and waterlogged wood. The Americans cheered her every shot, aching to intercede. The Guerrero missed again and again, until it didn't. A shrapnel shell struck the Tampico between the smoke stack and the forward bridge and she burst into flames. There was no water pressure to put out fires. A piece of metal wrapped itself around one sailor who tried to flee the ship and the Captain bid him stay and fight or die. He died. Cannon fire rained down on the boat again and again for the enemy had found the range.

The Rebels abandoned ship and raced their two lifeboats toward shoal waters. But within a half hour, the Guerrero caught the boatloads of men and let down ladders commanding them to come aboard. Abimiel climbed the ladder onto the big ship but looked back to see his Captain Malpica stand tall in the boat, his head high unable to accept the dishonor of having failed his mission to vanquish the Federal Navy and unable to fail the woman he loved. Abi and the crew called out to the Captain who, at just 24 years old, stood before them unrelenting in defeat. He pulled out his revolver, put the barrel into his mouth and pulled the trigger.

The Federal gunboat immediately half-masted her colors and the American vessels followed suit. Like a black cloud, sadness fell over the ships for most of the sailors on the gunboat had served with the hero from Veracruz. His body was taken to Mazatlán aboard the General Guerrero.

The Captain of the Guerrero ordered a table to be cut up to make a casket. Abimiel measured and cut the wood to fit his beloved Captain. When it was fashioned and lined with black plastic, Abi wanted to seize a moment of fun. Lighten the mood. Indeed, the men had been drinking the liquor onboard to ease the pain of so many dead, so much destruction, and especially the death of their hero Malpica. With all the crew watching, Abimiel raised his drink to his dead Captain in a salute. "My General My Commander. I want to lie down where you will be for all eternity so you will remember me." He laughed a bitter laugh and climbed into the casket laying out flat like Malpica and the casket closed over him. Everyone laughed some more. It is like that when everything dear is lost. People do laugh.

But when the cover was raised, the laughing stopped. Abimiel lay motionless and white, stricken with madness. The look in his eyes caused the sailors to shrink away from him. He shook his head trying to re-enter the world of the living. Finally, he climbed out of the casket, fingered the wood with reverence and helped place Malpica into it.

The General Guerrero steamed alongside Olas Altas into the harbor past the blackened forecastle of the Morelos protruding from the water like a silent monument to the sea battles of the Revolution and the valiant odyssey of Hilario Maplica. The hulk would remain there for three years, then like a ghost, the Morelos would rise to serve another master.

Federalists fleeing Mazatlan Aug 9, 1914 from a
hastily constructed pier on Olas Altas

The men aboard the gunship Guerrero under Federalist command collected monies to buy a plot in Mazatlán's graveyard for perpetuity and a plan was made to smuggle Malpica's body through Mazatlán still in the grip of the Federalists. In the dark of the darkest night, all the Tampico seamen who had survived carried their dead Commander ashore knowing that in order to avoid being shot, they must melt into the countryside held by the Rebels. Somehow, they succeeded and at the exact moment Malpica was lowered into the grave, a volley of gunfire was heard from the hills surrounding Mazatlán. The Rebels under General Juan Carrasco were fighting to win back the city just as Malpica had hoped to do. It was a fitting tribute to the cause of freedom and to Malpica who fought so valiantly.

Abimiel watched the Federalists flee for their lives as the rebels took back the city.

Though his heart ached for his Captain and the Rebel cause, Abimiel never fought another naval battle, but read the news of triumph. Headlines screamed of Pancho Villa's raids through Northern Mexico into America and on to México City. News came of the explosive revolt from the south led by Zapata from Oaxaca. General Obregón, appointed Minister of War, had shrewdly chosen to serve under Venestiano Carranza who became President of México. Obregón was wily and wise. He defeated Villa in the battle of Ceylaya and both Villa and Zapata were assassinated by Carranza who feared their power, while the most ambitious General Obregón became the President of México in 1920 after he broke with Carranza, and it was arranged that Venestiano Carranza would die. The great heroes killed each other. Abimiel wondered with all of México how the revolution would end and who would be the last man standing.

In time, Abi's skill as a carpintera won him a job in the Belmar. He took a room there, and because of the passion of his stories, it became known as the Captain's Quarters to honor Malpica. Abi often visited the grave of his Captain, and then one day as he approached the grave sight he caught his breath. There kneeling before him was the beautiful Maria Elena Suárez, come to meet her beloved in Mazatlán. Abimiel lost his mind the moment he lay in the coffin of his Captain ; his heart was broken by the grief of the brown eyed beauty Malpica had hoped to marry.

The spirit of Abimiel held in memory the life and death of the heroes of the Mexican Revolution, too big, too passionate to be contained. When he lived, he felt too much for his mind to fathom. He is the ghost who haunts the Captain's Quarters.

I thought Abi's story would tie in to what I was learning of others who had lived in the Belmar. Lived or died in the Belmar! And so I continued my research into the bloodbath called the Mexican Revolution. Who indeed would be the last man standing?

The revolution played out in a complicated manner full of ironies and icons during Abimiel's lifetiime. In 1920, General Obregón seemed safely in power, and a relatively stable government was at hand. In Mazatlán, Lewis Bradbury began building the Belmar, where, in 1922, Abelardo L. Rodríguez, sometimes called a puppet of General Calles, took up residence. He had come to rule Southern Sinaloa, living with his beautiful American wife in the new hotel. Within 90 days of her arrival, she committed suicide. Very soon after her death, the angel of Mazatlán, Juan Carrasco, ever faithful to Carranza, challenged Obregón's right to rule and was hunted down and killed.

In his first term as President of México, Alvaro Obregón empowered the unions, dismantled the church, reformed education and won the recognition of the United States for his new government. The USA joined with Obregón's Mexico to write a treaty concerning oil. This prompted a battle and the United States took Obregón's side and sent in 17 planes to bomb the opposition. Backed by Abelardo, Obregón won the Presidency of México again in 1928.

But before he could start this second term, José de León Toral shot him in the back of the head. Toral was himself executed by a firing squad after a trial that involved Madre Conchita, a Capuchin nun, rumored the mastermind of the assassination. Now the way was open for Obregón's fellow Sonoran, the General and former President Plutarco Elías Calles to become the de facto President of México for a period called Maximato. There were three Presidents during that time. Abelardo Luhan Rodríguez, once stationed in the Hotel Belmar, was the last one ruling from 1932-1934. He commissioned a beautiful monument to Alvaro Obregón in the very center of México City.

ABIMIEL

PANTEON Nº 2

UNVEILING LEGENDS

Mazatlán wears a coat of fog but the sun is breaking through warming the winter afternoon. I think it is like an unveiling. As I walk out onto the Malecón toward the Belmar, I play with the word "unveiling" and how it relates to the ghosts of the Belmar. As the fog lifts I am aware of tables on the sidewalk and people strolling by. Real alive folks enjoying the sun. Among them I spy my friend Wesley.

"Wesley, I need to talk to you."

"Well sit right down then and have at it."

He is sitting at his favorite table in front of the Belmar, sipping a beer, smoking the biggest cigar I have ever seen and reading a war novel about ships at sea. Holding court, too, as people pass by acknowledging him and sometimes touching his shoulder or sitting down for a visit. Today, his visitor is me. He has on his favorite cap embroidered with the name of a US Navy aircraft carrier, the USS Lexington, surrounded in golden oak leaves that symbolize the strong wood used in the wooden ships.

Wesley Holady, Navy man

"Your ship?"

"Yep, she is a museum now in Corpus Christi, Texas. I cried like a baby when I visited her. She was called the Blue Ghost by the Japanese. Tokyo Rose kept reporting she was sunk, and then — blue out of the blue— she comes sailing. She was the fifth ship bearing the name Lexington after the battle that kicked off the Revolutionary War. The fourth one was lost in the battle of the Coral Sea. They were built in the same shipyard twenty years apart."

He reaches into his duffle bag and pulls out a little blue book that looks like it has been to war and back, faded and worn with use. I read Salt-water Sonnets by Dan Mack on the cover. He says he brought it for me to read, and hands it over. It opens somewhere in the middle to the last stanzas of a sonnet about two marines who had gone together to heaven but couldn't stop fighting. Finally, in unison, they told Saint Peter:

We're sorry we've disturbed you
But we didn't know before,
That your rules and regulations
Wouldn't let us fight no more.

Please take your harp and halo
Let us go to other scenes,
For heaven surely is no place
For two old ex-marines.

"So Wesley. Do you think things like ships or maybe buildings like the Belmar here are alive sort of? Like they have souls?"

"Look on page 121," he says, and then he turns his gaze out to the ocean as I read, this time to myself, about an old sailor finding a ship he had served on.

The sides of which were rusty,
And whose decks were rotted through,
Her rigging bent and twisted
And her rail was broken too.

His eyes grew dim and misty
As he gazed upon the boat
He cried "Old pal, I've found you"
Then a lump came in his throat.

I look up at Wesley but feel he wants me to read on, like my question about the Belmar being alive might be answered by the poem, so I do:

To me you were a mother,
And a home and friend in one—
When tired I've often slumbered
On your breast just like a son.

"Take it home and read it. You will find most everything you are asking me in that book, or in that hotel behind us."

"Thanks Wesley, I will." I look inside the cover for the copyright date and see it was in 1930. "I'll take good care of it and get it back to you." I finger the cobalt blue fabric cover that is frayed to white in places.

"You must have read it a lot, huh?"

He smiles and puffs on his cigar and doesn't answer, so I change the subject to what I came about.

"I guess you have been talking to Cynthia. She says you thought she should stay in that room she's in. Since she's been there, strange things have happened. I'm worried about her. You know, her state of mind."

"Strange? Yeah, she tells me. Well, I have a friend, Michael Deane, who I see every week. He started to write about the Belmar years ago. He put me in his book, too, as 'the man in the panama hat.' We went up to the desk to get someone to let us into a room he heard was haunted, and Alicia at front desk says—now listen up—she says, 'Can't let you in.' My friend says 'Why not?' Says she in Spanish, El fantasma tiene la llave. I knew enough words to translate to Michael. She said ' The ghost has the key.' We just looked at each other. What a great name for a book.'"

"A great name for a book," I echo. "For sure."

Silence and more puffs of smoke.

"So, what do you think about the nurse who lived in that room then. Is she a ghost do you think?"

"Damn straight she is. You're talkin' about the Coat Nurse, famous all over Old Town. Doctors and nurses who worked the night shift at the Civil Hospital tell stories about their colleague working miracles at their side. So reserved and disciplined was she, her uniform as impeccable as her soul, that they held her up to honor like the saint she was. How many patients survived because of her dedication to them? The kind of passion to serve, selflessness, duty, devotion, whatever you call it, she had it, but it left her without family to die alone in that very hospital.

"Or did she now? For still today, in the operating rooms of our hospitals here, when things go bad in the rush to save a life, there comes this nurse working alongside the doctors. Quiet. Expert. Breathing life into the patient. And only after the rush of it is done and the medics are comparing notes, only then do they realize she's been there. It's her strange dress that tells them who she is. And some night you might be lucky enough to see her hustling along the streets, her coat floating out behind her, heading out to care for some poor devil."

I came for some kind of acknowledgement that maybe my friend Cynthia was over her head, under stress, or even "nuts" like she intimated, but here is another believer.

"Now Lori, you aren't a Doubting Thomas are ya? If ya are, let Cynthia know and she will get ya up ta snuff. Or me. I'm Irish ya know and we have a saying: 'An old broom knows the dirty corners best.' So, let me bring it home for ya.

"You know Niko, the Belmar bell-boy who's been there over 50 years? He tells a story about being at the front desk when a man comes down to check out. He says to Niko 'Many thanks for sending the nurse. The golden gates were half ways open but she got to me in time. Good on ya man. How'd ya know to send her? Strange get-up though. Looked kind of old fashioned, but sure as god made little green apples she saved my life.' And then Nicholas nods and smiles through the shivers up and down inside because he knows it's the Coat Nurse who came and she was not sent by anyone in the hotel.

"Your Cynthia got the best room in the hotel. She got it cus she knows. Yup, she knows." Reverence veiled in cigar smoke drifts over Wesley and me as he raises his beer to his lips.

"The Coat Nurse, huh," I say doubtfully. "Any chance you know her name when she was alive and living there?"

"I've got a historian friend who might know for sure. He's told me she had the de la Peña name, and they called her Lety I think. Her story goes all the way back to the early 1900s when Simona Bradbury already owned the beginnings of the Belmar. You know Lori, you really should meet Joaquín Hernández. He could help you so much. And he probably will. I'll ask him. He thinks we all should know about what happened here in the Belmar and all around it, and before they put the first brick into it. And he will know the story of the spirit Coat Nurse who was just a child when the Black Death came a visitin' to Old Mazatlán. And who knows what else. The seeking of one thing will find another. Leave it to me."

I say *adios* to Wesley and notice how bright the day is, unveiled by the sun. People like Jorge Puente and Wesley Holady have given me direction, shedding light on the writing of my book. And now, Wesley thinks his historian friend Joaquín might help me too. What could spirit life tell me about the history of the Belmar? According to Wesley, the ghost has the key! What secrets lie hidden behind locked doors?

14

THE COAT NURSE

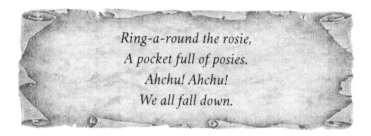

Ring-a-round the rosie,
A pocket full of posies.
Ahchu! Ahchu!
We all fall down.

I READ THE EXPLANATION OF THE VERSE ABOUT THE BUBONIC PLAGUE IN Wikipedia: The "rosie" is the rash and the "pocket full of posies" refers to the herbs used as medicinal protection. Sneezing and coughing happens before death which often comes within hours. In the end, "we all fall down." The line "Ashes! Ashes" in another verse of this little rhyme game refers to cremation of the bodies. Full body costumes and masks were designed to protect the doctors. These had giant beaks to contain the flowers whose scent was meant to filter out the spread of the Black Death, the Bubonic Plague. I find the image of the plague doctor horrifying. But so was the disease which killed 60 percent of Europe's population, or approximately 50 million people, in the 14th century.

The Plague Doctor

The locket left at Cynthia's room begs an explanation. Who was the nurse who lived in that room? What connection to the Black Death could she have? The plague doctors wore a mask that was symbolized on the locket left to Cynthia—the raven with the long beak. It was time to turn to history books to read what I could about the plague in México.

At the turn of the century, the trade of opium flourished between San Francisco and México's western ports. Beginning on October 13, 1902, Mazatlán's 20,000 people, a high proportion of which were Chinese, lived a surreal nightmare beginning when the ship Cacoa out of San Francisco unloaded riches from Chinatown as well as one feverish Chilean crew member who walked the town spewing crazy talk. The very sick man was taken to the Civil Hospital where he quickly died of something strange. There were no antibiotics. There was no cure save the grace of God.

The city named for the deer had terrible sanitary conditions. The population was steeped in superstition, the killing fields of the Revolution had sapped the emotional and financial resources to deal with an epidemic. It was the perfect stage for fear and pestilence to play out a tragedy.

At first, secrecy ruled and in the cause of commerce the busiest ports in western México and the United States stifled news that could cripple trade. But the truth was undeniable. People fell over in the streets, healthy in the morning, dropped dead by nightfall, their bodies swollen with black fluid filled buboes. Rainwater sat stagnant filled with garbage in large marshes next to the sea; fat rats scurried around and about. Toilets in peripheral areas were a dangerous source of infection. Panic set in like the Black Death itself and 15,000 people raced for the hills. At first they checked into quarantine stations before they were allowed to leave but the numbers were overwhelming. What to do?

Horrified, John Bradbury, the brother of Lewis Jr. who in 1902 had assumed controlling interest in the nearby mines, set up a $1000 fund. He then challenged the people of the United States to step up and join him with money and expertise, reminding them of the generosity of México to places like Galveston, Texas in the face of their hurricane disaster. Money was donated. Strong measures were taken to help the too-close –for-comfort neighboring nation. Because, well, what if San Francisco was infected? They could lose the whole West Coast.

As the danger was recognized, American harbors were closed to Mexican ships. Borders were enforced. The countries of Europe enjoyed the buffer zone of the Atlantic and they were stunned that such a thing as the plague still existed. It was a disease of the dark ages when Europe lost over sixty percent of its population. Doctors worldwide searched their records and modern medical science for answers. The response was epic. Back in Mazatlán blame was everywhere. 'It had to come out of the Far East. China. The bloody finger of opium use! Yes. God's retribution.' In the end, those left in Mazatlán closed their circle and grimly faced down the enemy within.

At first, it was thought that a special kind of malaria was killing people. The Governor of Sinaloa came to stay in Mazatlán for the duration of the epidemic, arriving December 20, 1902 to set up an autocratic government capable of drastic action, sometimes at gunpoint, using the military and creating a brand new Board of Charity. On December 24, the plague was diagnosed and medicine and the special Besredka serum were immediately ordered from Paris. These arrived toward the end of February,

1903. Indeed, spectacular order scarcely with a parallel in history ensued. Since the citizenry (what was left of them) refused to be vaccinated believing that the vaccination would cause the disease, brave leading citizens displayed splendid courage and were vaccinated in the Public Square, among them the local priest and Dr. Carvajal. Using phosphorus paste, fruit and tallow poisoned with arsenic and strychnine, troops killed the rats, incinerated the fleas, burned the garbage and drained stagnant waters.

The citizens left in Mazatlán were either brave, ignorant or too poor to flee. For those living in cardboard and tin houses, the dread of sudden death was added to the horrors of want and starvation. For practical purposes, all were imprisoned in the city. An isolation hospital, called a lazaretto, was hastily erected on an island in the harbor; all victims of the disease were hurried there. One report listed 20 people collected off the streets and 19 dead by the time they reached the island. The police were directed to search the houses of the poorer classes daily to prevent the possibility of concealment. The city was smothered with disinfectants.

Consoling thoughts were grim at best. The plague offered the shortest cut to another world available as patients passed away quickly. Then too, the bubonic plague promised economy as the expense of funerals and monuments was circumvented. And there was convenience as the Civil Hospital was only two blocks from a grave yard, a short walk for those who could. As soon as the victim stopped kicking, even while the bubonic swellings moved with micro biotic life, the dead were jammed into special shrouds and interred. Where? Well, the digging was constant and there were no monuments so location of the loved one was a matter of conjecture. Hence, survivors were spared grave site visits.

Doctor Martiniano Carvajal demanded extreme measures. All local doctors were vaccinated in a group to settle the fears of the population. Any house that could not be perfectly disinfected was burned. Rigorous cleaning for each person and each house was mandated. Along with strict isolation of the sick, those tending them were also to be isolated. All the landfills were burned, all drain pipes disinfected, bodies were buried in a sheet soaked in bio chloride of mercury then placed in a deep ditch between two layers of quicklime. In addition, the port was closed and people going in and out of the city stayed in strict quarantine for ten days. By April of 1903, hundreds of houses had been burned and everyone had been vaccinated. After that, deaths from the bubonic plague declined. It took three years but there was success due to efforts that once seemed impossible. All was documented in the Doctor's book called The Plague in Sinaloa.

The plague killed without discretion but there were those left behind not knowing how or why they still lived. The streets of Mazatlán became the home of many orphaned children. They lived in alleys like feral cats with no parents to love and care for them. Romanita de la Peña was 25 when she began to collect these children. When she was six, Romanita had suffered the loss of her own mother and she felt a special empathy for displaced children. At 15, she had joined the Ladies of the City Committee comprised of Mazatlán's influential and elite women. They went on to establish and construct St. Vincent's Hospital where the poor people of the city were given free health care. Later this hospital would become Father Hogar's Home For Boys. In 1903, several servant girls working for the de la Peña family died suddenly of unknown cause and Romanita took their children as her own to raise, giving them her bed.

Lety was six years old when she found herself living on the streets, her parents dead, her home burned, lost with no one searching for her. By now child survivors were regarded with suspicion as carriers of the plague that was ravaging the city. Hungry and desperate, Lety was at the mercy of fate. Lady Fate smiled on her when Romanita de la Peña, on a walk with her new children at her side, saw Lety begging and took her home. That year Romanita married Carlos Careaga and the couple had eight children of their own.

Romanita de la Peña and the Orfanatorio Mazatlán

Lety learned compassion from Romanita and as she grew she learned selfless devotion to service. They worked raising funds to pay for a new orphanage, and kept their focus even though money was needed during the Revolution. Indeed, when the law, the soldiers and a General demanded the money for war, Romanita said a respectful but firm "No." Because of her passion and the strength of her focus, wealthy businessmen contributed money, Architect Balthazar Inzunza oversaw the construction and even the workers gave their labor, until finally Orfanatorio Mazatlán was built on the street named after the man who had given land to the ladies, Germán Evers.

By now Romanita was a certified normal school teacher and Lety was a trained nurse. They were friends of the Bradburys who had created the fund for Mexican relief when the plague was first recognized. Lewis Bradbury Jr. assumed control of the mine property from his mother and built second floor guest rooms above mine offices on the property Simona had purchased. Lety expressed her gratefulness by looking after Lewis and those who stayed with him on business. He expanded the Tajo Mine offices on the street of gold into the Hotel Belmar, and she took a room in the wing above where she lived while working in city hospitals.

I had the history written down, safely contained in the past. But past, present and future seemed to blur in the Hotel Belmar. I know that Cynthia wants answers, but I am beginning to want some too. She is living in a room hinting at paranormal activity. Why her? Why now? What is the full meaning of her being able to see the 'other side?' I think there are some things Cynthia has not told me. "When the time is right," she says. "Hmph."

Our friend Wesley admits to knowing ghosts first hand. Really Wesley? The ghosts have the key? He must be kidding. I am looking for a voice of reason. No more myths and fairy tales. Wesley did point me in the direction of a Mexican man who is an historian and perhaps knows more about the Coat Nurse and facts to explain the Woman in White about whom I have serious questions. I see the way the stories are connecting around the Belmar Hotel, like it is a sort of portal. So much is unanswered... and I intend to find out.

COAT NURSE

CLASSMATES

15

JUAN CARRASCO

Of chivalry, revelry, honor we sing;
of loving, and warring, his legend takes wing.
Outflanking confronters. Out foxing his hunters
Playing music to dance life away — on
his fleet-footed dappled grey.

I WAS AT A LOSS AND CONSIDERED WESLEY'S SUGGESTION THAT I LOOK UP
Joaquín López Hernández. Another friend, who knew Señor Hernández
well, told me to make contact on Face-
book. Facebook for goodness sake! I
found him. He calls himself "the history
detective." Perfect. Miraculously, he mes-
saged a reply. "Let's meet tomorrow!"

When I first meet Joaquín, I immediately know he has been sent for me,
or on some level, I have called him into
my life to help me research the Belmar.
It is like a door opened to me and I felt
drawn in, just as I had that first time I
entered the old Hotel Belmar. It is as if
Cynthia's father were alive again telling
us stories while we sat close as we could
to the fire, bewitched by dancing flames.
Only this master of tales is the historian
from Teacapán, a University professor

Joaquín López Hernández
before a map of Ciudad
y Puerto de Mazatlán

and the author of articles about Simona Bradbury and the origins of the Belmar published in the Viejo Mazatlán newspaper and on the internet. His stories are passion and spirit captured in words. And with his dark Spanish eyes and Mexican charm, he weaves the separate yarns I have found into a tapestry.

On the way to my various meetings, I usually walk along the beautiful street named Gral. Ángel Flores. Today, choosing a route past the family home of Romanita de la Peña, I pause at the corner of Benito Juárez and Calle Constitucíon to look at the house and reflect on the influence Romanita had on orphaned children and the Coat Nurse. Joaquín tells me later that Juan Carrasco had purchased this very house from the de la Peña family, now lovingly restored as Hacienda El Recreo. I cannot linger here for long. Joaquín will be on time and I do not want to be late, especially since we will be discussing General Carrasco.

The coffee shop Allegra is on Sixto Osuna Street several blocks inland from the side entrance to the Belmar. We meet at the door at 3:00pm and easily find a table away from people. It is not crowded here and quiet this time of day. I have my notebook to record words and my impressions. I order coffee Americano plain and black and he asks for caffe latte with un pocito de chocolate. Even the aroma is delicious.

My curiosity sets the tone as I try to figure out how he thinks of things.

"Joaquín sir, I am knee deep in ghosts over at the Belmar and wondering how you feel about that. Do you believe in ghosts?"

"My first wife was a medium and my grandfather was a shaman of the Huasteco tribe. The Mayans spoke the same language. I am an historian who studied at USC Berkeley and learned to read English understanding the essays of the Mexican writer Octavio Paz. "

"Yes," I say, not fully understanding. Joaquín smiles, reaches into his bag, and offers me a book containing the Labyrinth of Solitude by Octavio Paz, winner of a Noble Peace Prize in Literature. It must be a precious book to him for he has carefully wrapped it in plastic. I thank him, and say I will read it over the weekend. But I also read amusement in the toothy white grin he flashes, even more dazzling against sun-bronzed skin.

"What I believe is unraveling as I go back to my roots," he says.

"Oh," I say, and guess that this explanation is fuel enough for several books. But I hope Joaquín will help me zero in on what Cynthia has experienced so I continue, curious about what has not been said.

"When I read an account of the life of Abelardo Rodríguez, there was very little to learn about his wife dying in the Belmar where they had settled. Only that General Rodríguez had been seen strolling with his beautiful American wife along Olas Altas beach out front and beneath the very room where she met her death. How tragic that she should commit suicide and so soon after the marriage. And in the next sentence or maybe even the same one, I read that Juan Carrasco had been killed."

Juan Carrasco

We both sip our hot drinks. Joaquín looks away frowning and I see cognition in the grim set of his mouth. But when his eyes find me again, his sad smile tells me that the name of Juan Carrasco, like the chocolate in his coffee, adds sweetness to a bitter brew. I am encouraged. I tell him what has sparked my interest in the man.

"Since I once raised and raced Arabian horses," I explain, "I was excited to read that Carrasco was an expert horseman. They say about him, in song and story, that he danced his dappled grey horse to the 'wild melodies of the terroir.' I looked that up, and it means to 'the beat of wild abandon, wine and the earth that receives us all.' I am especially interested in him because of a ghost Nicholas describes that haunts the Belmar. This apparition has been seen dressed in the suit of a charro sometimes wearing the ammunition belts of a Rebel fighter across his chest. Could he be Juan Carrasco?"

"Yes. You describe him exactly," Joaquín says. "And what a stage to dance upon. The Belmar was Mexico's palace of glamour and love, of bloodshed, celebration and war. The hotel favored by the rich and powerful was, in 1922, the exclusive meeting place for the commanders who survived the Revolution. From your reading, you found that it was General Abelardo Rodríguez who Obregón installed in the Belmar, and you guessed that he was sent to fulfill a mission: to find and kill Juan Carrasco, the People's General."

Joaquín sums up the man as if he has known him personally and is speaking his eulogy.

"Juan, Mazatlán's native son, was a major figure of the Revolution. A farmer, a rancher, a fighter. Intelligent, brave and honest."

The professor sits tall in his chair, remembering the way Juan commanded his forces: "If in battle he was pursued, ...Juan would choose to attack."

A breath of fragrant steam curls up from his cup like the circling of his thoughts. When he speaks again, it is to understand fully what Nicholas has told of haunting within the Belmar Hotel.

"And you are telling me the ghost of such a one as Carrasco, who in life embodied the spirit of México, this legendary warrior on horseback or in hand-to-hand combat appears in the Belmar where Abelardo once plotted his killing? Sinaloans called Juan the 'Knight of the Noble Heart' for his love of women ... Now that is something. Oh that would be such a story. Perhaps if you can write it, the telling will satisfy his spirit, although he has good reason to be an avenger. Hmmmm. I have a rare book, the only biography I am aware of, and I will share it with you. But to begin, let's start with what I have words for."

I open my notebook, pen poised for note-taking, ready to fill pages. Joaquín is animated, his voice so expressive that very soon I get lost in the story and forget to write.

Joaquín seems to enjoy the topic and begins with one of the many stories he knows about the General. This one comes from a boy who had visited the General in the hospital where the local hero of the Revolution lay broken in pieces, even one eye almost lost from its socket. What happened?

"The story behind Carrasco's injuries took place during the siege of Mazatlán when the Federal gunboat General Guerrero shelled Mazatlán just as Juan led his soldiers across the Juárez bridge. An exploding shell literally blew him off his horse and then he was dragged for thirty meters. The boy was so horrified that he told everyone he knew how terrible the injuries were. How could anyone survive such wounds?"

But Carrasco did not stay down. He returned to the cause of freedom. Mazatlán was liberated, the Federalists were driven out, killed in battle or shot by firing squads. The streets were stained with the blood of those who once slaughtered protestors or anyone who sided with the rebels. In this terrible time, Juan Carrasco dispensed mercy in a city ruled by revenge.

"Carrasco," continued Joaquín, "was nothing if not loyal. Loyal to the core. In this case his loyalty was to the Presidency of Venustiano Carranza called the First Chief of the Constitutionalists. But when Carranza could not succeed himself in office and still tried to maintain control, northern Generals urged on by Álvaro Obregón caused him to flee for his life toward Veracruz. Carranza was ambushed and died in the mountains, perhaps by his own hand. Then Obregón revealed himself as coveting the Presidency for himself. He easily won."

Joaquín explains that the iron clad authority of Álvaro Obregón did not allow questioning, but Juan Carrasco did just that. He wrote the "Manifesto to the Mexican People" that ignored General Álvaro Obregón's Presidency. He signed it June 22, 1922 at his ranch. By November he was dead. Did he realize that he was signing his own death warrant? Probably.

"You must understand," pointed out Joaquín, "that we Mexicans remember our friends. So it was with Juan who would give his life for his people, and he believed that those who give light must endure burning. Obregón was different. He tasted power and it made him thirsty for more. He became mighty like a great river that rolled over obstacles. Even his boyhood friends met their maker if they threatened his political ambitions."

In order to prepare for our meeting, I had researched Juan Carrasco. So, I have questions.

"A couple of things, Joaquín. First, I read that Juan could not read or write so how could he write or sign anything? And then, are you hinting that his friends looked out for him? I read that General Ángel Flores was Chief of the First Division of the Northwest, which included Baja California, Sinaloa, Sonora and Nayarit. Juan was killed under Flores' watch yet he had once commanded him. They fought together and shared friendship. Friends don't kill their friends. Or do they? "

Joaquín looks out the window. He seems to be considering my question and I cannot read his thoughts. The questions must be hard to answer, for he sips his chocolaty-coffee considering. But when he is ready, he puts his arms on the table leaning toward me and shares Juan's story with conviction.

"As to if Juan wrote the Manifesto himself? His father died when he was eight, and so just as he was to begin schooling in Mazatlán he was summoned to work in the lime fields. They called him El Calero, "the Lime Burner Boy," at home in the saddle, working cattle, playing the guitar and drinking like a man. He was eager to learn. As he supplied the lime burned down from stone, he listened to the news of unrest that shopkeepers and businessmen in Mazatlán

Charro and Warrior Juan Carrasco

120

shared. He mastered the language of literate men, knew well the bluster of ruffians, sang the songs of revolution and echoed the refrains of the drunks. Infused with the spirited body language of animals, he was elegant, daring, and street smart. Happy to serve. That was Juan. He was a candle in the winds of change, burning himself to share his light with his beloved México. Did he write the words of his Manifesto? In some accounts, riding alongside the General or marching among as many as 800 of his men came his 'secretary.' In any case, the words were his.

"Whole armies, as many as 1500 armed men, marched in pursuit of him, but were defeated by his knowledge of the lay of the land, his genius, and the will of man and beast to fight under his command. He was a most exceptional man, beloved by women, the hero of Mazatlán."

"Do friends kill friends?" mused Joaquín, turning back to my question. "One exception I mentioned was that of President Obregón. And since you ask, I give you the case of the brilliant General Ángel Flores who also relished power and became hungry for more. Hungry enough to eat the heart of a friend? Who knows? Some would say the intelligent thing is to turn a blind eye. To pretend you do not see certain things to save yourself. Juan Carrasco was not a pretender and power did not tempt him away from his convictions.

"General Ángel Flores is said to have been ambitious and smart, though his education, like Carrasco's, was in the school of life. His battle-field experience began under Carrasco's command but Flores won favor with Obregón, a fellow Sonoran, who called him the greatest general of the Revolution. Already in the battle to liberate Mazatlán, General Obregón had appointed Flores as Colonel and Commander of the Sixth Battalion, while Juan Carrasco of Sinaloa wore the golden eagle of the General. Carrasco knew the terrain, so used guerilla tactics and Flores, a man of the sea, bombarded the gunboats and Federalists in the port. They were both self taught and brilliant together, but Carrasco was far more popular with his troops and fellow Sinaloans. That, and the loss of an election galled Flores into withdrawing from public life, sad and depressed, to lick his wounds and plot his course upwards.

"By the time Flores opposed Carrasco for political power, the rift between them had deepened. The people had begged Juan Carrasco to run for office, and he would have won except that the First Chief President Carranza, a personal friend whom Carrasco supported, was assassinated. Then Juan withdrew, ever faithful to his friend and to the law, protesting politics that killed its best leaders. He had tasted power but it never seduced him."

Professor Joaquín picked up the story again, referring to México's historical figures by their first names, as if they were old friends of his.

"With Juan stepping aside, Ángel Flores became the governor of Sinaloa and the Commander of the Northwest Military Region. Juan, manly and honorable as he was, would not bend to pressure from Ángel. He now mistrusted the government and his Manifesto proclaimed it. Soon, high level decisions were made in Mexicali on the Baja between Obregón, General Ángel Flores and General Abelardo Rodríguez who ruled that part of México, and out of that came the assignment of Abelardo to Mazatlán. He came to kill the patriot called Juan who, out of modesty and loyalty, had turned down opportunities to advance himself. Was it revenge? Jealousy? Or perhaps just another chapter in the bloodbath called the Mexican Revolution?

"In the end, when Ángel Flores made a bold move aimed to attain the Presidency of México for himself, like Obregón thirsting, indeed hungering for supreme power, he dined on poisoned food. How ironic. He died in agony. Ah. It is said that 'Revenge is the pleasure of gods and man.' Ángel Flores died lacking money and friends.

"After the siege of Mazatlán, Culiacán was made the capital city of Sinaloa. Although no longer the capital, Mazatlán remained the heart of Sinaloa. And her native son Juan Carrasco, who answered to simply "Juan," became famous. Common folk told his story to one another through the Mexican corridos, the poetry, press and propaganda of the country. These ballads portrayed him as "Juan Without Fear." Women loved him for his colorful image, his passion, and chivalry; men for his heroism and humanity. And his tornillo horse arched her neck in pride to carry such a one, dancing to the beat of life on a razor's edge. It was said that Carrasco's body was covered with the scars of battle, but his spirit was unblemished. He became famous for his boundless joy: singing, dancing, boozing in parties that seemed never ending, while on the battlefield he enjoyed the comradelier of men who would die for him.

Illustration of Carrasco on cover of a poetry collection of Carlos McGregor Giacinti

"The ballad of Juan Carrasco begins:

'Juan Carrasco wanted freedom for his people,
and shouted to them "If I don't succeed I'll hang.

And ends :

'Fly, fly little dove and rest upon that rock.'"

"All across Sinaloa, corridos told his story in song. The body of Juan Carrasco was exhibited, flower petals and sunflowers all around, on a rough straw stretcher in his hacienda. In keeping of the tradition called velorios the people of Mazatlán arrived carrying the candles of their families. They encircled in light "Their Candle in the Wind" called simply "Juan," picturing him dancing his silver roan horse beyond the mountains of perdition. They consoled themselves with his example: "those who give light must endure burning."

"Among them was a man who, as a boy, had seen Carrasco almost destroyed in the battle to free Mazatlán. He looked upon his General again in disbelief. And the smoke, fragrant with incense, heavy with prayers, rose up around his savaged body bearing his spirit upwards. They came. They saw. El Calero was dead. Or was he?"

JUAN CARRASCO

16

EPIPHANY IN THE GARDEN

LONG AFTER THE SUN SINKS INTO THE SEA, TURNING CLOUDS GOLD, orange and red in a spectacular sky, the city is alive and kicking. Laughing, screaming, yelling, singing, the whole population of Old Town seems to parade below Cynthia's window along Sixto Osuna Street on the way to or from the beach, to or from the party. Always loud. Always street noise: the thunder of motorcycles, the squeal of tires, revving engines, backfires and fireworks punctuated by an occasional scream, and constant music. She hears whole conversations in Spanish, dogs barking, always the dogs, the sound of sirens and the offensive burps of police car wigwags that say "pull over." All of these and more, until after two in the morning when night noises begin to die down, a rooster picks up his cue and finally the coo-coo of the morning doves. But in an odd way, all of this is comforting to Cynthia who lays awake waiting.

Every night she opens her mother's Bible and reads words so familiar she knows them by heart. She likes to hold the book, it smells of her mother's roses, the pages are worn by her mother's loving touch, and now she uses the holy card of the Queen of Hope to mark her favorite passage: "Yea, though I walk through the valley of the shadow of death, I will fear no evil: for thou art with me."

Stay close. In case Roy finds me here. She holds that thought as she sets her mother's Bible in the safest place she has, under her pillow, and goes to the door. The time is 3:00 in the morning and the band outside has stopped playing at last. It is a moment in between night and day to visit the dominion of the "in between."

The locket of the Coat Nurse lies on the table she has confiscated from the pile of discarded furniture in the garage. Cynthia has never worn it, but this night she will. Why? "Thou art with me," she says aloud. She opens the locket and sees her own skeleton face take on flesh and come alive in the mirror. Snapping it shut, she puts it around her neck and sets the silver clasp. The burning cross shines in the hotel lanterns.

Out the door and down the stairs into the garden thinking what it must have looked like. Simona's garden. Lori has told her about Simona Bradbury. How she originally purchased the property where the side entrance and cemented over garden is now.

Joaquín had shared a copy of the Viejo Mazatlán magazine, the issue where he wrote about Simona, the Cinderella of Rosario, the maid who married a millionaire. Whether it was what she read, was told or imagined, it comes crystal clear in the night air. Cynthia remembers the details exactly. The Poet Amado Nervo saw Simona at a New Year's Eve party given for the high society of Mazatlán called pata-salada or "salty feet." The hosts were from Rosario and had been dubbed chupadiedras or "stone-suckers" to even the score. This gala event was attended by wealthy people lavishly dressed, but it was Simona who enchanted the evening. Writing for the Correo de la Tarde under the pseudonym of Adan, the poet called her "Royally beautiful. She wore a diamond-studded star on her forehead." He wrote that seeing her awakened memories of fairies dressed like that in the beautiful illustrations of the children's books of his youth.

Cynthia sits on a bench by the old well all alone and stares across at the expanse of empty cement where once exotic bushes and trees had been. Fairies. Yes, long ago she imagined them flitting like humming birds about in the lilac and white spirea bushes in her mother's garden. She can even smell those flowers now, the lush pinnacles of lavender laced with the tiny white blooms exuding the fragrance of spring.

She is startled by the sudden presence of a woman wearing a gown of night magic. The colors periwinkle blue shimmer violet to deep purple as the heavy satin material ripples to catch light and shadow. Roses of pink to red are embroidered on green and gold vines that adorn the mantle and a ribbon of shell pink over a gossamer white border whispers around her wrists and her ankles so that the lady seems to float on a mist. Cynthia knows she is looking at Simona and panics for a moment, feeling small and unworthy but her fingers reach to touch the burning cross brooch so warm against her skin and immediately she is comforted. The lady smiles in understanding—indeed glows. All around her are flowers turned toward her as if she is their sun.

They speak in the language of knowing only diminished by words. What Cynthia learns from Simona she will remember. Indeed her life will be changed by it. No longer is she a victim of violence living in the room no one else wants. Breathing deeply, she accepts the gift Simona offers, feeling like the queen Cinderella became. In her mind, Cynthia revisits the monument to the women of Mazatlán on the Malecón entering the beach of high waves. Bare breasted, with arms flung wide to take everyone in, the bronze lady exemplifies the soul of Mazatlán's women and with Simona's visit, Cynthia fully becomes such a woman. Gone is the anger and resentment she had toward Lori. Gone is the fear she had of Roy.

The sun is turning the sky into shades of pink. Another day is dawning and for Cynthia, it is a new day.

SIMONA

WOMAN POWER AND FORGIVENESS

I AM SOMEWHAT SURPRISED WHEN CYNTHIA ASKS ME TO BRING EVERY-thing I can find about Simona Bradbury and come visit her in the Belmar. Much is written about Simona's husband Lewis L. Bradbury and about their son Lewis who built the hotel, though little is written about her. But she has Joaquín's story of Simona and I have found and printed out information from the family records and from the "Find a Grave" site on the internet.

By now Cynthia has a little desk and two chairs that are good enough to sit on. Perfect. When I spread the internet pages out, Cynthia right away picks up a page that includes a picture of Simona's Memorial show-case. Inside is a serene portrait of her and two of her dresses.

"Oh look at this. Yes, this is what Simona was wearing. And the lantern lights in the garden made that satin dress look like the Northern Lights. Remember them, Lori? Remember how we used to stay up on clear cold nights, black velvet nights they were. And the colors, how they danced across the night sky?"

"What are you saying Cynthia? Did you see this dress before?"

"I saw Simona wearing it last night in the Belmar garden. She is more beautiful than this picture shows. And all around her I saw the most gor-geous plantings. That garden must have been something to see when it was hers to tend!"

"Okay, Cynthia. And next I suppose you will be telling me you and she had a conversation."

"Yes. Well, we did. Only without words really. I never told you about my new talent I got in place of dancing. Guess I was sort of ashamed of it."

Cynthia gets up and walks to the window looking out. I see she is wearing her silver looking glass pendant and not just displaying it. Ashamed? *Shame never did much for me.* I notice she seems different. More confident. And she has lost that gaunt, hunted look. So I lean forward and nod at her when she turns around, like I am ready to hear.

"I'm all ears."

"I should start from where I left off about the kidnapping and my jump out of the car when I banged up my knees and hip that ended my dream of a career in dance. I would never dance professionally again. But also, I hit my head very hard and jarred my brain. I had all those operations that restored my face, but *voilà*, I could now see what most people can't. The ghosts of dead people. It's a mixed blessing, believe me. I wear dark glasses most of the time because my eyes are so sensitive. Oh, I guess lots of little kids see ghosts, but they get told they don't exist and pretty soon they don't see them anymore."

"And they talk to you?"

"Sometimes. Roy, the man who attacked me, blamed me for what happened to him. My testimony sent him to prison and he died there. But right away, his spirit showed up at my cabin in Colorado threatening me, saying 'You'll pay, I'll haunt you to death.' Both my parents were ailing by that time so I got out of there and went home to Wisconsin. But he followed me. It was terrible. How could I explain? The dogs knew when Roy came. They barked at nothing my parents could see. Things broke, so much went wrong. My coming home to help probably scared my poor old mom and dad to death. I never burdened them with my story. They didn't need to hear what happened to me knowing they worked so hard to give me that chance. I kept that secret. Lots of secrets.

"But my mom knew I was afraid. I have her Bible and she had a passage marked. Let me show it to you. I read it every day:"

Matthew 10:26-28

"So have no fear of them, for nothing is covered that will not be revealed, or hidden that will not be known. What I tell you in the dark, say in the light, and what you hear whispered, proclaim on the housetops. And do not fear those who kill the body but cannot kill the soul."

I read the passage aloud. The part about killing the body makes me shiver and I don't find it consoling. So I ask Cynthia about her new passion for religion.

"Since you have come, you have told Bible stories several times. I never remembered that about you when we were growing up. I guess what you have been through was such a trial. Did religion help you through it?"

"Religion? No. The Bible helped me. Like I took what had inspired my mom for myself. She read that book over and over, and you know how I love stories? Well, the Bible has them all. And on top of that it was my mother's. It sort of speaks to me like the ghosts, I guess. When I put on the locket left from the Coat Nurse, I feel her spirit of service to others. I get out of my own self. Yes. And now that I live in this room here, her room, I feel close to great women. I mean great not in money but in spirit. I think maybe it will be okay here in this old Belmar Hotel, living in the room of the nurse, in the hotel begun and inspired by a woman. For the first time I have hope. And now I want to set things straight with you too."

I look at Cynthia and see that she is holding tight to the locket around her neck as if it is giving her strength. But I don't have a locket or a ghost to talk to or a mom's Bible. I am afraid of what she will say next.

"Lori, it was my last option to get in touch with you. It should have been my first. We used to be so close but then there was what happened with Glenn. Glenn and I had been sweethearts since first grade and you knew it. But when I left for Colorado, you dated him. I couldn't believe it."

Well here it is. The Bible verse she had read comes clear for me now: *What I tell you in the dark, say in the light, and what you hear whispered, proclaim on the housetops.* Perhaps I can argue my side, but no—I will hear her out. I owe her that. She is sitting next to me now. Not standing, or pacing around me like a lion ready to pounce. She is speaking low and soft. Her glasses are off. I see her eyes.

"He wrote to me and told me. Said he was confused. But it was just too much for him and so he up and joined the army. And the rest you know. He was killed in a helicopter crash in Korea."

"Cynthia, I know. It is the thing we have never spoken of. It was not my intention to betray you. He was my friend too and we met up because we both loved you, and then, well, we began doing some fun things together. You know, skiing, listening to music, swimming at the lake. I didn't mean to betray you. In fact, I believe women should not ever do that to one another. And I am sooooo sorry. Never, ever again."

"Well Lori, I have forgiven you. There is a song that says it all and I played it over and over and even danced to it, but only now do I understand it. It's all about love. The song is *Love is a Rose.*"

"Yeah, Linda Ronstadt sang it and it was a Neil Young song. I listened to it too." I pause for a moment, remembering. The song said that like a rose, love only grows when it is on the vine. When it is claimed as "mine," like the picked rose it dies leaving behind the pain thorns can cause. Pain. Oh the pain of loss. I look at Cynthia and meet her eyes. Because I don't read blame in her expression, I dare to say:

"I thought you would want to go to the funeral."

"Nope. Too mad. Just couldn't do it. But lately Lori, I've learned a lot of lessons, I'd almost lost hope, but that shrine by the Belmar front desk is the picture of hope, *de la Esperanza de Macarena*, Our Lady of Hope! And last night was the clincher. Simona in her garden. Now there is a woman. She just made things beautiful all around her. She gave and gave and gave and didn't get caught up on keeping it all for herself. I thought you should know. And I thought we should do the research on her together. You know. Get high on the spirit of Cinderella of Rosario who built an empire. I got stuck in resentment and anger as if in the red mud of Lake Superior land. But that was then, this is now. I don't know where this book of yours is heading, but I'm ready to add in my talent to make it a best seller. Everyone should know what women power can do."

I look at Cynthia through tears in my eyes. She reminds me of someone I once knew and loved —the Cynthia of long ago when she was a girl pumping higher and higher on her swing until she could see Lake Superior and beyond. She is back.

CINDERELLA OF ROSARIO

Cynthia and I pour over our research on the lady in the garden, Simona Martínez Bradbury, the heiress to a mining empire. She was born in Rosario, Sinaloa, in 1846 of what was described as "humble parentage." Joaquín had done research of birth documents and theorized she might well be descended from black slaves who came to México. The Spaniards kept slaves and brought them with them into New Spain, as they called México. One leg of the American Underground Railroad ended in México where slavery had already been abolished for a third of a century. Two of México's Presidents were of black heritage.

José Maria Morelos, a Roman Catholic Priest, perhaps the most brilliant strategist of the battles for Independence México fought against Spain, abolished slavery in 1810. After he was captured by Spain and executed for treason, his black first lieutenant by the name of Vincente Guerrero continued the fight and abolished slavery all across México in 1829. The State of Morelia is named for Morelos whose picture is on the fifty peso note.

I had already researched the Federal gunships of the Mexican Navy christened the Morelos and the General Guerrero which had both shelled Mazatlán. The exploding shell from the General Guerrero had blown Juan Carrasco off his horse as he led his army to free Mazatlán from Federalist rule, and the Morelos was sunk on a reef by Stone Island for years. I could not believe how all these stories came together through the spirit life of the Belmar.

And now, Simona Bradbury was about to add another chapter. One that begins with her as Cinderella in a storybook romance and ends "happily ever after" as she takes her place as one of Mazatlán's legendary women.

Her story begins with the discovery of silver in Rosario.

> Legend has it that a certain herdsman was searching for one of his cows and nightfall found him on Loma de Santiago, where he built a roaring fire to warm himself. It was the morning of August 4, 1655, when he scattered the ashes and—lo and behold—molten silver lay underneath.

Was it a stroke of luck or God's gift to the city that sprang from this discovery? To answer, the grateful city chose its name to be Rosario for the rosary left by the herdsman to mark the spot where silver from *Mina del Tajo* bubbled up from the mother lode. *Tajo* is Spanish for "a slash." And slash they did. Over 230 years of mining, 43 miles of tunnels were carved under the town built on that site. When an especially rich vein of silver was mined away, the church built above it began to sink. It was disassembled and rebuilt on solid ground.

The Bradbury family, along with American folk hero Paul Bunyan, was from the area of Maine prospering from lumber. They had descended from English and Welsh families many of whom held the ideas of Free Masonry popular with American leaders like George Washington, Abraham Lincoln and in México, Benito Juárez. The idea was to embrace God as a free thinker. Lewis L. Bradbury's father died when he was only four years old, but his mother later remarried into the Smith Family and came to reside nearby in California. She lived over 84 years. Lewis came from wealth, brought it with him and worshipped in the church of Capitalism.

Already a millionaire in his 30s, Lewis L. Bradbury left Oakland, California for México in 1862 and began to acquire *barras* or "shares" in the mines. He bought them from the English consul with the surname of Kelly. Lewis was comfortable in the company of the merchants of

Mazatlán like Melcher, Claussen Lejarza, Felton Paredes, and Norris Coppel, for they all dealt with his partner Thomas Bell, the owner of the San Francisco Bank.

It seems the affluent free thinker who settled in Rosario had the Midas touch. But then, when he hired a maid named Simona Martínez, Lewis discovered a treasure more precious than silver and gold. Like the warmth of the Sinaloan sun can melt glacial ice, the golden skinned maiden disarmed the man from the righteous land of his Puritan fathers.

Love, like that legendary fire warming the night on Rosario's mountain, began to rage within him. It was not just her supple delicious curves or the grace with which she moved; not only her wildly curling hair tumbling fragrant across her shoulders, black as the dark of her eyes; surely it was not only that she sensed his every need. So much more than her service to him, it was the exuberant joy with which she worked, her vivacious loving ways, deep humility, and the devout spirituality he had somehow missed.

Simona: a stroke of luck or God's gift? She was everything he longed for. Lewis Leonard Bradbury 45, single still and without an heir, took 21 year old Simona Martínez as his bride in January of 1867. In October, just nine months later the first of six children was born.

By 1873, Lewis L. Bradbury held a controlling interest in the Mines de Tajo. Four years later, he wrote in his journal that he could feel revolution coming and in 1876 Porfirio Díaz seized control of the government and ruled it for 35 years. Early on, the policies of President Díaz favored foreign investment. But México was increasingly concerned about foreign control of resources and Lewis L. Bradbury worried that the mines would be nationalized. In 1879 he transferred the

Simona Bradbury

majority of shares in the mine to his wife, a Mexican national, for security reasons.

Lewis L. Bradbury died in 1892 and Simona presided over the family businesses for the next ten years before her death in 1902. President Díaz signed mining claims between 1897 and 1909 and with Simona's death, the control of the properties passed to Lewis Bradbury Jr. The business, incorporated as Bradbury Estates Company, purchased parcels of the Copala mines in 1927-1928. Litigation was filed by family members

Portrait of Simona

involving mine management and ownership. Lewis Bradbury Jr. died in 1948 and the business was dissolved in 1965.

Simona. Along with birthing six children over 14 years, Simona assumed control of property in México in 1879. At that time the Bradbury estate was valued at $2.2 million. In 1880, the Lewis Leonard Bradbury family built a mansion on their Duarte Ranch which covered 2750 acres. Already invested in railroads and with plans to lay tracks to forests of the Sierra Madre, they were represented by Judge John Bicknell, the same person who represented the interests of railway magnate Leland Stanford.

Quick to learn high finance, Simona gained fame with California's high society. Indeed, even the press termed the parties held by the Bradbury Family as simply the best. Simona was glorified as the "vivacious daughter of a leading Spanish family in Mazatlán" by the *Los Angeles Times* which also characterized her as a "Sterling and Able Business Woman," noting the development of both her understanding of the English language and her amazing grasp of business practices.

Conceived as an office building around an atrium of light and wrought iron, the enormous Bradbury Building at 32rd and Broadway is a National Historical Landmark, a Los Angeles tourist attraction and a prime set location for various TV shows, music videos, literature and movies. It is featured in many movies including *Blade Runner, 500 Days of Summer, Chinatown,* and *The Artist.* LL. Bradbury never lived to see it finished.

The style is a testament to his vision, the skill of architect Wyman, unknown at the time, and of Simona's love of the art form called architectural design. She oversaw the final construction and went on to commission the construction of the Tajo Building in Old Los Angeles.

How did Rosario's Cinderella learn Mexican baroque and classic form? Two years before he died, Bradbury sent his talented wife and all six children on a luxurious first class tour of Europe. Simona went to the Vatican and met the Pope, then traveled on to Florence to enjoy world-class art and to order sculptures of Italian marble.

But long before that, Simona was a student of Méxican design. New Spain was inspired by European design, enlivened by the Aztec civilization of the great Mexican Valley. Early on, she learned art of form and space in Rosario. Founded in 1655, Rosario was for 250 years the most important mining town in Northwestern México and one of the richest. The stunning church Our Lady of Rosario was built during the years 1731—1759 in

Golden Altar of Nuestra Señora del Rosario
Church in Rosario, Sinaloa, México

an elaborate Baroque style, and the fantastically intricate carved altar was gilded in pure gold. Simona's love of art and architecture began the first time she looked at the golden baroque altar of Nuestra Señora del Rosario in her own home town.

Mazatlán's streets had different names in the 1800s. There was no Playa Sur and the Customs House was located on Arsenal Street, presently named Venustiana Carranza, right in front of where shipments came in through the natural harbor to the little pier. Simona had acquired plots and structures in Mazatlán. She had become a Catholic in 1890 and her altruism deepened as she became more devout. She donated a house and property to the city to make a road called Ancla which provided a direct route from Olas Altas to the Customs House in 1885. Simona sold a residence in 1891 on the corner of Arsenal and Ancla (now DR Gonzalez Street) to the operators of a commercial warehouse just in front of what is today the Museum of Art.

By 1900, Simona was the administrator of an estate valued at 100 million dollars. She had become one of the richest and most influential women in California. In control and on a roll. Her next acquisition, two years after her husband died, was a construction next to the Muralla Sports Club on Sixto Osuna Street in October of 1894. The seller was Carlos Woolrich, Vice Consul of Great Britain. This property was to become the Belmar entrance into her gardens, a grand entrance today, bearing the Bradbury coat of arms. Alongside the 14 foot high ebony doors is another door, the first much smaller door that led to the offices of the Mina del Tajo on the ground floor.

The Belmar was a labyrinth to me, and I was groping my way through it. In terms of my Catholic upbringing, it was a seven story mountain. Certainly the ghosts were like the masks the Mexican people wear to tell the world who they are. I was literally finding masks of the conquerors and the conquered, masks of healers and killers, of chaos, violence and fiesta.

México favors the mask of motherhood. Many practices were adapted or forced upon the Mexican people, but the pre-Columbian culture spawned the Goddess traditions that are the roots of México's veneration of women. She is, of course, the focus of romance but also of beauty, mercy, culture, grace and spirit. No other country reveres the Holy Mother as much as México does! Our Lady of Guadalupe appears in shrines all over México, even on my street in Mazatlán. With Simona, I found the lover unmasked. Out of her came life. Behind any mask she chose to wear— that of a wife, a business woman, executrix, artist, or mother —there was Simona as Cynthia had described her the night she appeared in her garden, "glowing like the sun."

Octavio Paz, Mexican author and Nobel Prize winner, wrote eloquently of what it means to be a Mexican woman. Should she aspire to be an object of man's desire, perhaps to be owned and cast aside? Or maybe the spirit of the earth, receptive and fertile? The womb of creation? Inspiration? What?

In the end, Simona found her identity in devotion. How fitting that the patroness of the Hotel Belmar is *la Esperanza de Macarena de Sevilla*— Our Lady of Hope. Simona's six children made her dream come true of building a church to honor the Holy Mother, donating the land and paying all the costs of construction for the Church of the Immaculate Conception in Monrovia, California. In this way Simona was able to tell her story of love. Immaculate conception means "full of grace from the first moment." That is how I think of Simona.

19

TO CATCH A MOONBEAM
IN A BOTTLE

IT IS A NOTION, NOT A PLAN THAT BRINGS ME TO THE BELMAR TODAY. I will pop in and surprise Cynthia with a little gift I found in the local *bazaar*. But as I approach the front desk Nicholas comes down the stairs. He gives me a smile that would cheer a cloudy day and I forget all about Cynthia.

"*Hola, Loritita, mi amiga,*" he croons. "Where you go? I take you."

"Why *hola* back, my amigo Nicholas. You are looking *muy bueno*, very handsome today. You know, *wampo.*"

"*Guapo? Si. Gracias. Hoy es mi cumpleaños.*"

"Cump-lee-anos? Ah yes, your birthday. You're working on your birthday?"

"Working? No Señorita Loritita. I bellboy *para mi amigos. Es mi casa.* No work."

Like as if I'd planned it, I give him the gift meant for Cynthia with a flourish. I justify the switch with the thought that, after all, she has that gorgeous locket and has made close friends out of everyone I know, and besides that *she* can see ghosts and *I never have seen a single one.*

Nicholas takes the gift to the front desk with the excitement of a little boy at Christmas, saying *tengo setenta años.* I ask him to write that out, and it seems it is 70 years that he has. He says "*comienzo*" which I can recognize as "commence to work when he had 20 *años.*" Even without paper and pen, I can do the math. The dark eyed beauty at the front desk

THE LITTLE GIRLS

shrieks with delight and produces scissors to cut open the wrapper. Alicia appears from a door-way to a side office along a staircase to the mezzanine to see what the excitement is about and translates the message on the little plaque. It is an Irish Blessing on green glass to hang in a window that says in an Irish font: *May your home always be too small to hold all your friends.*

We all agree Nicholas has made many friends at the Belmar over 50 years. Alicia will be retiring next month after 25 years. I make a mental note to get a 'little something' retirement gift for her.

In a playful mood, I tease Nicholas about his *muchos amigos* that even include the Belmar ghosts, and he readily agrees. He says they come up around him while he is working in some dark corridor of the hotel. He feels them and shows me his arm indicting the hair standing up, and then he says to the ghosts in Spanish, "Oh, it is just you, my friends."

Alicia, joining in to the fun, laments that she has never seen a ghost but both her and Nicholas point at the lovely expressive girl behind the desk. The young lady immediately begins waving her arms and speaking with wide-eyed passion. Alicia translates that "one night she opened the door behind the desk." I have never noticed this door before as it completely blends in with the wood panels there. The girl swings it open, showing how she entered and I see another staircase, one I didn't know exists. She shows how she started up and then ran screaming back and slammed the door and locked it. She put her hands over her heart acting out the scare. She starts to explain.

"*La niña...*"

Both Nicholas and Alicia indicate the size of this child phantom and Niko says, "*Tiene nueve años.*"

"Yes, nine or ten years," Alicia says, and the check-in lady who has disclosed the sighting throws herself into the chair behind her desk, her hands over her head like she is protecting herself from an attack. I gather from her animated Spanish that the child was on the stairway motioning her up.

"*Sube! Sube!*" Aiheee!"

"I remember the night that family on the second floor checked out," Alicia says. "That same *niña* say 'come' to their ten year old. She invite her to play in ocean tunnel." And Niko also remembers, nodding, rolling his lips tight like it was not a happy time.

So that secret passageway exits, I think. Wow. I am all caught up in this and blurt out:

"Well, two little girls drowned here in the old pool, didn't they? I guess the hotel doesn't like to admit anyone died there. I thought that was why they redid the pool."

Everyone nods "yes," like they understand everything I have just said, rolling their eyes at each other.

Instantly, a question slips out of my mouth.

"I wonder how many people have died in that old Belmar pool?"

They all talk in Spanish at once and don't even try to translate for me. It is like I am not even here, but I can gather the numbers adding up.

"There was the man at the bottom of the pool one morning," Nicholas puts his hands down to floor level, his eyes and mouth scrunched in horror, and the one he found floating, his hand waves like water, and, and... Alicia is gesturing at rooms upstairs and I just don't want to know. Seeing my dismay, Nicholas starts telling about all the ones he himself has rescued. Oh my.

Alicia and Nicholas at the
Belmar Front Desk

Alicia and the girl at admissions become very excited, their voices rising, Spanish words tumbling about faster and louder as they urge Nicholas to tell what happened one night when both he and Alicia were not there. That night they had been scheduled to be on duty but called in sick and others were found to take the night shift. Alicia shows me where the safe used to stand behind the desk.

"Robbers came with a knife," she says, demonstrating the deadly strike that killed the man standing in for Niko. She puts both her hands against his arms in a kind of embrace, squeezing him with her hands, distraught, eyes closed.

"You would be dead too," she sighs and everyone moans his name.

Whew. We have just relived 50 years of angst. I think the mood is lifting as the hotel staff resumes their professionalism. I have forgotten why I came, excuse myself with an appreciative pat on Nicholas's arm, glad he is upright to see 70, and with a *muchas gracias* to the staff, I take my leave. Clearly this hotel is a place of drama.

As I walk out alongside the dark library toward the sunlight shining on the sidewalk at the end of the corridor, I relive the experience I had when I was wondering if there really were ghosts in the Belmar Hotel. I made arrangements to tour through the hotel with a Medium who was visiting from Canada this season. Vibrational Energy expert, Debbie A. Anderson, said she would be happy to do a 'walk about' the Belmar on her visit. It was such an opportunity for me, and she did not disappoint. Debbie went on to describe the crowds of people coming and going in the Grand Belmar Hotel, walking through walls that were erected in later times, and the lush gardens, the ballrooms with people swaying to the big band music, the busy corridor coming in through a heavily protected passageway to the giant vaults, tennis courts and even a secret escape way to the ocean. I walked along taking notes and seeing not one thing she described. I envied her the ability to see ghosts. And, I envy Cynthia though I know it was tragedy that brought her that ability.

When I reach the sidewalk, I turn and look back like I was able to see into another century—like I am looking back through the gigantic old wooden doors through a portal to another time, another space, another reality.

In order to fully view the Belmar, I cross to the other side of the street.

Distance gives perspective, senses give me information. Sure enough, I see the size, shape and color, have experienced the sounds and smells of the hotel and think that the construction is mud bricks mixed with straw and dung, cement and iron plastered and tiled over, enhanced with artistic expression. But there is more to the Belmar than the structure before me. I am finding that the circumstances of México, the aspirations of foreigners, layers of philosophy, and masks of the people have shaped the hotel with meaning. It is a combination of ideas from the Americas, European and Eastern civilizations. No wonder after a hundred years, people explore these corridors hoping to catch the energies of thought, labor, violence and love.

Could those very energies manifest as ghosts? It is like catching moonbeams in a bottle, only I can't see them. Cynthia can! I want to glimpse something lasting, meaningful and beyond this world!

I decide it is time to enhance my view of the hotel, so I ask Joaquín to teach me. After all, like the Mexican writer Octavio Paz, Joaquín left México to look back and see it better.

In previous conversations, Joaquín had shared that he sold a lucrative business, left himself no safety net, and traveled to San Francisco to study the philosophy of language under Werner Erhard and later under Fernando Flores. He knew he could learn history, but could he learn a way to express thoughts and creeds. How to catch a moonbeam in a bottle!

Today he tells me this book has come along so he can infuse it with what he has learned. History. Philosophy. Spirit. So I ask him:

"Joaquín, help me understand. I want to write down the philosophies of México in this book. I want to tell the Belmar story. But I am American, a foreigner. Give me your vision of this old hotel, the whats, the whys and the wherefores."

And so he begins.

"México has philosophy that was generated from within: the roots of the indigenous people all the way back to pre-Columbian culture when the woman was the Goddess. Remember that even today, México is eighty percent indigenous. Today we still have this veneration of women, more then any other nation, as a mother and of course as the focus of romance. Of beauty, mercy, culture, grace and spirit.

"But today we know that what defines mankind is not race. In fact, we think the idea of race itself is a myth. It is culture that tells the identity of a nation. Because the indigenous peoples recorded their history in images and conquering forces burned these records thinking they were of the devil, we have a problem of identity. This has happened all across recorded time as one culture copied and erased what came before it. The Aztecs did that to the Toltecs. Language carries ideas forward. Languages change and the ideas are lost in translation. But people carry everything that has gone before them inside somehow.

"We are a superstitious people. We believe in the sacred and kept ceremonies around old beliefs just calling them with new names. Here in México, there have been brutal assaults on what we think of as sacred, an attempt to turn this country into a place of atheism and socialism. But not so fast. For there is this philosophy that life is a kind of death and death is the dream we realize. There is this 'other side' which will not be denied. We believe in miracles, angels, and flowers. Do you know why you bring flowers to a wake?"

"No," I reply. "You described the *velorios* ceremony where burning candles surround a body at the wake. But the flowers?"

"The flowers are the symbols of our wounds. We love our wounds."

I nod in agreement having seen so many front page newspaper images of dead people lying in pools of blood.

"Okay," he continues, "and it is said that the flowers are the clothing of our resurrection. Petals from the golden flowers show the way back for the departed on the Day of the Dead. Think about the huge coronas they construct at the flower market. Go and look at these crowns for the head of the dead person, the place of the brain. But the mind? Where is the mind?"

Now I sit and think. I realize this last look at the beloved departed covered in a sweet smelling halo is a promise of glory that trumps memories of suffering. And his question of where the mind is hints at immortality.

"So Lori, I want us to go to the graveyard and there among the memorials, I will tell you more of the way Mexicans think of life and death. We'll arrange that for later.

"There are many Méxicos," Joaquín continues. "Many philosophies of México were not generated but acquired. They came with the people from other lands. The riches of Mazatlán's mines drew peoples of Spain, France, Germany, the United States, China and Japan, all bringing their traditions and cultures. This hotel contains a little of all of them. And of primary importance was the philosophy of the Freemasons that spread throughout the Western World. Think of it! Man can directly relate to God as he mastered levels of morality and education! The promise of freedom from oppression for all peoples. And here in México, freedom was honey for the starving."

"I read that in Nahuatl culture, the term *macho* means 'the enlightened one' and had nothing to do with being male or female, but how did it evolve into the word *machismo*? The Belmar displays two large posters near the bar. One is of the bullfighter, the other of a female Flamenco dancer. Did gender stereotypes come with the Spanish?" I ask.

"How interesting that the words are similar but the meanings are so different," Joaquín replies. "In Peru, *Machu* means ancient. In Spanish, the word means 'manly.' Again, the language carries the meaning. The culture and the original meaning were lost in translation. Fighting the bulls goes all the way back in time to Mesopotamia where the bull was sacred. Today it is still practiced in Spain and Portugal and even in México. It is a dance of sacrifice and death. It was thought of as an art form and the word 'Machismo' is portrayed by a good matador. The two pictures you mention are perfect for the Belmar where acts of passion and desire transpired over a hundred years."

I had done considerable research on the foreign influences on México that affected the building and success of the Belmar Hotel on the world stage and found some surprising facts. Together with information from Joaquín, I wrote down many of the ideas of foreign nations. México embraced some, rejected some, and thus formed its culture.

The French influence on Mexican culture began when the French occupied México pretending to collect debts incurred in Mexican wars. But the Civil War in the United States and wars in México against the French were really all the same war. It was supposed to be about slavery but in México it was more about French ambitions. France under Napoleon hoped that Jefferson Davis's Dixieland, eleven slave states in the South of the USA, would join with Northern México to be another country under France. In order to facilitate this grand plan, the indenture system was instituted in Northern México, a sort of reversal on slavery to be in sync with slavery in America. But Benito Juárez sided with Lincoln, a fellow Mason, and it didn't happen.

Cinco De Mayo celebrates the 1862 battle when out-numbered and poorly equipped Mexican fighters defeated the French in the Battle of Puebla, but the French sent more soldiers. After the Civil War ended in America, the USA assisted México with arms and sent 50,000 troops to the border as a warning. The French troops withdrew in disgrace and México under Benito Juárez tasted victory.

But the romanticism of France lingered in México. French baroque architecture and later Art Deco became popular, both ideas present in the Belmar. Fine French cuisine was featured. The *bolillo,* French bread, became the bread used for *tortas. Pan dulce,* sweet breads became Mexican breakfast treats. Also, the music used at weddings under the term '*Mariachi*' was adopted.

American influence was invited by President Díaz who came into power and ruled México for seven terms until 1911 when thoughts of Revolution began to boil. His philosophy was a kind of survival of the fittest that was called Positivism, a Capitalist leaning that encouraged foreign investment. He signed papers declaring the mines that built the Belmar were legally in the hands of Simona and her children even though they had been purchased by Lewis Bradbury, a foreigner. America and México came together under the law.

The Germans began their considerable influence in the country when México was again offered the spoils of world domination, this time by the Germans as they fought World War I. The Mexican gunboat Morelos, sunk on Stone Island during the Revolution, was refloated and refurbished in Mazatlán Harbor. She was to be a supply ship for submarines of Germany bent on world domination. México was offered Texas as her reward if she would only help Germany win the war. The Casa Melchers warehouse for Melchers Sucesores, known all around the world, was right next door to the Belmar. Most of their buildings still stand. Look around Mazatlán's Old Town and you still see the German homes and stores. And Mazatlán with its fabulous port, gold and silver, and its German population that all but ruled the city, was ripe for harvest! México did not take up the offer.

Today's local industries such as cheese making and beer brewing have been heavily influenced by the Germans. Popular beer brands such as Negra Modelo and Dos Equis Ambar derived from the dark lagers brought to México by the brew masters of Vienna.

Germanic music caught on due to the large numbers of German people in the 1930s. German accordions were marketed and German music styles developed under different names: *tejano, conjunto, Tex-Mex, quebradita, banda, ranchera,* and *norteño.* Music in Sinaloa had for centuries been dominated by the tambora drum which was a large drum covered in animal hide that made a loud bass sound. Coupled with the new Germanic sound, the music

Tambora-Sinaloense was born. Such bands often played in the Belmar.

The iron rule of Obregón cooled the Revolution in México. He was a self-educated man, but he had studied in the United States, and he brought in José Vasconcelos, a Mexican philosopher who changed education in México. Music and art flourished, the walls were opened to mural painters and in Mazatlán the rich decor of the Belmar reflected the pride of Sinaloa's old families in their grandest hotel. A playground. A showpiece.

"Eat Drink and Be Merry for Tomorrow You Die" is a cliché taken from Bible verses. It seemed appropriate at times of war and prohibition in America. Party time! Even today Cerveza Pacífico is México's gift to the brewing of beer. But in 1921, American prohibition caused U.S. breweries to shut down. What an opportunity to augment the Diaz de Lion Brewery, the other brewery competing in Mazatlán. Immediately, the Melcher Group geared-up to supply the thirst of Mazatlán, Mexico, America and the world, by buying an entire brewery in Milwaukee, Wisconsin, dismantling it and shipping it to México piece by piece, adding lager beer to the Pacífico Line. Let the good times roll! México, Canada and the United States all working together to make Mazatlán a destination. And along came the Belmar, just in time.

In the early 1930s, Mexico's Genaro Estrada whose family lived in Mazatlán on the street named for him, wrote a doctrine that changed México's standing in the world. His doctrine stated that México would not judge the governments of other lands. México claimed neutrality recognizing principles of self-determination and non-intervention that are considered essential for mutual respect and cooperation amongst nations.

Modern art and culture began to take hold in México City in the early 1900s. México City with its palaces was famous the world over. In 1912 at the Palace of Fine Arts of México City Tiffany created a landscape of the Valley of México from a million fine crystals. People traveled from other countries to see this crystal curtain and the works of Rivera, Siqueiros, Alfaro, Orozco, O'Gorman and Tamayo on the walls of the Palace. Yes, México City was filled with fabulous art, folk music, new music and the operas. The Italian operas were beautiful for the sound of their language and the melodies of longing.

"And we know longing. We love passion," declared Joaquín on the subject of opera.

During those halcyon days, Mazatlán on the Pacific Ocean was a place to vacation with the same sort of emphasis on the arts plus the drama only the ocean can bring as it crashes and sparkles. Here the sunsets were unmatchable, the moon above the restless sea reflected intuition and mystery. Famous poets and writers, philosophers, and artists came here.

Mexican opera star Angela Peralta sang her last song in Mazatlán. She was never recorded but it has been said by those who followed the voices in song of all the great divas, that she was matchless. The best. The sweetest.

And the stars of Hollywood and Mexican movies checked into the Belmar as well. Why? To taste the elegance of the Belmar, designed by the son of an American multimillionaire and his Mexican wife. They built it and the world came to luxuriate, to savor and enjoy the spirit of México.

"Ah, yes, Simona Bradbury," I agree, "one of the ghosts in the Belmar that Cynthia was so excited about. And the other ghosts? They exist as spirits but why are they here still in the Belmar? And why can't I see them?"

"Ah Lori, my impatient American friend," chides Joaquín. "Tell me. Did you read the *Labyrinth of Solitude* by Octavio Paz?"

"It says so much," is all I can muster, but a term from the books has stayed with me. "The masks. The masks of México are...."

Joaquín interjects. "Like the ghosts. Each one showing something to the world. Each one with unfinished business. And you? Perhaps as you work through putting your book together, as you tell their stories, you will be able to look behind the masks. Writing a book is a kind of solitude isn't it?"

"Yes. All the arts require alone time to consider choices. It's like finding a way through a labyrinth. Kind of like life. Going forward by looking back."

20

THE ASSASSINATION OF THE GOVERNOR OF SINALOA IN THE BELMAR

WE ARE MEETING IN THE BELMAR ITSELF. NICHOLAS HAS JUST SHOWED ME the bullet holes, hidden beneath a picture, from the bodyguards shooting at the assassins of Governor Loaiza. We pass the giant posters of bull-fighting and flamenco dancing and take our seats in a quiet corner of the famous Belmar Bar. There is a party of revelers near the window. They are talking busily, leaving us to enjoy our privacy. We order drinks. I have my notebook, but set it aside early on as taking notes interferes with enjoying Joaquín's stories. He begins.

"Before I tell you about The Gypsy in the Belmar, I made a mark so I would remember to tell you some horse stories. I know you love horses. You told me you used to raise Arabian horses, no?"

"Yes," I say meekly, realizing he listens to my babbling.

"*Lista?*" he asks. "Okay. Here are two stories and then we will talk about The Gypsy.

"My first story is about the horses we have here. I suppose you have noticed some of our horses have Arabian blood? The French brought them to ride in battle. In one instance, a Mexican peasant mounted on his rough pony tried to retreat. The battle was lost and he didn't want to die, but behind him and closing fast was a French officer on his magnificent pearly white Arabian stallion and he saw the sword extended out ready to cut through him. What could he do? No use to run, his horse had no "go" left but he had a great "stop," so precisely at the moment of impact he pulled him to the side and up short. The Frenchman careened by, the peasant leveled his gun and, well, he came home with the stallion, the sire of so many beautiful horses we have today. See them in parades, their great dark eyes and little black noses, dappled grey or white and prancing under silver saddles, wavy manes to their knees and tails flying high as a flag. All chutzpah, power and pride."

I have tears in my eyes thinking of my Arabian horses from long ago and the way the world looks from the back of such a one—the little tipped ears tuned to catch anything moving that would be an excuse to run. Like riding a thunderbolt.

Joaquín pulls my attention back.

"And now my other horse story. True also, about two drunk Mexicans riding horses on Olas Altas beach and into the Belmar."

"Into the Belmar?" I murmur. In my mind I hear the sound of horse-shoes on marble and smell horseflesh entering the world of perfume and flowers.

"They rode right into the Belmar through the big fancy entrance doors past the great glass windows of the dining room, the mirror, wrought iron and stained glass where all those rocking chairs are now. Nonchalant like trail-riding, clip-clopping past the grand ebony reception desk and the tiled shrine to the Queen of Seville, and then into the luxurious ballroom Patio Andaluz and right here into the bar past the *touristas* and clients.

"Those with glamor and class were stunned. The bar-flies grabbed up their drinks and made for cover. The drunks, they whirled their horses around and laughed and spurred them up so that they kicked out and reared, and chairs fell over as the customers dodged the hooves.

"Ahhh. The horses were so good, better than the drunks. They showed the whites of their eyes, but they kept their heads down, so nervous they whipped foam from the silver bits all around the bottles on the back bar. The glasses spun and tipped but the bartender threw his arms around them so nothing broke before the onslaught. But when his arms came out, the horses tossed their heads, ears back, snorting like he was the enemy, and he ducked and hid. The drunks ordered drinks. 'Ya,' they yelled. 'Ya,' called the patrons. And the bartender came out scared, but fired up too, and poured them faster and faster.

"Oh the mood was crazy fun. They threw some pesos at the bartender. *Bravo. Caramba*! People were singing, getting in a good rowdy mood and clapping, so the horses arched their necks, so proud they were, and sidestepped all the way out, the great glass chandeliers jiggling above like diamonds in the wind and echoes of iron shod hooves tap dancing staccato all up and down the shining Belmar corridors while the people cheered. Singing loudly, the horsemen rode onto the street in front of the Belmar, and then they traveled the road to the infamous Honolulu Bar near the inner harbor spreading bar to bar merriment."

" What a scene." I am breathless. Joaquín is quiet as a cat playing with a mouse, so satisfied with himself for spinning such a great story. I seize the moment to share that I have ridden horses weekly for years from the Hacienda Las Moras around and about the tequila factory north of Mazatlán, climbing zigzag trails into the mountains of purple and yellow flowering trees, higher and higher until a vast hill and dale kingdom with no end in sight is spread out below, all of it covered by powder blue agave plants.

Joaquín describes the production of mescal to the north of Mazatlán, south of the town of La Noria and near El Quelite, and I am already familiar with where the blue agave grows. I also know, having read factory literature, that fifth generation Osunas are restoring their family's business with permission from the President of México to produce and distribute their product under a name other than tequila.

Joaquín begins another story, saying I will soon see the connection to the assassination of the Sinaloa Governor. Nothing seems simple in México, everything intertwined like a web.

"In 1864," Joaquín says, "three Osuna brothers emigrated from Spain and began commercial growing of agave, opening the Vinata Los Osuna and tequila factories that by World War II rivaled the factories of the neighboring State of Jalisco. A prominent member of the family, Justo

Tirado Osuna, a rich and widely respected man, held the prestigious title of the *"Cacique."* At that time land owners had a system in place, a kind of government from ages past. Hacienda owners of northern Sinaloa grouped themselves around the leadership of a *Cacique.* Such a leader was very powerful.

"Justo Tirado's son, Alphonso Tirado Osuna, called "Poncho," became Mayor of Mazatlán, beating out a member of the ruling PRI Party. This so enraged the Governor of Sinaloa he sent an army of 320 men to confiscate and seize the Osuna properties. But Justo hired a forty man mountain militia and the battle was on, with the militia sustaining only six deaths while the defeated Army Cavalry lost 206 men. Think about that for a moment. Can you imagine such a victory as that?"

I do try to imagine it but really can't. He continues.

"Alphonso Tirado ruled as Mayor of Mazatlán for two years. He never took a salary and was extremely popular. So his fans turned out in droves to urge him to run for Governor when he left office to run the family's tequila business.

"But in 1938, at the Morelos Hotel in the capital city of Culiacán, a gunman assassinated Alphonso. The State Police Chief who killed him claimed he did it over a barroom fight. The chief got a light sentence. Most people believed it was part of a plan by Alphonso's political opponents.

"Alphonso's father went to the President of México, Lázaro Cárdenas who had the support of the PRI. The *Cacique,* Alphonso's father and leader of the people, was not heard. Six years passed and with a transition to the Presidency of Manuel Avila Camacho, México along with the USA entered World War II.

"Fast forward to 1944 in the Andaluz Ballroom of the Belmar. Sinaloa's Governor Rodolfo Loaiza, who was believed to have ordered the killing of Alphonso Tirado, was shot and killed. This same Governor had pocketed the money sent to turn a blind eye while the poppy harvest was on, and then had mercilessly persecuted The Gypsy and gangs that protected the fields. So, who was to blame?"

I look blankly at Joaquín and sip my margarita. He smiles and holds his drink up so the light shines through the golden, icy brew.

"In any case, there was retribution. In 1949 it was decreed that tequila from only a few selected regions, primarily in the State of Jalisco, could meet the Standards of Tequila Classifications and most of the Vinatas in Sinaloa closed, including the Vinata Los Osuna."

I pull myself together remembering we came to talk about The Gypsy. I can now understand several reasons the Governor might be a target.

"Okay, Joaquín. I bet you can describe the whole thing. Right? What happened that evening?"

"There are many versions of what happened that night," he explains. "The problem was the confusion of the crowd. The dancers were all in costume. By the way, that is not allowed anymore at indoor Carnival events.

"So, we have The Gypsy with the body of a football player, dressed in a brightly colored shirt with flaps at the wrists and neck like the Huichole Indians wore. Cowboy pants, holstered guns, high boots, baggy and unbuttoned shirt across his massive chest. His heavy black mustache and dark curly hair so thick he had it pushed back with a rolled bandana under his sombrero. And he watched, just steps away, as the Governor socialized in the patio of the Andaluz. Waiting for a time when the Governor's bodyguards were not attentive, and he had been assured that moment would come.

"The Governor was having a great time, even singing his favorite song 'El Quelite,' laughing and chatting with politicians, journalists, landowners. And the band was playing. The beautiful Lucila Medrano had been crowned Carnival's Queen of the Floral Games and of course the Governor was sidling to her side, his bodyguards giving him privacy to tease her, enjoying her closeness. They were laughing over the compliments he showered upon her, she being coquettish, looking at him sideways with her radiant smile.

"The band struck up an exciting song, 'Los Coyulitos,' the crescendo choruses of coyotes. The beat picked up, the clarinets sounded, and just at that moment The Gypsy threw down his sombrero. *Boom, boom, boom,* thunder split the night. Three shots, the Governor slumped, the clarinets howled, and there in the lap of the Carnival Queen lay the dead Governor of Sinaloa, his blood staining her long white gloves dark red.

"Four men wearing sombreros dashed out among the costumed revelers, firing their weapons. Through the screaming crowd they ran out toward a car gunning its engine. The door guard heard the screams, the gunfire, the crowd charging the exit as he drew and fired at the men racing past him. One of the assassins was hit. A bullet in his back. The assassins half carried and dragged their injured comrade and dove into the car, doors slammed, tires squealed. They were gone in a blaze of bullets.

"The crowd poured out onto the bloody street tearing off their masks almost tripping over the body of a boy named Ruben Brooks, an innocent passer-by. An American pilot from Tucson, out for a walk that evening, also fell dying onto cobblestones amid chaos all around. Later, when the father of the pilot was notified his son had died in a shooting, the man keeled over with a fatal heart attack. Another death piled tragedy on tragedy, and who was to blame?"

Joaquín pauses. The people who had crowded the window table are filing out with furtive glances out the window, sliding by quiet as mice. Joaquín finishes his drink, watching them go, and when we were all alone he continues in a low voice.

"Here is a little known fact. Mysterious hands broke into the official residence of Governor Loaiza in Culiacán while he was in Mazatlán attending the Carnival. At the very moment of assassination, they stole and ransacked his property.

"Meanwhile, The Gypsy fled in the dark of night to the graveyard in La Palma near the tequila factory where you tell me you rode horses. That was where Alphonso Tirado was buried, and now there was another dead man to put into the earth. They dug a grave next to Alphonso's and made a sign. It said in Spanish *Eres Vengado,* 'you are avenged.' History shows that The Gypsy killed not only Rodolfo Loaiza but the government, the state and civilization. He could go where he wanted and do what he pleased and not the military, civilians, peasants, cowboys, merchants, politicians, even other murderers like himself could not stop him."

I am sober and quiet. Joaquín notices but presses on.

"You are researching you say? Then find out who was to blame for this if you can. It is a matter of controversy. And let's meet soon again over at our coffee house. My challenge. Your opportunity."

THE GYPSY

21

THE QUEEN JULIANA AND WHO IS TO BLAME

"Joaquín," I greet him in the doorway of the Allegro all excited. "Wait 'til you hear the story I have researched about who killed the Governor!"

We are meeting at the coffee shop. I have my arms full of pages and pages of research from the internet and what I have written from dozens of books I am reading. I never worked this hard at University.

We get a table around the corner where it is quiet and sit down. Our table is completely covered with all my pages of research I want to show him, but I forget all about that very soon and start writing on the back of the pages so as to record what he is telling me.

"I traded one hundred of my books for two pictures of the ballroom where the Governor was killed, the banquet table all set, and the people seated around it. I am the only one who has these pictures. We need them for our book."

That takes my breath away. I look at the man. Like many Mexicans, despite big families, walking miles, bus travel, in some cases less than an ideal laundry or none at all, I see the shirt he is wearing is blindingly white. That very fact says it all. I wish I had taken more care about my appearance, but I had all those papers to bring for goodness sake. I try to organize them, shuffling them like cards, as I notice he has only a little bag with him to carry a small notebook he has carefully written notes in. Everything is in his memory.

Noticing his eyes are on the volumes of research I have brought, I get right to the point of our visit. His research assignment.

"Joaquín, I read the interrogation of The Gypsy by the courts. It's all right here. Even the mention of a General who ordered the death of the Governor."

"Ah yes, your research that blames The Gypsy. And the General was Don Pablo. Good that you found mention of the General, most stories just end with The Gypsy. Much easier to blame him.

"Yes, there was a time when all the states of México were headed by Governors who had been Generals in the army. It is fascinating, this blame game between the Generals all looking for political power after the war. I will tell you stories about who The Gypsy was and I am curious to hear who your research blames for the Governor's death. One time years ago now, we historians met in Aguacalientes and shared what we knew. There were maybe fifty of us, and one man had a whole file box full of documents. It is important to us that details are correct."

Joaquín raises an eyebrow at the tall pile of documents.

"You remember last time I asked you to remember the mountain militias hired to protect the landowners in my story about Alphonso Tirado?"

"Yes," I answered proudly, "they were called *Los Dorados* or *Los del monte* because they took refuge in the mountains where they were protected."

"And the white guards? Did you read about them too?"

"I think they were the same people called by different names," I reply feeling unsure.

Joaquín reaches up toward the ceiling.

"They were tall, well built men and these mountain giants had lighter skin than the coastal people. It was a joke among the Indians that they would come down out of the mountains and eat us. Who knows.

"Well, The Gypsy and his father and his father before him were built like football players and they were valuable as guards and workers. In Aguacalientes, the Valdez family chopped sugar cane. They were magnificent men who towered tall and strong.

"José Valdez, The Gypsy's grandfather, was especially handsome and caught the eye of an American woman who met him in nearby Concordia. In those days, Concordia was the very center of commerce in the mountain towns. The lady was Carlotta Newman whose mother lived in Mazatlán. José courted Miss Newman, and she was tempted for he promised her a life of adventure. But her mother wanted the proper young woman to live with her in Mazatlán, for she was almost blind. In those days the stage from Concordia had its first stop at Aguacalientes on its way to Mazatlán."

Joaquín reaches down and extracts a newsprint article carefully folded and wrapped in plastic. I wait, and he hands it to me.

"I have here an article from the *San Francisco Chronicle* that tells how The Gypsy's grandmother came to Aguacalientes, where it all happened."

I read the article. The title is "Delightfully Romantic." It describes four armed men stopping the stagecoach from Concordia and hauling off Miss Newman who "begged to be saved." While the driver and other passengers watched, she protested with pitiful shrieks and cries as she was being thrown over a horse and tied down. But Miss Newman recognized the big and magnificent looking man directing her kidnapping as José Valdez her rejected lover and, as the article puts it, "discerned the plot."

Half way through my silent reading, I look up, one eye scrunched shut with puzzlement. Joaquín notices and clarifies.

"In those days, in that place, a kidnapping was akin to eloping."

I read on aloud. "When the stage reached Mazatlán, the news of the kidnapping prostrated the mother. A party of *rurales* was sent to capture Valdez who was described as 'a dare devil and spendthrift who was from a fine family but had a very bad reputation.'"

"Yes. That was true enough," Joaquín agrees. "Carlotta was taken to Aguacalientes where José hid out in a secret cave until those who pursued him gave up and went home. He used that cave all his life when he needed to disappear.

"Later, a Mexican woman of Carlotta's age became her best friend. This woman, named Maria, was betrothed before the gypsies arrived.

Again, the background...When the gypsies came to town, life got interesting in Mexican towns. They camped by the river in colorful caravans and had parades through the towns with dancing bears and monkeys. The women danced in the tradition of old southern Spain."

I interrupt. I cannot help myself because I have researched this very thing and so I finish his sentence.

"...whirling to the Andalusian deeply romantic music that culminates in wild passionate whirling skirts, the men dark and flamboyant wearing baggy trousers and a silk sash, silver earrings, headscarves and tassels like the Moroccans. The women told fortunes, played with cards, and the men stole what they could, even the hearts of the local women!"

"Yes. Such a thing happened. A thing of legend, it was. Carlotta's friend Maria, already betrothed as I said, fell in love with a gypsy man who romanced her, and when her *novio* confronted her, she confessed. He pulled his pistol brandishing the weapon and told the world that 'if she would not have him, she would have no one.' He then shot her in the head, she fell in a pool of her own blood and then he shot himself in the chest, his beautiful Smith and Wesson hand tooled gun falling to the dust beside him. So tragic. So dead."

But that was not the end of Maria, according to Joaquín's story. Although her blood flowed, Maria did not die because Carlotta ran to the woman, tore cloth from her own skirt and wrapped Maria's head wound tightly. Cleverly, Carlotta tucked the gun in her waist and took Maria to the gypsy camp where medical secrets saved her life. Maria lived to wed the gypsy man of her fantasy, and Carlotta adopted a new lifestyle, one her poor mother could never have imagined in her worst nightmare.

Carlotta learned to tell fortunes, dance the wild dance, ride a horse, play cards to win, cheat, drink like a man and get thrown in jail like one, too. She became a *pistolerra*, a sharp shooter. And in the holster on her hip was a beautiful Smith and Wesson hand tooled gun. She was hooked on the feel of cold steel in her hands and fear in the eyes of anyone who faced her. She was legendary. She was blond. She was American, and she was the grandmother of *El Gitano*, The Gypsy. He took his nickname from her.

"Carlotta's grandson's full and proper name was Rodolfo Valdez Valdez which meant his parents were first cousins, a prevalent marriage tradition around the south of Sinaloa, explained Joaquín. " The Gypsy's father was Fortino Valdez of Aguacalientes. Marrying into the family was an idea to keep fortunes from being dispersed and was much more convenient, as travel was time consuming and it kept power at "home." What it did for The Gypsy is a matter to study. True enough, some of his children had blond curly hair, 'bred in' so to speak, even occurring in later generations. Perhaps a psychological probe into what inbreeding did to The Gypsy's personality or mind would be interesting, but it is not my aim."

I desperately try to bring order to displaced pages on the table between us, hoping I have them straight and inwardly feeling confused. So while I shuffle papers, Joaquín orders coffee for us both. His with chocolate, mine Americano black, both steaming hot, delicious.

Joaquín notices my dishevelment, decides a little background history of México is called for, and elaborates on the years the Gypsy was a young man living and working in the Sinaloa Sierras .

"By the 1940s, more than half of México's cultivated land was held by the *ejidos*. But not in Sinaloa. People who coveted the land came from the south, the land of Michoacán and the home of President Cárdenas. They were called *agraristas*, and under the pretext of enforcing the Agrarian Provision Act of 1934, they committed all kinds of abuses with landlords and small agricultural owners.

"You see, conditions were different in Sinaloa. There were no lands to distribute as was intended for massive and extensive agriculture, since most of them were temporarily irrigated or were in the mountains or near the sea. The land was already plotted in the south since Colonial times and in the north, the great expanses of estate land, the *latifunda*, were not productive. Landowners considered it as graft to take them under Federal Law. Violence by the *agraristas* was vigorously countered by the White Guards and armed gangs hired by the landowners.

"The landowners' way of life was profitable because of the new crops in the north: marijuana and then poppy for the opium the United States requested México to grow to deal with the wounded coming back from World War II. The USA financed a great hospital near Zaragoza Street and the Malecón to be specially constructed to deal with all the wounded. Thousands of them. It was recently taken down and a park is being built there."

"Yes. I know just where that place was. And is. I researched it when I heard about the Coat Nurse thinking it was the Old Civil hospital."

Joaquín seems undeterred and continues instead by taking that bit of research as reason to go off on another tangent.

"President Cárdenas wanted to avoid another uprising that might lead to war, like the recent Christo Rey Catholic war that had killed 100,000 people and caused five percent of México's population to flee to America. It was still costing one third of his budget. And to top it off, there was civil war in Spain. Wisely, he slowed his seizing of land and saw to it that Communism was forbidden to calm the fears of landowners.

"In the meantime the government of Spain, fearing the rebels there, sent treasury money to be sheltered, much of it coming in through Veracruz traveling to fill the great vaults of the bank in the Belmar Hotel in Mazatlán, the financial center of the Northwest created by Abelardo Rodríguez. Then, in 1940, México had a new President, Manuel Avila Camacho. And that ends my story of the politics of México, meaning it only to be background for the shootout in the Belmar."

"Before we get to who is to blame for that shooting, Joaquín, tell me please more about The Gypsy and his fight against the Governor. It seems to me he had personal reasons for killing him. Am I right?"

"Well, during that time period Mazatlán was at the center of the settling of accounts. The Town of the Deer had become the City of Massacres. To each murder of *Los del monte*, the *agraristas* hit twice as strong. The shootings were endless, night and day, in the streets, in the mountains, in the hotels, in the markets. The Gypsy hired out to Pedro Aviles, the main grower of poppy and marijuana from the Sinaloa Sierra. Doggedly pursued by Governor Loaiza, The Gypsy always managed to escape because in southern Sinaloa he was feared and admired for all his bloody confrontations with federal and state forces and he could always flee into the mountains. As a last resort, he had the cave in Aguacalientes which to this day contains items of his occupation.

"But in 1943, a year before he was killed in the Belmar, Governor Loaiza appointed Colonel Salustio Coto, called "Colotta," a ruthless torturer who specialized in killing bandits. They said Coto "loved his Smith and Wesson 38 revolver as much as his wife." The gun was unique, had gold scales covering the grip, encrusted diamonds, and on its barrel was engraved the name "Queen Juliana."

"Really Joaquín? There was a gun in your earlier story. And I believe I have heard of this gun somewhere."

"Yes, really. It is a legend and wait until you see who ends up with it.

"The Gypsy made a perverse plan to deal with Coto. From the haciendas of Concordia, he led a gang of killers mounted on horseback. They rode boldly into Mazatlán to slaughter two policemen by the light of day. The horrified Mazatlecos bolted their doors and stayed low until The Gypsy rode out of the city headed down a road he knew well. At a certain narrow and disadvantaged place, he lay in ambush for the inevitable pursuit of the arrogant Coto who was convinced he was dealing with an ignorant barbarian. When Coto and his men drove their vehicles through the narrow point of vulnerability they met a rain of bullets. So ended the torturer, two of his lieutenants and fourteen soldiers.

"All the equipment now belonged to The Gypsy and of course the gun engraved as Queen Juliana would be his. It is said that 'she (the gun) scoffed at the number of victims killed by her bullets.' The Gypsy was so impressed with the

Precious hand tooled Queen Juliana revolver

title that he had his name engraved on his bullets from then on. He was inspired and so was Governor Loaiza who, when apprised of the massacre, described the attack as 'an act of wild animals' and then, throwing down the challenge, the Governor vowed to capture and execute the murderers before concluding his term."

We sit for a moment as I think about it. I have my pen in hand to write everything down, but already forgot to do it several stories back.

"What a story, Joaquín. But they caught The Gypsy. My friend Jorge Puente said they had him in jail here in his neighborhood at the top of the hill. Remember, I have in my papers here," and I gesture at the pile of research, disheveled again, "a report hinting that a General gave him orders. General Macías who they called a Don —Don—"

"Don Pablo," Joaquín says.

"Strange about that. I think that General Macías, the Don, was the same General who relieved General Abelardo Rodríguez in Mexicali on the Baja, assuming his responsibilities so that he could come to Mazatlán with his wife who died in the Belmar. Let's see, I have it recorded in my research."

I paw through my papers, but Joaquín continues so I stop to listen.

"Yes, The Gypsy surrendered to a posse in 1947 after a three year chase. And he was sentenced to 27 years in prison. So you might think he was to blame. Right? But in your research, you say that you have the report of his interrogation, and it was rumored General Macías gave The Gypsy the order to kill Governor Loaiza. A rumor? The next sentence would have been, 'that was most certainly false.' No?"

"Why yes, how did you know?... Oh now I remember. Ha. You told me that is the way such things are written." I smile a sad smile and put down my pen. What's the use of taking notes. I have given up trying to figure out who is to blame.

But Joaquín is enjoying being a history detective.

"Go back the three years it took to catch The Gypsy and see who became the new Governor of Sinaloa replacing the dead Rodolfo Loaiza.

"General Pablo Macías Valenzuela, or Don Pablo, had sworn to return to Sinaloa, aces in hand, to be Governor of the state but before that, in the election of 1935, he had tasted Loaiza's dust. This time though he had the full support of President Camacho and his political party and was already challenging Loaiza when the assassination occurred. Three other candidates withdrew, and Macías won.

"But soon after the followers of Loaiza and the *agraristas*, as they say, 'stirred turbulent waters, deep, dark and dirty.' Macías wisely headed for México City and the protection of his friend President Camacho, even abandoning the train he was on when warned it would be stopped by a militia with orders to apprehend him. He got off in Tequila and escaped to safety by car."

As for The Gypsy? He came to trial in 1947. It was reported that "everything had been thoroughly investigated. It was a long process, but in the end the verdict was in." The motives of the crime in the Belmar and the name of the murderer were clear at last: Rodolfo "El Gitano" Valdez Valdez and his accomplices were definitely to blame.

It was now impossible to implicate Macías but perhaps a scandal would unseat him? Sinaloa had a law that the Governor must come from Sinaloa. Ah—the game of politics rocked with rumors to challenge the Governorship of General Macías, among them the question of his birth certificate. Could it be true that the border of Sonora split the very home he was born in? But Macías proved he was born in the south room, and subsequently, he was ruled a native son of Sinaloa.

Then Miguel Alemán, the Attorney who became President of the Republic in 1946, aimed another slander, this time in the biggest headlines of the National Press, stating that Don Pablo Macías Valenzuela was 'head of the drug trafficking in the northwest.'

"I am lost," I confess as I try to piece the stories together. "Confused as the crowds in the Belmar that night in the ballroom. But, as you said, it marked a watershed moment didn't it, when more than the Governor died that night. And the blame for the killing? More unclear than when you began your stories and I began my research."

"Of course you are confused and it is best that you know nothing, and remember that rumors around power are most certainly false. As I said, politics is not of interest to me. No, my story is about The Gypsy.

"Within two years, 1950 it was, it was arranged that he could escape from jail on Cerro de Vigia, Lookout Hill, located on military property where the fortified cannons towered above the ocean. Once at water level, The Gypsy hid in a cave until nightfall and then made his way up the hill looking for food. The Mazatlecos closed and bolted their doors when they heard The Gypsy was out.

"But he fled to the mountains. Road excavating machines such as power shovels, bulldozers and graders were up on the Devil's Backbone, the road to Durango. The Gypsy hid himself well among the workers in their construction sites, and soon he was back guarding the juicy business he knew best.

"It wasn't until 1959 while trafficking cocaine in Guadalajara that he was caught again. He had been watched for a long time and finally a trap was set and two Federal Agents closed in. He didn't go quietly and in the shoot out he killed one lawman but took a bullet to the eye, falling to the floor. Much like her gypsy great grandmother, his blond daughter fired Queen Juliana at the remaining agent to protect her injured father, but it was no use. They were surrounded by Federalist lawmen. This time The Gypsy was sentenced to 14 years, but he was to live under the custody of Leopoldo Sánchez Celis, the Governor of Sinaloa. The Gypsy, *El Gitano*, died in 1963 of natural causes."

Prop gun used in the movie "The Mexican"

And now the rest of the story. Governor Leopoldo Sánchez Celis had long ago lifted a young man living on the streets out of poverty and raised him to become his bodyguard. Felix, the bodyguard, was street smart and loyal and in time became the godfather of the Governor's son, Rodolfo Sánchez Duarte, who by now owned the beautiful pistol engraved with the name of Queen Juliana. Felix went on to head the Blood Alliance later known as the Sinaloa Cartel.

And the Queen Juliana? Well, legends are made into movies to entertain. Movies such as "The Mexican" about a certain famous gun. Here in México, rumors are most certainly false but stories become legends.

22

TERROR

I FIND CYNTHIA IN HER ROOM. SHE HAS IT PARTIALLY FURNISHED NOW with a refrigerator, a desk, and some equipment she has hanging on pegs in the kitchen space. She says her neighbors have given her most of it. I also have my arms full of things to give her. A table cloth I bought in Guadalajara in rainbow blocks of color, a little bedspread, better pillows, and a little fancy leaf plant. But she is mostly interested in telling me her news.

She gestures at a chair and I slide into it across the table from where she sits. The seat is polished slippery with years of use. The style is simple and plain but sturdy. When I compliment her and tell her she is the scrounging queen, Cynthia tells me some history of changes at the Belmar.

"This chair is the best one I could find. All the fancy old furniture was carted out of here in the 1960s when the Belmar was remodeled. So much changed at that time. The old swimming pool was very deep and was a diving pool and it was replaced by the pool that now takes up some of the old Andaluz Ballroom."

Her mention of the old pool jogs my memory of rumors I've heard. Bad things happening in the Belmar are very difficult to research. Such secrets are kept quiet for good reasons. I remember what my friend Clyna told me about the drowning. And she used to sneak into the Belmar to swim with the guests. She knew about the two little girls who drowned in that old pool. Definitely a bad thing to happen at the Belmar and maybe a good reason to change the depth of the water, but she told me it was an accident.

I ask Cynthia: "Have you seen these children, the ghost children I mean, the ones Nicholas says drowned in the pool?"

Cynthia has the same expression on her face Nicholas has when he speaks of the little girls' ghosts. Like naughty children, they are impressive and funny at the same time. She raises her eyebrows and nods.

"No, but I hear them. They are giggling together and lots of strange things happen like they are playing pranks. Others have seen them by the pool or even in the pool. They seem to haunt that area of the hotel. The story goes that their mother drowned them. I don't know. They play hide and seek with me but I haven't talked to them. I saw a picture of the pool with the caption 'The Phantom of the Swimming Pool.'"

"I'd like to see that. Where is it? Were the ghosts in the picture?"

"I was looking at reviews of the Belmar Hotel on the internet and there it was. Sorry, no ghosts in the picture. But I did see the Woman in White again."

This must be her news. I lean back in my chair, grounding myself for the inevitable change of mood that comes over Cynthia when she speaks of the woman. She gets up and walks around the room. I see her glance down at the Bible she keeps close to her bed. It is open with a ribbon marking the page and she carefully closes it. Then, maybe fortified to tell me more, she continues.

"Just like the last time, she was coming out of the bar with her room keys on the way up the golden stairs. Remember, last I saw her she was so sad I tried to keep her with me. I just didn't want her to go up to her room. There was no way I could stop her. But like Mary in the Gospels of Luke who kept things in her heart, she had things she hadn't expressed, things important to be told, and so before she ascended the stairs as she must, she told me something of what sent her to her death. Something of her terror."

"Really! She confided in you?"

"Yes. Well, some at least. It started out that she had such high hopes. She was a princess. She came from a close Jewish family that lived in San Diego where Abelardo often traveled on business. They met and he was enchanted with her beauty. He courted her. They danced. They dined in elegance. The wedding in February of 1922 was all crystal, satin and roses. Nothing but the best, and in México, why, there would be fiestas, pomp and circumstance. How romantic and exciting to be wed to this dashing Mexican General who held the prestigious title of Chief of Military Operations for all of Northern Baja. Why, he had made Mexicali famous single handedly. The city was jumping with excitement over the construction of Casino Caliente. Soon the world would come to gamble and imbibe the finest spirits. It would be the destination of the fabulously wealthy. And when they celebrated, how his military friends adored her. How safe and honored she was on the General's arm. And this magnificent man loved only her. Such a feeling—to have power over a powerful man like her General."

Cynthia gets up and paces around the room again. This time she gets a handkerchief and wrings it in her hands. I see her distress and almost wish she didn't tell me more. I am silent when she sits down again. She is so diminished. The emotion is so palpable I can feel the loss of a dream. Is she speaking about the woman or herself?

"But soon after, he hardly ever offered his arm," she told me. "He had no time for her. Suddenly he was reassigned to far away Mazatlán on a mission to kill an enemy of General Obregón, Juan Carrasco. Surely the news that she was pregnant would make him decline the position. But no! Oh, he was happy that she might give him a son, but the news fell flat, leaving her alone with fear of the unknown. Alone with no friends. Her husband was in meetings planning attacks, putting down wars, keeping the barbarians at bay.

"But he promised it would be better when they got to the glamorous Belmar, seat of luxury, the finest hotel in México set on the ocean at the curve of the "Bay of High Waves." So she packed trunks full of her beautiful dresses and jewelry and followed him, hopeful but afraid into the unknown.

"Once on the train, she felt safe at last and she had him to herself. They were making love one afternoon in their room when the train jerked and shuddered, the wheels churned backwards squealing, sparks smelling of burned coal and metal rose up hissing in a cloud of steam that fogged the windows. And there they were stopped. In front and on both sides were ragged horse soldiers loyal to the dead President Carranza, some of Juan Carrasco's men who Abelardo had been sent to kill.

"Her heart stopped. There were so many of them and just General Abelardo, his bodyguard and her, traveling undercover so as not to draw attention. She thought they would blame her husband for killing President Carranza and she began to cry. Abelardo turned to stone as he looked out at the soldiers. In a gruff voice, he told her he would handle the situation. 'Pull the curtains, stay down and stay quiet.' Through tears, she watched her brave husband go out alone to speak to the soldiers. 'Alone.' She kept saying that. 'Alone' She was sobbing now, feeling terror so strong it paralyzed her being, killing her dreams.

"Panic and fear closed her ears to escape so she could not hear Abelardo convincing the soldiers that the train was filled with armed soldiers and that it would be sure death to attack his train. He raised his hand in a salute to the memory of their heroic President Carranza and to México, telling the soldiers the next train would have the killer they were looking for. The soldiers returned the salute and turning their horses around, galloped away. Abelardo gave the signal for the train to start forward."

Yes, I thought. The General did have the reputation of being a professional in words and action. Cold as the scales of a snake or the steel of his gun.

Cynthia continues the story. "The couple left the train in Culiacán at the Headquarters and decision center where Abelardo was named Chief of Military Operations of Southern Sinaloa. It was June. By the time they reached Mazatlán, the Woman in White was in the throes of a miscarriage. Their little daughter was dead. Ninety days later so was she.

"And that's when she got all strange."

"What do you mean—strange?" I asked.

"She put her hand up like she was trying to protect herself. And her face. White for even a ghost and big eyed like she was looking at something coming at her. Again, I didn't want her going up to her room. But she covered her face with her sleeve and was gone.

"This time, the smell was different. No more perfume. Instead, pure terror. Like the smell that makes the hair stand up on your arms or that prickly, icy feeling up the back of your neck. I wanted to tell her. I wanted her to know I'd been scared like her. You know, so she wouldn't feel so alone. But then I realized she wouldn't be telling me these things except that she already knew what happened to me and that I had felt it too. Maybe she wants me to get over my own fear. Without me telling her, she knows about Roy."

We both sit in silence. I contemplate the despair of the feeling of "alone." And how do you deal with it when you are alone with no friends in a foreign land? I think again of Cynthia in the mountains of Colorado. She surely felt the terror the Woman in White showed her. Was she a mirror to Cynthia's feelings? There is the aloneness that we are born with and die with. But how alone must Cynthia have felt struggling to escape from Roy on that lonely mountain road? And the year it took to reconstruct her face! The disgust of those who saw her. Oh Cynthia. You told me the story, but I am only now beginning to feel it. And the terror of Roy still chasing you down. No wonder you continually watch for him. Finally, I ask:

"Do you have a sense of him following you here? With all the ghosts you have seen, no Roy. Right?"

"Well, but you're never going to believe this."

So this is it. The news she has been hinting at. And it can't be bad news. She has set down her handkerchief. Her eyes sparkle with the kind of hope I have not seen there since she arrived in México.

"Try me. I want to hear."

I am straining forward in my chair. Cynthia is animated, using her hands and body to act out what she describes. For a gal of Finnish descent to show this much excitement, it must be something very special she is about to tell me.

"I thought I saw Roy yesterday," Cynthia begins. "He was standing outside my window looking up, like Romeo come to serenade me, only his was a song of threats. He wanted to scare me to death. I froze solid—didn't breath. But along came this man swaggering up the sidewalk. I took my eyes off Roy to see him, his presence was so strong.

"He looked like he was coming to vacation in Mazatlán. Big white western hat, yacht pants, boat shoes and a light overcoat like maybe a gun was under it. I could see a belt when he pulled it to the side and his right hand is ready. There was that way about him. In Westerns I've seen it a thousand times.

"The stranger stopped and stood looking at Roy, taking his time lighting a cigarette. Watching. Watching, then he sauntered over right in front, between Roy and my window. And he was tall. So tall he towered over Roy, and he blew a cloud of smoke over the ghost of the man I have been so afraid of, so that now I no longer can see Roy. Like this stranger is disappearing Roy right back to hell where he belongs. And sure enough, the pavement beneath my window was empty when the drifter in the white Stetson turned to face the ocean, and sauntered on up the street, walking that familiar walk, and turned right along Olas Altas just like he was coming to the entrance of the hotel.

"Lori, it was" ... and we say the name together, for although I did not see the man, I know him from what Cynthia is telling me, from the movies I have seen, what I have heard, and what I have read.

"John Wayne."

23

HAUNT OF SUPERHEROS

CYNTHIA AND HER NEWS. AS I WALK THROUGH THE CONCRETE GARDEN and take the route through the cavernous storage area that was once the Las Palmas ballroom of the Belmar, I think it all seems like someone else's dream. Maybe I am jealous. Suddenly I realize I am. I haven't seen any of these ghosts except through the research I have done. Well, I started off to write this book about the Belmar and got waylaid by Cynthia and the ghosts who indeed have the key to the history of the Belmar and to Mazatlán, and to her too. The stories they tell are far more interesting then the bit of fluff I had intended to write. But how about me? I am doing all this work and for what?

The Belmar was at the center of things. Joaquín has a letter from the manager of the Belmar from 1938 to 1950 by the name of Roberto Gorostiza. He stated that all the Governors of Sinaloa had stayed within these very walls. And the Presidents of México came here too. Miguel Alemán came during his campaign and stayed here when he was the President of the Republic. The Generals. Yes, especially in the 1920s and 1930s this was the place the Generals called home including General Pablo Macías who became the Governor and Governor Loaiza brought his wife and family here. General Cárdenas, later the President of the Republic, stayed here with his family when this was the headquarters of the Pacific Military Region which included representatives from the United States. I haven't scratched the surface really with the Carnival celebrations. I remember with chagrin all the files Encarnación has sent to me from the Archives. What have I gotten into?

As I come to the mural with the old grandmother pulling the rebellious child up the hill I stop and breathe. I feel lost in the writing. But like the headstrong child, I must go where I am led. Presently, that is toward Cynthia's news. She has seen John Wayne, and he has even done her a favor and dispelled the ghost of Roy. For now? Forever? What good would it be to dwell on what may never happen when grandmother and me are almost to the top. Another breath and I wonder what the view will be like when we get there, Grandmother Belmar and me. I like this mural. It stops me from feeling sorry for myself. It keeps me climbing.

I need to know more about the movie stars that came here and it looks like I should begin with John Wayne. I decide to run this past my old friend Wesley Holady who has become a major advisor to Cynthia. He is one of many people who have watched the comings and goings of people and happenings in the Hotel Belmar, and he holds court right out front. I find him reading a book, sipping a beer and happy to talk, as usual.

"You've inspired me," he says. " I've started writing my memoirs." He opens his notebook filled line after line with handwritten reminiscences. "I've been sitting out here for forty-five years after my time on a Navy aircraft carrier."

"Well Wesley, let me 'cut to the quick.' That's an old expression. Those of us who know about horses' hooves know all about what that means, and you Navy guys probably don't. So I'll use your lingo, let's trim the sails."

"You mean cut the bullshit?"

"Yes. Have you ever heard of John Wayne's ghost? I mean has anyone seen him here in the Belmar since he died? They say he kept a room here in the hotel for at least ten years and I thought if anyone had heard that sort of news, you would have. Especially since you told me about the Coat Nurse."

Wesley has an all knowing smirk on his face and I find his expression aggravating in my present "poor me" mood. He leans back in his chair looking me over like I am an open door.

"Well, you've come to the right place. Me being Irish as well as one who enjoys his *cerveza*, now that should be good for a grand gossip of mermaids, if'n you want to know about the ladies of the sea that sing to tempt men. No? Or today would you be after a rally of hobgoblins, you know, spooks like for Halloween. No? Or is it to be a league of superheroes like John Wayne or Errol Flynn? Both of which show up now and then, back in their stomping grounds right here in the Belmar. Yes? Is that it now? And you aren't asking Cynthia? Why not?

"Well, since you think I know better than your bestest friend, I'll tell you about one fellow who sat in the very chair you're warming up, and told me he had a grand talk with the Duke. Went on and on using expressions Wayne used like, 'We're burnin' daylight!' and 'no handouts for sittin' on yer backside.' That feller didn't know whether to be upset or amazed when I told him the Duke had been dead since 1979.

"Are ya lookin' to get an interview with the big man himself, or them's that's seen him? Have you talked to Cynthia for instance? She's got the kind of grit he likes in a woman. One of my favorite quotes is from the Movie True Grit: John Wayne playin' the lawman Rooster Cogburn says of 14 year old Mattie, come alone in the winter to avenge her father's death: 'By God! She reminds me o' me!'"

The word *sisu* occurs to me. I think it over to myself and nod agreement with Wesley. He seems ready to stop his teasing about the *marvelous* Cynthia who confides in him, but in me—not so much. Ah well, He knows I want to hear about Wayne and Flynn, both dead for years and still appearing in this hotel that they favored, And I do like sitting with him. He makes me feel not so crazy. His smirk has changed to a wide smile as he thinks about John Wayne, and he puffs at his cigar like the king of the sea he is. Two puffs and he continues.

"Okay then. When you're ready, we can talk about Flynn. Are ya old enough, do ya think? Grow up fast. Get shed of rules of morality and such. He had his own. And pretty fair too. He was a bad-boy by self report. He said he had a highly checkered career. Ha. Well, his yacht was parked out front of here frequently for years and he kept a room in the Belmar too. Room number 35 I think it was. Ask Nicholas, he will remember. Later, when no one could stand to stay in it, they demolished and renumbered it.

He loved the house of delights over on Icebox Hill called the Stratosphere owned by Carlos Borba. The most elegant place in town famous for its banquets for politicians.

"Lots of stories there. Tell you what. I'll start gatherin' up tales of Flynn in his Belmar days while you chase after John Wayne. A tall order I'd say."

"Wesley, you're the best. You sure have pointed me in the right direction over and over again. But for now, if you were going to tell about John Wayne, you know, write about him here in the Belmar, how would you do that?"

"Well, I'd start with Tim who lives in the old John Wayne room. He's been collecting Wayne memorabilia for years. That room is a museum to John Wayne. And Tim is famous too. Look him up on the internet. Everyone knows Tim in the Belmar, the cab driver from Boise. Hell, he's been there nine years. You know him, don't you?

"And by the way, in all seriousness, I'm privy to why you are so excited about John Wayne right now. Cynthia told me that she has seen the Duke for herself. And you haven't I take it? Well, when yer ready. In the meantime, you can ask her what he's like. I know what yer doin'. Ya can't fool an old Navy man who can find the evening star on a cloudy night."

I ignore Wesley's dig, hoping no one else has noticed my frustration over not seeing any of the ghosts, thank him and explain that I have known Tim since he first arrived in Mazatlán. I decide to go up and see his famous room again. It keeps evolving just like him.

I cross over to the Malecón and stand gazing at the Belmar. I can see the balcony where Tim lives on the top floor in the room John Wayne kept. Maybe he is there right now looking down at me. On the other side and a floor below is the room where the Woman in White died, and further to the right facing the ocean is where Errol Flynn and his wife, Lili Damita, frolicked. I have learned so much in my research and from Joaquín, but until now, all of it is still in my head.

Suddenly, standing across the street from the Belmar, I see it in a new way. Like an epiphany, it strikes me. In the background the ocean waves crash, eternally washing away and renewing, while in front of me

Belmar Sign

is the giant Belmar façade tarnished and changed over a hundred years. I see the broken twisted pillars added to give it a Moorish look, suggesting adventure and romance, but I know the Freemasons use the image of broken pillars to show severed vision into the next life.

The physical appearance of the structure is not all there is to this hotel. Before me is a living, breathing history of México, the art and aspirations of foreigners, layers of philosophy, and the masks of the people. The building combines the ideas of the Americas and Europe. No wonder after a hundred years people explore these corridors hoping to catch the energies of thought, labor, violence and love; hoping to glimpse

something lasting, meaningful and beyond this world! The past, the present, and the future are wedded in this building, and now more than just hearing about it, I feel it. I know it for what it is.

And Tim? Yes, we are friends, but his is a personal story. A love story he has trustingly told to me. Will he allow me to share it? I would need the help of John Wayne and the power of the broken pillars and maybe even Cynthia's Bible, her locket and her holy card of the Queen of Hope. But I think the answer will be "yes."

Sue Carnes and Tim O'Brien in front of the Belmar Hotel's Room 48

24

SPIRITUS CONTRA SPIRITUM

THEY SAY THAT NO ONE DIES IF YOU REMEMBER THEM. FUNNY. THAT thought has occurred to me again and again, maybe because I have been writing about the ghosts of the Belmar Hotel, telling their stories and some history to boot. Today, I am on my way to see Tim O'Brien who lives in the John Wayne Room. Of course I want to talk to him about the Duke and see what Tim has done since last I visited him in his room. Has he acquired new memories of John Wayne to display?

Last year when I visited him, Tim was at a standstill. Isolated and depressed, he had no plans to move forward, actually no future. He even handed over to me everything that was dear to him like he didn't need anything anymore. He was diagnosed as having only days to live. But this year, still alive, he is out and about and talking to people. I hope he will tell me about what almost sunk him and what is making him want to see a tomorrow. The ghost has the key? Alicia at the front desk spoke those words when she had no way to open the door to a haunted room. As it is with all the spirits Cynthia has encountered, would it prove true yet again?

So as I trudge my way up four and a half floors in the Belmar. I remember how I had met Tim the day he arrived in Mazatlán nine years ago. He had taken a "good enough for me" room at the Belmar and strolled over to the Puerto Viejo Bar where we were socializing, hoping to see the green flash as the sun set. That night, I missed it because I was looking at Tim.

He was a slim, tall, and fit western sort of dude. With a smile that lit up bright blue eyes, a handsome face framed in lots of curly black hair,

I thought he was striking. He said his name was O'Brien. Tim O'Brien. Irish like my dad, I thought, which to me meant full of fun and tales.

Only, Tim spoke softly with care and I sensed there was something about him...not so fun. Maybe because he had endured army service in Vietnam? Endured. Or not. I remembered the Drill Sargent's motto of "what doesn't kill you makes you stronger" and wondered about Tim for I didn't think that was true of him. Was it that his military bearing was a little tarnished or was he missing something? Was it pride? What? He didn't stand as tall as his six foot frame would have allowed. He said he was a cab driver from Boise, Idaho and thinking of moving here for the winters.

A friend from Medicine Hat, Canada came to our table just then, met Tim and together we extolled the virtues of Mazatlán repeating its reputation as a happening place drenched in beer. My Canadian friend sang and played his guitar at the local Canucks Restaurant and needed someone with a camera who liked music and could help him arrange his gigs. Tim was his man. They became drinking buddies.

Tim soon heard about John Wayne staying at the Belmar and wanted his room. In fact, he wanted everything about John Wayne, aka "the Duke" and King of the Belmar. He began right then to surround himself with Wayne memorabilia.

At first Tim gave parties in the John Wayne Room that were well attended and the booze freely flowed in the suite once occupied by his hero. He collected pictures of Wayne, articles and verbal memories of the Duke in Mazatlán. He was excited to be the one to tell the story of John Wayne and bring him alive again.

But Tim had a private life that was fast becoming too private. When he first came he spoke often of his beloved friend Darby, his therapist, who had helped him over the trauma he had suffered in Vietnam. He brought Darby to Mazatlán on several occasions. She wrote a tribute to him about his John Wayne Room and his talent of taking pictures. It was well written, and Tim was proud of it. He realized how talented she was, her writing good enough to be published. How kind she had been, how gentle was her touch, how carefully she listened, how warmly she held him close as he told her of the horrors of Vietnam and the anguish of combat. And he let himself love her even though he was afraid of love. Afraid of the pain of loss, afraid to feel again the loss of someone dear.

But that is what happened. Darby was diagnosed with cancer. She was brave. She fought it alone but when she could no longer do it, Tim went to Florida and brought her home to Boise with him, and they fought it together before she died. And then he drank. Tim used alcohol to dim his pain of loss, grieving alone. Increasingly alone. Until there was only one life left for him to lose—his own.

When I went to see him last year, he was fresh back from the hospital. He had been counseled that he needed people. "Alone" was not working for him. John Wayne smiled down from heaven and sent people to see Tim's room. When I visited him, Tim was cordial as always, invited me in, and was game to show it. Every inch of wall space held pictures and memorabilia, but I was drawn to a decoupage on wood, framed and labeled with the title "Palomar." It was a spoof of the Last Supper. Marilyn Monroe sat centermost where DaVinci had painted Jesus. Her hands were out in a fetching pose, her beguiling fingers soliciting a visit. On both sides instead of the disciples were all the movie stars in Marilyn's world, many who visited Mazatlán and stayed at the Belmar. Together, we named the Hollywood Stars: Laurel and Hardy, Elvis, Clark Gable, John Wayne, Charlie Chaplain, Marilyn Monroe, James Dean, Humphry Bogart, Fred Astaire, Gregory Peck, Boris Karloff and Marlon Brando.

Renato Casaro's painting of the Last Supper with Marilyn Monroe

"As soon as I saw that, I had to have it," Tim said. "Emilia and I were eating lunch in a bar when I saw this plaque on the wall. She went back later and bought it for me and we hung it over my bed."

Emilia. A Mexican woman who became his best friend, spent time with Tim, cared about him, and reminded him that his life mattered. In the solitude of each night as he lay in his bed, Marilyn kept a vigil. Glowing golden, she shone her light upon him like a beacon bright. And his darling Darby came to him, telling him she loved him, speaking words of wisdom and pushing him to live for her. Love. Spirit. What was it that Carl Jung had written to Bill W.? Yes. The answer is *Spiritus contra spiritum.* Jung prescribed "a protective wall of human community." Spirit counters the spirits. Perhaps another way of saying the ghost has the key.

Tim asked me to find information on the meetings his counselor had prescribed. The meetings could make a difference. I said I would find out and it did not take me long to get the information. Mazatlán has gatherings of every kind, and the meetings Tim referred to were advertised in the papers, on the internet and on public displays. I wrote everything down and went back to the Belmar. But in the fourth floor lounge where I would ascend the last staircase, I had a most amazing encounter.

I had seen him outside the Belmar for years, this leprechaun of a man named Jimmy. The first year, as I passed by the hotel, he sat like he was comatose, a little man in a big chair, unmoving, while people passed him by. The next winter season, he followed me with his eyes. On the third year, he spoke to me saying things like "Where's lucky?" referring to my partner Bill.

Then last year when I returned to the Belmar with the information Tim had asked me to gather, there was Jimmy sitting like he was waiting for me, up in the fourth floor lounge. He was humming a song. I politely greeted him and he gestured to me to sit down. He explained the beer on the table next to him.

"I am a maintenance drinker. And I suppose you are here to see Tim. We are all worried about him."

"Yes, how did you know?

"We are a retirement community here in the Belmar. We look out for each other. Tim thinks he's all alone, he keeps his door closed most of the time, but we are all around him hoping he'll let us in. The trouble is we all are still fighting our own wars. Yeh, that's it. So maybe we are alone together."

"Of course. Alone together. Hmmm." I shift around uneasily in my chair. But a bright thought comes to me and I say:

"Tim lives in the John Wayne room. It's sort of a spiritual thing isn't it? I mean living with John Wayne as a roommate. True Grit. Right?"

"Oh, Tim never told me any such thing. Maybe now he thinks that way. Now since he got back from the hospital. John Wayne was a sort of war horse now wasn't he. Tim and his private war living with a war horse. Ha. Maybe now."

Then, a sly grin crossed his face.

"Here, we got it better than in this tune. Listen-up. You must know it."

We regarded each other, my eyes widening as he began to sing a Beatles song sitting like an elfin minstrel on the old Belmar couch. He watched my look of surprise, his eyes keen and shining. The song bounced around in my memory as he crooned familiar words about "Eleanor Rigby who died in the church. She was buried along with her name... And nobody came."

I thank him and move, this time determined to leave, but he sang more of the song: "Father McKenzie, brushes the dirt off his hands from the grave," and then, entering the staircase to Tim's room, the last words of the verse, "no one was saved. All the Lonely People."

Today, as I pass the fourth floor lounge and head onto this same staircase again to see Tim, I see the empty couch where Jimmy sat only a year ago. He died last spring after I left for my summer home. I heard that he grieved over his wife who had died before him, and was determined to make it across the broken pillars to the other side.

I miss him. But he left me with a conviction. The Belmar is a community one can belong to. I mean it is a dichotomy of good and evil, dazzle and decay, ruined and rich. Maybe in this place of brokenness a person might reach some kind of wholeness with a little help from a friend. And a nudge from a warhorse like the Duke. Reminding myself that late last night Cynthia saw John Wayne on his way to the hotel, I telegraph my thoughts to the Duke: *Tim needs spirit to replace the spirits he has all but drowned in.* And there ahead of me, at the end of the hall, I see the door to the John Wayne room is wide open. Like maybe Tim has decided to live, open to what a tomorrow might bring.

"Mr. Wayne, are you here?

Immediately there comes an answer, the words of John Wayne:

"Tomorrow is the most important thing in life. Comes into us at midnight very clean. It's perfect when it arrives and it puts itself in our hands. It hopes we've learned something from yesterday."

JOHN WAYNE

25

THE DUKE IS LIKE THAT

IF YOU THINK THAT ALL JOHN WAYNE DID WAS PLAY HIMSELF, YOU'D BE right. But also, you'd be wrong. In 1979, a tearful Maureen O'Hara testified before a House subcommittee of Congress pleading with them to strike a medal in his honor.

"John Wayne is not just an actor, and a very fine actor, John Wayne is the United States of America. He is a hero and there are so few of them left," she said.

On the Duke's 72nd birthday, the White House sent the medal. He himself said how he would like to be remembered—well the Mexicans have an expression, *Feo, Fuerte y formal*. Which means: ugly, strong, and dignified. He loved the poetry of Walt Whitman, a favorite passage was: *I contradict myself? Very well...I contradict myself. I am large; I contain multitudes.*

I didn't have to research Duke Wayne. I grew up with him. Harry Carey Jr., one of the great Western horsemen, said of him, "Directors needed a Western canvas to keep him from filling the screen." Wayne wanted to do his own dangerous stunts and Harry taught him how. Yes. For real, Wayne could tame a bucking horse, jump from a horse onto a train, fall over and under a horse, and take a horse over impossible jumps and down death defying slides. Oh to be able to ride a horse like that and live to ride another! It takes bravery to try again after taking a fall. John Wayne did that and respected that kind of gumption in others. It makes sense that he would appear to Cynthia. She has Sisu which is Finnish for true grit. I wish I could see him like she can. I feel a now familiar pang of jealousy.

And John Wayne loved México. He loved Mexicans and married two Latina women.

Early on, I was surprised by an amazing coincidence, and felt his blessing for the writing of this book. While typing the name of Mazatlán's Pedro Infante, a famous Mexican movie actor, flyer, and singer, I carelessly misspelled Pedro's name in the search engine on the internet. And up in the search came a "pink elephant in Mazatlán." Suddenly the screen filled with an excerpt from a book called *John Wayne American* by Randy Roberts and James Olson. On page 119 was a story about a trip on John Ford's yacht, the Araner, to Mazatlán.

John Ford, the Duke, Ward Bond, Henry Fonda and Dudley Nichols sailed on the Araner fishing for bonito, dorado and marlin, drinking tequila with beer chasers at night and telling lies. When a week into the voyage, Ford, no doubt influenced by too much alcohol, claimed he saw a "green slimy vicious" sea serpent and Fonda challenged his story, the Duke and Bond backed him up. Then Fonda insisted he saw a "pink elephant."

With luck they reached Mazatlán, one of Duke's and Ford's favorite towns and went ashore. Here they went barefoot and unshaven, dressed in work khakis spotted with fish blood, and listened to mariachi bands playing in the saloons and whorehouses. By afternoon they had been thrown in Mazatlán's jail and, as noted in the logbook of the Araner, the jailbirds "had been invited by Mexican officials to leave town."

Drinking, carousing, and storytelling led Ford and the Duke to found the sarcastically titled "Young Men's Purity Total Abstinence and Snooker Pool Association, " a club for men who were wise enough not to join any clubs that would have them for members. John Wayne kept these friends all his life. He was like that.

In time John Wayne had his own yacht, the Wild Goose. It was anchored near the light house in Mazatlán's harbor while he made films in Durango. He would fly his plane down to Mazatlán every chance he had to fish and vacation between shooting films.

Joaquín had shown me a letter from Roberto Gorostiza who managed the Belmar, saying that Wayne became a close friend of his wife Ann and their children Roberto, Ana and Patricia, a great customer, sometimes pretending to be a vendor in the employ of Roberto. They laughed a lot and met many stars through the Duke. John Wayne came to their apartment in Olas Altas to celebrate the last Christmas night of his life before dying of stomach cancer. He was like that.

John Wayne held certain things sacred. One was friendship, the other was his country and he was talented beyond belief. He became a leading man in movies, influenced by those he admired, like Harry Carey, who gave him the pattern for his dress and acting style, and his no-nonsense, no-show business approach to life. Wayne loved Ollie, Harry's wife who chain-smoked, swore often as necessary, and always spoke her mind. When he announced that he wanted to play all kinds of roles, character parts, heavies, whatever, and avoid being type cast as the hero, Ollie told him that people had accepted him into their hearts and liked him as a certain kind of a man. The studios thought so too and used him, as they did Errol Flynn, in ways that made them money.

The true capability of men like these two will never be known. But many who worked with John Wayne thought it a shame the public didn't get to see how well he could act. He seldom was stretched toward his potential because he was so good at what he did. He was able to fill the bill and go along and he always needed money. Always. His money was spent to make others happy. His parents, his mother, his wives spent all his fortune. Like his father, he was so generous he left himself without and he worked until the cancer was so bad he could not get out of bed. In the end, he was barely ahead of the bill collectors. He was like that.

In many ways, the Belmar Hotel is just like John Wayne. It has the right stuff. It is large. It contains multitudes. All nations are welcome here. The Duke would feel at home here in this room Tim has refurnished for him. It's a man's room with many of the varieties of fish this sea holds, swimming just below the ceiling. Women are featured here too. The picture of Marilyn Monroe is still on the wall with Hollywood's favorite stars gathered round her, friends of John Wayne, and this year, Tim has found another classic Marilyn picture to display.

While I am admiring that, Tim gives me the letter his counselor Darby left him.

Tim O'Brien at the entrance to the John Wayne Room in the Hotel Belmar

The Permanent Tourist
By Darby Thomas

Some people just aren't comfortable anywhere. Tim O'Brien, a frontline combat Vietnam vet, was one of them. But that was before Mazatlan... On the tip of the Pacific, perched above cobblestone alleys and outdoor cafes, he has found a resting place. His is a most unusual nest.

Think 80 year-old vintage hotel. Think pink. Visualize twenty-foot ceilings, the painted tiles of old Spain, rooms, once inhabited by globe-trotting '40's glamour. From the moment you turn off the shoreline sidewalk, a deep and dare I say it? —mysterious atmosphere envelops you, promising more. And more is coming.

This is, after all, the Belmar Hotel, once established and exotic, now just finding its way out of crumbling plaster and neglect. As the savvy arrive, rooms and suites are being reborn, redesigned for today's traveler, and the haunting poignant sense of dramatic history—being destroyed? Not a bit of it. The current management seems to understand how badly we want the witness of the past as much as the postmodern comfort.

So, exactly where is Tim? He has taken the fourth floor sea view haven that once belonged to no

less than John Wayne. Yep. Icon of the West. Tim took one look at the uninhabited studio, thick with dust, cracked walls and ancient light fixtures. He also pondered two massive four-poster beds, glass-brick bath, and balcony smiling out to the bluest of seas.

Now I should admit that Tim is not your average, wandering, uncreative expatriate. Oh wait! I forgot there is no such thing. The expats I know usually recognize a good thing when they see it.

Tim, however, is a true artist, with background in photography, watercolor, and furniture design. He met this room like an old friend. It more or less demanded that he bring the space back to life, cherishing its solid masculinity and shameless romance.

Within a month, Tim, with the help of his friends and the Belmar staff has done exactly that, culminating in a grand party. Flaming florals, a hand-tiled table, freshly plastered walls and Hollywood Wayne posters recreated the ambience. Party goers brought the freshest of homegrown goodies and a momentous time was had by all.

Make no mistake. The Belmar is not for the sybaritic, but if you are the pioneering, independent type, it could be an opportunity to manifest your new past.

Somewhere, John Wayne is smiling.........

"Put this into your book," he says. "Darby sure could write. Now others will know—not just me. I think she'd like that."

I think that "somewhere" is right here. The ghosts have the key to this room. How many hours did the Duke spend looking out over the sea from Tim's balcony? Of course he is here. The military characters Wayne played would not abandon this man who served in the hellhole that was Vietnam in the last days of the war. Tim who says he loves projects has made a shrine of the John Wayne Room.

And Darby? Surely she is here too. Tim has kept her letter in the safest place he has. Now it is being published, and her picture is going up on his wall. He is decorating again. Collecting. Last year, he had given away his phone, his camera, and his computer, but there, on his desk are these items that spell communication, and he is giving me his phone number. He now has a cat and many new plants to care for. He is going to live to see a tomorrow.

Emilia is still his friend. The power of masculinity is a dead end without the spirit of the feminine. Unless life itself is a dead end, it extends across the broken pillars to the realm of the dead. Together they make up a protective wall of human community, this *Spiritus contra Spiritum*.

I remember Jimmy who last year sang to me of "All the Lonely People." He was dying to be with his wife again. Could he be looking back over his shoulder at his friends who spent his last days with him in the Belmar? I can almost hear him singing a different tune to his lady with kaleidoscope eyes. "Lucy in the Sky With Diamonds."

26

PROGRESS, DISASTER AND THE PASSAGE OF TIME

JOAQUÍN AND I ARE MEETING FOR COFFEE OUT IN FRONT OF THE BELMAR discussing the way the hotel changed over time. I know from reading and talking to people that when new roads made passage easier, Mazatlán developed to the north and other hotels became popular as the Belmar aged. I decide to see if we can piece together progress with the story of the hotel.

Joaquín slowly stirs his chocolate-laced coffee.

"Well," he says, "the story of the hotel is much like the story of the man who built it. Do you know much about him?"

I am ahead of the question because I have been researching him on the internet. About the same time that he built the Belmar, he also built a home for himself in Santa Monica. It was finished in 1922. The style of both the hotel and his house was Spanish Colonial Revival. That very house was just sold for $12 million dollars. It has 14 bedrooms and sits on a cliff overlooking the ocean. But, with all this real estate, he never married and had no heirs.

"Let me tell you more about the man, Lewis Bradbury Jr. We will put it together with the hotel after I tell you how he fared in the face of progress.

"Want more coffee?"

"I'd love another cup," I answer as Joaquín catches the waiter's eye and motions for a refill.

"So Lori, I look at you right this moment as being like Lewis Bradbury

LEWIS BRADBURY JR.

in 1922 with a full cup. Plenty of money, he hired Benito Rodil as his Hotel Manager, and traveled the world collecting antiques for his hotel. Bragging it up on his travels. He is responsible for many Europeans traveling to México and vacationing in Mazatlán, of course to stay in the Belmar where he had incorporated furniture and art from the best of what they have in far away lands. It all sounds wonderful. Right?"

"Well yes," I say drinking my coffee, emptying my cup a little. "But, my daddy told me that one generation makes the money and the next one spends it. I suppose that is what you are getting at."

"Yes, just as you drain the coffee from your cup, Lewis spent his inheritance that came from the mines. You see in México we have an expression. 'In order to have a mine, you must have a mine.'

"Do you know why a mine is expensive? No? So many disasters. There is a diary in the Bradbury family papers from the managers of the mines who told of problems such as assaults, flash floods, employee inebriation, accidents, amputations, smallpox, gangrene and lock jaw. Terrible things, all of which happened at the mines."

Despite the calamities, records show that beginning in 1910 Lewis Jr. bought more properties, incorporating them. He even bought a controlling interest in the mines of Copala in 1928. This expansion was just in time for Black Tuesday, the fall of the stock market on Wall Street that began the Great Depression in the United States. Things became so bad that 300,000 Mexicans left the United States to move back with family still in México.

From 1932 to 1938 inter-family litigation took place between the six children and various grandchildren of L.L. Bradbury over business and financial management decisions and the disbursement of funds. On top of all this, mining profits were down because now the Depression was in México, and also because of conditions in the mines. It was a perfect storm.

Lewis formed a Sport and Hotel Company and convinced the mining company to sell the Belmar to this company and write it off as a loss.

"Lewis Bradbury Jr. had a severely diminished bank account and little coming in," Joaquín points out. " He didn't have many shares left in the mines, and the whole industry was failing. In 1937, he could not cover his debts and ran a deficit of 50,000 pesos. The Commercial Pacific Bank took the Belmar over in the midst of all these troubles. After foreclosure Rodolpho Coppel and Silvario Trueba owned the hotel. It continued, still splendid and popular in spite of natural disasters and World War II, but by then it was not the new kid on the block anymore. Progress."

"Speaking of natural disasters," I interject, "consider this story from my research on hurricanes in Mazatlán."

On the 9th of October of 1943, Walt Disney and the entire crew of his "Greetings Friends" movie that had just wrapped up filming in México City were on board a Mexicana Airlines flight to Los Angeles when they faced an essentially undetected tropical cyclone that sprang up in their flight path. It became the most savage hurricane ever recorded to hit Mazatlán. It was measured at "as least a Category Four," with winds over 219 k/h, but the anemometer itself blew away in the storm so no one knows how savage it really was. The hurricane was bad enough to kill and injure over 200 people, leave a thousand homeless, destroy the towns of El Roble and Las Palmas, half of Mazatlán and wreak deadly damage on Olas Altas and the beautiful Hotel Belmar.

Walt and Friends put down in desperation at Mazatlán's small airport as the hurricane ripped a wing off their airplane propelling it onto the roof of the office. They hunkered down in the plane— what was left of it, hoping that no more of it "took wing" but they were totally soaked by the driven rain. For a week a radio in the plane provided the only communication available in the city.

The Belmar to the rescue. Walt Disney, his wife Lillian, Lucy and Desi Arnaz , the three superstars, Norma Shearer, Patricia Morrison and Kay Francis and the rest of the production crew somehow were transported to the hotel for perhaps the worse night of their lives.

The hotel was a disaster and completely full of others taking refuge and those who had booked in for pleasure. No luxury could be offered the illustrious visitors who dropped from the sky. All the windows of the ballroom were blown out to the street and the tables set for breakfast had lost the plates, tablecloths, glasses and cutlery completely. To this day, no one knows where they all went. Perhaps they landed in Kansas. The entire roof over the kitchen and the dining room was gone and the floor of the patio was painted with abstract designs of tiles, wood and plaster from the ceiling of the hotel. Stained glass, priceless antiques lay in ruin.

Hurricane in 1927 hits Hotel Belmar

The Hotel Manager Roberto Gorostiza created sleeping quarters, rented cots and brought out the driest blankets available in a supreme effort of imagination, cashing in on the good will he built over the 12 years he managed the Belmar. The Disney production gang cooked what they could find for themselves with whatever was still usable and helped make their own breakfasts the next day. So grateful were they to be alive, no one complained, but it was like camping out at a landfill.

What had Walt Disney been doing in México City? He had just received The Order of the Aztec Eagle, the Government of México's highest honor ever bestowed on a foreigner, for his efforts to foster beneficial international relations with México by making popular propaganda films in México during World War II.

Hurricane Olivia in the News

The hotel manager lost no time in rebuilding the Belmar, especially since there was now competition from the Hotel Freeman constructed on Olas Altas beach. Much of the best of times happened in the 1950s. But disaster struck again with the hurricane of 1957, a Category Four that collapsed the baseball stadium and once again bombarded the Belmar.

By the time 1975 rolled around, Mazatlán was a tourist destination and had a Golden Zone to the North with another big famous hotel called the Playa Mazatlan.

That year, another hurricane struck Mazatlán and this one had a name—Olivia! Hurricane Olivia had a 20 foot storm surge flooding the city causing what today would be $91 million dollars of damage. Olivia struck Mazatlán on October 23, destroying 7000 houses and leaving 30,000 homeless. Thirty people were killed, 20 of them drowning in shrimp boats. Winds were sufficient to put a ferry and tug boat high and dry up on the wharf, and the Angela Peralta Theater was almost completely destroyed. Today in the Belmar, a solid surface rims the patio, once all sunlit glass shining across casual dining to the ocean. On it is a mural chronicling the ancient history of Olas Altas and later, the original Belmar on the beach. It is temporary. Aren't we all temporary? It is a kind of story to remind us how things change.

Joaquín tells me what Olivia was like for him. He lived through it. All of Mazatlán was devastated, terribly wounded. He says it was the worst storm he has ever seen. A harbor of sunken shrimp and sports fishing boats, and sailboats too. He lost a brand new speed boat.

"There was not a single tree left in Olivia's path. No sand on the beaches, large boulders rolled down from the hills and blocked the water front. Freight train cars were pushed into the bay. Some had people who took refuge in them, and those people drowned. A large ship wrecked herself upon the side of Deer Island and was there for months.

"It was impossible to drive," Joaquín continues, "but I was able to move around thanks to my dirt bike. I was motoring through the wrecked city when I saw a beautiful red classic Ford Mustang convertible, immobilized by the storm. Standing beside it was its owner, a drug lord of his time. We said hello, we were both going to the only boaters club open in town. Politely, he asked for a ride. Wow, all that power, unlimited money, and I had the only decent means of transportation, a dirt bike. On we went, with me in disbelief. The most powerful man in town was riding on the back of my dirt bike, parading through Olas Altas, past the Belmar while people pointed at the only moving vehicle and its passengers.

"Disaster, like death, has a way of making everyone equal. There are no borders or stratifications based on wealth, heritage or position. Again I remind you, we love our wounds. When we tell such stories, we get moving again. We realize we are all in this together, this thing called change."

Again the Belmar had to be rebuilt. But this time, big changes were made. It was very expensive to rebuild with the materials that were first used. So many tiles were destroyed it was decided to take down much of what was left. Mid Century Modern architecture was in vogue, not Spanish Restoration. Living modern meant flat planes, geometric lines, flat roofs, changes in elevation, large sliding glass doors, dark wood paneling on one wall, use of new materials, a sleek industrial look. The hotel was expanded and new materials were used. There should be integration with nature, so straight line balconies were created, and multiple access points. No more arches and carved furniture. Instead the Belmar was furnished with simple pieces that were inspired by Danish modern ideas.

"I guess that is progress, huh Joaquín?"

"Yes, that is progress but progress is not such a good word. Here in Mazatlán those who love the grace and beauty of the old craftsmen are not inclined to opt for cheap and common. And I am of the belief that we must go backwards to find our singularity if we are to understand our history. And it is this singularity that tourists come to enjoy. Not another flavor of what they have at home. Am I wrong?"

27

SIROCCO WINDS

I ASK NICHOLAS ABOUT ROOM 35. NIKO CONFIDES THAT MANAGEMENT AT the Belmar knew they could never rent the room at the end of the hall where Errol Flynn once stayed because the would-be occupant would always come running to demand a change of rooms. The ghosts in that room made it unbearable to stay inside and no one wanted to go inside to clean that room. Because of that, rooms were reconfigured and re-numbered in a renovation. But still, no one wanted to brave the dark hallway late at night alone. Something strange lurked and played there. Sure enough, late at night many have seen an exceedingly handsome well dressed man come from where Room 35 used to be, headed down and out on the town for adventure.

That would be Errol Flynn at the top of his game, when he lived first class, best and front of the line, and that was the Belmar Hotel in her Golden Days.

Errol Flynn seemed to have it all. Superb good looks. The kind of handsome that turns heads all around the room, makes the ladies swoon and the men sit up to notice. He loved to fight. I mean, FIGHT, and al-though he and most every star in "tough man roles" mixed it up, Errol specialized in barroom brawls and almost always triumphed, but reg-ularly checked into emergency rooms for repairs. Once, after a gossip columnist insulted Errol's dog, our hero tracked him down at a dinner club and leveled him with one punch but took a fork in the ear from the wife. They sued him for assault.

Errol kept in tip top form by sparring twice a week both with street fighters and professionals who taught him the right moves for the honorable or the dirty opponent. And because he constantly jabbed people, he frequently used this skill. David Niven, a close friend of his for a time, said of Errol: "You always know precisely where you stand with him and he always lets you down. He thoroughly enjoyed creating turmoil for himself and his friends." Errol labeled himself a "rake" and others added "of the highest order."

No wonder Errol Flynn still has an international fan club even though he died in 1959.

When he was 26, it was a very good year. In 1935, fresh off his success as a corpse on a slab in the Warner Brothers movie "The Case of the Curious Bride," the actress Lili Damita invited him to her place named The Garden of Allah. He was captivated by her hourglass figure and the music of her rustle when she walked or seated herself daintily, spreading her skirts. No one rustled like her.

She knew important people and they soon were invited to visit with Diego Rivera at his fantastic home just outside of México City. Out Diego's window was the magnificent volcano Popocatepetl. To the left was a pyramid built by the Aztecs, and close up was a glass topped convent covered in bougainvillea, ginger and the flowery cactus tree. All of these nuns and novitiates right next to Rivera's arty Bohemian radical center from which Rivera led the Communist movement in the Latin-American world!

Soon Diego Riviera introduced Errol to marijuana so that he could "hear México speak to him in simple paintings of a woman on a mule moving through a field of cacti or of peasants at their labor," and he suddenly saw, felt, and heard an indescribable song. He was hooked on exaggeration. The tequila they had been drinking made a matchstick on the floor look like a log. And so when dinner was announced, he shouted to the heavens:

"Food!" His arms up imploring heaven, "I sip no sup and I crave no cup, while I cry for the love of a ladee!"

Diego took an instant liking to him. México became a favorite place for Errol to come to enjoy passion, color, exuberance, and excess.

He had to have a boat or he felt bereft. Soon his yacht, named the Sirroco after the wind of Northern Africa that drives men mad, was a familiar sight anchored out by the Mazatlán light house. And the Belmar Hotel was the place he brought his Lili to. She taught him erotic lovemaking, purely animal, ravenous woman-tiger sex. But he was a voracious reader and her eyes glazed over at cerebral exercise. Also, she had an overpowering possessiveness, as he said, "like a blanket or an oxygen tank." Icebox Hill in-

Errol Flynn as Captain Blood

creasingly drew him away to sample the delights of Mexican women at the Stratosphere club, but he had to be careful no lipstick of any shade but Lil's was on him. And so he fought with Tiger Lil and made ferocious love in Room 35.

Errol was not a tame kind of man. He loved tigers. He was an Australian whose upbringing had been in Tasmania and New Guinea, deep in its jungles, steeped in its raw terror, at home with its natives, in love with its amazing creatures not found anywhere else in the world.

Along with criminal exploits and exotic travels, the real history of our Tasmanian Devil was misrepresented and ignored when Warner Brothers, in all their wisdom, described him as a "veteran of the theatre" and "more Irish than the Irish potato." Characterized as a spud, Errol still became a swashbuckling star, epic for misbehavior, outlandish pranks, and self destruction, who did his own stunts.

He said that his most strenuous role was in "The Charge of the Light Brigade" when he and the whole cast toughed it out in tents after a fire burned their hotel in Bishop, California. They persevered on site, shivering in their tropical garb before freezing winds off Mt. Whitney, the highest summit of the United States, and the whole Sierra range. One man was killed. So many horses were injured that Errol became an animal activist. Along with him, the animals themselves rebelled. He and David Niven trampled and trumpeted their way all over the set in a basket on top of an elephant trying to rub them out, gone berserk under the lights and sounds of filming. Finally it became so intolerable that the "location" headed down México way to avoid constraints of the law and publicity around the shooting. México was fast becoming a favorite destination for Errol Flynn.

Women claimed they knew who Errol was. They swam out to his boat moored in Mazatlán, begging him to take them aboard. Letters came daily claiming he had fathered, or would he please father children with this one, or that one, or no one he knew.

Lili took him for everything he had, including his home on Mulholland Drive. He was broke, a bum and questioning everything. Just when his continuing search for himself was stalled at base level, Universal Studios sent out a scout to see if Errol could still pull himself together and play a part in a movie set in Turkey. Errol agreed, fantasizing a romantic sail across the Mediterranean, minarets, old mosques, temples, veiled ladies, a whole harem flashing their black eyes at him. But no. When understanding of what he had agreed to hit, he came with reluctance to make "Istanbul" in a studio lot in Hollywood—the last place he wanted to be.

It was then that the producer Darrel Zanuck showed he knew who Errol was, and so did John Houston. Errol Flynn was starred in "The Sun Also Rises," he played his friend John Barrymore in "Too Much Too Soon" and he alone thrived in the filming of "The Roots of Heaven" made in French Equatorial Africa that sweltered routinely in 135 degree temperatures, during which there were 900 sick calls from a cast of 120.

What was lacking in Errol? He had talent beyond belief, looks, courage, the drive to make and waste fortunes and exhaust everyone around him with his excesses. But it was never enough to this charming, engaging, and self destructive man. Errol liked first class. Still, no amount of pleasure satisfied him for long. Was he seeking punishment? Maybe. For although he was never humble, he could not assuage the longing, the emptiness inside. He tried all the drugs to do it, mainlined heroine, and used cocaine on his penis as an aphrodisiac.

But his loyal friends, convinced he was worth rescuing, saved him from himself. He suffered gamely from withdrawal, malaria, hepatitis, various venereal diseases, arthritis in every joint, terrible injuries, tuberculosis, cirrhosis of the liver, and fears of every kind, but he never let on, never gave in. He was a voracious reader, always curious to find answers. He forever was fascinated with convents. And churches. Was it the innocence of the young women inside, or had he caught reverence for the grace of motherhood, indeed the spirit of a woman México reveres in Our Lady? The mother he never had? The Bible became his last best read before a heart attack claimed him at age 50.

28

GIRDING FOR BATTLE

CYNTHIA AND I HAVE BEEN INVITED TO A PIZZA PARTY ON THE UPPER terrace of the Belmar later this afternoon. Afterwards we plan to watch the Carnival Naval Battle fireworks from the best vantage point in town, the roof of the Belmar Hotel in the middle of it all.

It's only late morning now, so I sit down with Wesley at his table by the street out in front. On this Saturday of Carnival week, Wesley looks ruggedly handsome in his panama hat. Wesley had lived a life on the ocean and what better place to settle down and marry than Mazatlán by the sea. He said he was successful at it because he had fallen in love many times over, always with the same woman—"Cha Cha Cha." He is reading a Star Wars Book called *The Return of the Jedi*. His ready smile invites me right on in to hear his stories. I'm glad he's Irish, a man of the sea and such an articulate man.

"Wesley, can I see the cover of the book you are reading? Ah yes. That's Luke Skywalker with his light saber. It's blue in this picture but green in the movie. I remember that this book was the best selling novel of the year it was written sometime in the early 1980s."

"Well sure. We are all looking for something to believe in, aren't we? The Force has a nice ring to it. Maybe you're a believer too if you know about Luke Skywalker. I see every movie. Did you know that the Walt Disney Company acquired Lucas films to keep the stories pure? There is a sort of Bible they use with Canons in it. Not the shooting kind but the truthful kind. Now they've put the Canons into what they call the Holocron. They paid dearly, something like over $4 billion dollars for the rights. Walt Disney loved these kinds of stories. He came here and stayed in this hotel behind you. Quite a story that one."

I grew up watching the Disney movies, so can converse with gusto.

"Of course Walt Disney would want the Star War films," I chime in. "They are all about the fight between good and evil and Luke Skywalker is my man. I even dream about him and I can hear the sound of his wand like when he had that light saber duel. The light saber was made with a crystal. No one could have those crystals except those in power. They were outlawed and Skywalker had to make his own using old knowledge almost lost. Guess that's why we want to read history. Just in case we need it."

Wesley smiles at that idea.

"Sure. Well sea goin' folks like me, we use tattoos. See here is my tattoo of an anchor. With this on my arm I always knew I would never drown at sea."

"Good to know that. For a man sailing to the far side of the earth, it is comforting to have something to hang onto, but I should think the tattoo would be a life ring and not an anchor. An anchor takes you down—no?"

"Ah well, the anchor just brands me as one with the sea and the clouds so drowning isn't necessary, see? The pirates used to pierce their ears to show they had crossed the equator, wear golden hoops for the luck of the world and tattoo a star for the North Star that shows the way home. When there is no land in sight, ya gotta know the rules. Like in that holocron I told you about. We had rules."

"Rules?" I searched my mind and came up empty except to watch out for the warning of a red sun in the morning.

"Sur'n, there's loads of 'em. Like this one that is longer than I remember without thinkin' on it:

When all three lights I see ahead,
I turn to Starboard and show my Red
Green to Green, Red to Red,
Perfect Safety—Go Ahead

"And then we always said to one another, 'no whistlin' lest you whistle up a storm.' You know, make the wind mad. Except the cook. He can whistle cus it keeps him from stealin' the food."

"Oh, I love your stories. And this being Saturday of Carnival week, tonight is about the battle by sea for Mazatlán, and of course Mazatlán won. I bet you, being a seaman yourself, know the history behind the fireworks. I'd love to hear your take on it."

"Ah, well good on ya then. Your friend Cynthia plays chess with Abimiel in the Captain's Quarters. I suppose you know that. And after all this time, you know the story of Mazatlán in the Mexican Revolution, but tonight is about what came before. That's what we're celebrating tonight. Mazatlán's first victory over the French. And Abimiel was there to see it. Abi would be, let's see, somewhere around 165 years old now. And bein' the ghost he is, he told Cynthia that they never buried him right. Didn't put that silver coin in his mouth or his eye so's he could pay the ferryman to cross the River Styx that flows between the living and dead.

"But Cynthia says it's all about how he laid himself down in his Captain's coffin. Being cursed to be undead, he just set up his haunt at the Belmar after the Revolution. That's where he tried his hand at dying of old age. He shoulda died in battles cus he saw or fought in the worst ones on the Pacific Coast, he did. Do you know he carved a coffin and kept it in his room to remind him how he is tied to his Captain? Lordee, how he loved his Captain."

"Cynthia told me some of the story," I reply. "I guess you put her to looking up Abimiel in the Captain's Quarters, and he told her all about the gunship Tampico and his captain Malpica. But the coffin in his room? Oh , that's creepy. The Mexican Revolution just blows my mind. It is so hard to understand. And so tragic. "

"Right you are. Like a terrible wound it was. But tonight is about a ship-to-shore battle that happened before the Revolution. It's about girdin' up. And Abimiel can tell the story of the fireworks from when he saw it as a ten year old! So if you want to hear it, I'll repeat what I can remember of it. You'll be gettin' it from an Irishman as told by a sorta-dead

Mexican, and elaborated on by what he told yer friend Cynthia, who is Finnish, right? All of us people of the sea. So sit down here land lubber that ya are, and like we Irish would say whist ya now. Listen-up."

I whist right up and he begins.

"Ah well, it is hard to know how far back to go. I'll just feather the nest for Abi's story. You know the streets of Mazatlán are named for all the Mexican heroes, and you've been hearin' about who they were. Benito Juárez for instance. He was a Mexican lawyer and politician of indigenous Zapotec origin from Oaxaca."

"Yes," I said, then continued, glad to be able to add my two pesos to the conversation. "Special enough to have his statue over in the Glorietta at Paseo Claussen Avenue. And all the streets named for him in every Mexican city I've visited. And cities named after him, too. I heard he was a freemason and married a white woman. He got to be the President of México."

"Yah, and we call men like him shit disturbers. Benito Juárez started at that even before he got to be the provisional President of México. He represented the common man and was liberal, which upset the conservative Roman Catholic Church that held fully one third of the land in México at first. Juárez separated church and state and took property back. The Conservatives were horrified and ready to fight. So were those of pure Spanish blood who wanted a monarchy. There were all these factions, maybe forty or more like the Republicanos and the Centralists, all fighting each other. Mazatlán was peopled by Europeans as well as Méxicanos, all wanting to rule. Juárez promoted civil liberties and freedom of speech, you know, a free press. Before that anyone of a lower class had to be careful or they got dead. One way to criticize the elite was in cartoon images—like making them look like skeletons. Catrinas. And they got by because the cartoons seemed in good fun."

I relate to that and happily add, "Like the jesters that survived while they criticized the Kings. Only those clowns sometimes got roasted for dinner in the olden days."

"Exactly," Wesley grinned. "That's why they were boney. No meat to eat. Huh, never thought of that. I always figured they were skeletons to say that everyone is equal under the skin, but maybe they were talkin' like ghosts from the other side with nothing left to lose.

"But whist ye now, try to stay on course. México was heavily in debt to France and England over the wars for independence from Spain. And then war began with the United States in 1846 after México abolished slavery. You see, Texas wanted to join the Confederate States and keep its slaves. Oh, México remembers the Alamo better then we do!

"When the dust settled, México surrendered to General Scott who had taken México City for the USA. Americans occupied all the ports on the Pacific, even Mazatlán, the prize. They left after treaties gave the USA over half of México's territory for $15 million dollars, or $415 million today, and the assumption of some debt México owed. Why, just the silver coming out of our local mines in Copala and Rosario produced ore worth over five million dollars every year. Just think of it. México lost what we today call California, Arizona, New Mexico, Nevada, Utah, and Colorado. Over half of the territory they once had. And it would never have happened except that México was divided internally. And the same thing with this city. Mazatlán fell to France because Mexicans fought with Mexicans. Had they united, France would never have conquered Mazatlán."

"Yes, nation building can be painful and usually involves battles and lots of bloodshed. That's a story in itself!"

"Well, sure. Whether it's nation building or even with each of us finding our way. Now you're on course by my compass. Ya, but here's the skinny. Or I could say, here's the Catrinas now. Right?

"Remember how I told ya about Benito Juárez? Well, he was elected a full President in 1861. Imagine that. Of peasant stock and partly Indian, but he had gotten training in law, became a Mason and friends with Lincoln to boot. Lincoln was also a Mason, liberal and for people's rights. He was a Republican as was Benito Juárez, both of 'em tryin' to glue together States into a Union.

"But right away Benito suspended the payment of interest on the debt owed to foreign nations. He had gone and stirred the pot again, and sure as death México was about to be stewed in the soup. It is one thing to rip off the Catholic Church and even to give peasants a voice, but welching on debts to France, England and Spain is quite another.

"France decided to make México its own colony. You see they wanted Mazatlán's famous port and its mines. It was all about money."

"But Wesley. We in the United States had the Monroe Doctrine. We would have defended México in their fight against European rule."

"Ah but ya see, there is the timin' of it. Lincoln and the USA had gotten busy fighting the Civil War and could not enforce the Monroe Doctrine which, yer right as rain, would have protected México from France takin' it over. México had been battling for years for independence and was now fighting over how to govern itself. Infighting was fierce. Europeans had flooded our good city, fleeing wars, seeking wealth. Many still nursed allegiance to their European roots. Many poorly paid soldiers were battle weary and just wanted to go home to their families.

"The time was right for France to strike. The way the French were able to take Mazatlán, the most fortified formidable city on the Pacific is an example of the bitter brew México was into. Lincoln got assassinated, and the best the United States did to help was to fish the Mexican sailors out of the sea when their ships were sunk and to leave guns and ammunition near the border for the resistance."

I nod remembering my research. In fact, I had read just last week that France was conspiring to form a new nation with the south of the USA and asked Benito Juárez to throw Northern Mexico in on it. But he declined the offer. When the Civil war was over in America, it was then that American Presidents helped México fight out from under French rule, but not before all the cities to the south of Mazatlán were burned and many animals and Republican soldiers were killed in battle or executed in Mazatlán streets, now named for the commanders who defended the city such as General Morelos and General Rosales. In the meantime, arms from the United States were smuggled across México to General Corona's guerilla army. There were terrible battles in the mountains along the

Devil's backbone and finally, in 1866, the French lost control.

That defeat humiliated Napoleon and weakened his position for his next battles into Russia. Europe's old families were horrified when Maximilian I, an Austrian royal, refused to flee the México he had claimed and was executed. Benito Juárez let that happen as a consequence of, as Wesley said, building a nation.

The conflicts did not end there, however. Other nations still wanted a piece of the pie. Mazatlán was such a prize that the English blockaded the port next, and even the Americans came briefly. Only under Porfirio Díaz did things settle down, and he ruled México for seven terms trying to encourage foreign investment instead of domination.

Then in 1914, the city where Germans had settled and won influence became a battleground once more in the Mexican Revolution. Again México was asked to join with a European nation, this time on the German side in the First World War, to take the United States from the South. Again, México declined.

Finally, in 1920 when Obregón took over the Presidency and prohibition began in the United States, a period of peace and prosperity came along. The nest was built and ready for the Belmar Hotel to hatch in it. And it was a golden egg indeed.

"Think of it," Wesley says pointing out to the ocean, "here we will be celebrating tonight the first battle with the French in 1864, a triumph for México that every Mexican remembers with pride. It is like armor. Like girding up for the bloody years ahead. That was 153 years ago. And Abimiel was there seein' it for real. Him just a boy wait'n and watch'in, to see what was comin at em out of the sea.

"Tonight, I want ya to picture that French war ship now will ya, her mast coming out behind Deer Island and all the Mexicans gawkin at her. Oh, they knew she was a comin', she had been maraudin' up and down the coast and now here she was and up to no good. It makes my breath stop to think of that moment.

"When you see the fireworks and hear the music they put together tonight to tell the terrible time it brought to Mazatlán, remember that the battle was won but the war was lost, for Mazatlán fell to the French and later to the Federalists that represented foreign domination.

"And Abi saw the beginning right here in Mazatlán. Right here on Olas Altas beach. He saw the executions of those who wanted home rule. He lived to fight in the Revolution that set Mazatlán free again. Oh history is grand, this breaking open that makes a nation."

Wesley stops talking like he has another thought. He takes off his hat and runs his fingers through his hair like he was letting the idea see the light of day. When he puts it back on, he sets the hat down firmly with a yank on the brim and looks right at me with his sly, teasing smile.

"Say, I bet Abi will be watchin' it again with you tonight. Did you think of that? Could be quite a night."

We sit for a little while I digest all of that. I am finally beginning to see the big picture—the nest, as Wesley called it, feathered-up to hatch the "golden egg," the Hotel Belmar. He speaks so easily about the ghosts and I know Cynthia is confiding in him. I decide maybe he knows a lot more than just history, so I ask him some questions that have been nagging at me all along.

"Wesley. Why is it Cynthia can see the ghosts—can talk to them and now you tell me, play chess with them? And you too? Why can't I?"

"Oh you ask such questions, my friend. Such questions. Well, let's see if I can explain it. It's like breaking a shell. We all do that, put up this shell. Maybe we are just too tender we think. Maybe we've gotten hurt and now are afraid. But life happens and our shell gets broke. And that's when.... Well, you think on it. You know your Cynthia. She told me enough so's I think she's been dealt a tough hand. A broken shell, a broken heart if you will, can make for a different view on life and death. Kids see ghosts because they haven't built their shell yet. Haven't decided what is real, maybe have one foot still back in another life. But later when there's a break-through—great expression that! Well, it's like a wound that never heals. And that's the opening you see. The ghost has the key? Aren't you going to use that name I told you about for your book? Use it. It's true. Think on that a little.

"Remember, all the ghosts have unfinished business. Cynthia's here for a reason and you are too. Did ya ever think of that? This hotel behind us here, this place is like a stage and we are all playin' our parts, us the living are playing the script written for us, or by us, and maybe some of the players are coaching from behind the curtain. Think on that awhile. Ya never know when there could be a guest performance from the other side! And remember, nothing is by accident. Not Cynthia's comin' here. No accident I'm tellin' you.

"But, this isn't all about Cynthia like you think it is. You ask great questions. So ask yourself what brought you here to Mazatlán? What made you want to write this book about the Belmar? You wouldn't have some unfinished business of your own now, would ya?"

29

FIREWORKS

But she comes from nowhere. The nurse dressed so strangely.
Her coat floating behind her, a cross on her breast.
She tenderly holds him. She speaks softly to him.
She breathes life into this man bent on death.

PIZZA NEVER TASTED SO GOOD AS THE ONE BAKED IN A KILN BUILT TO COOK pottery on the terrace of the Belmar. As the time for the fireworks nears, Cynthia and I thank our hostess and make our way up the stairs to the hotel roof. We have to unlock the padlock on the barricade as people are not allowed on the roof anymore, but Cynthia has arranged with the manager to get a key for just us to go for an "up close and personal" private showing. *Guardar el secreto.* I am excited that we share this secret 'in house' privilege. *At last, my chance for adventure!*

We enter an unlit, seldom used staircase to the roof, tripping over electrical cords and stumbling into cement barricades, find the lock, click it open and as we promised, fasten it again behind us. Now we are looking out at the Pacific Ocean and Deer Island, just the two of us, feeling small in the vastness and grateful to have found the best seats in the house.

The open sky is filled with moon and stars, the air smells cool and shimmers salty with sea spray. Below this vantage point, waves roll in overlapping circles of blue-green edged in foam against a softly lit mysterious silver arch. Crowds of people spill over the streets below and the music from many bandstands splits the night. From near the island, we see the lights on a ship slip silently into position to fire.

A cold shiver rustles through the hair on the nape of my neck as I feel a whisper, soft as a goose down feather, brush by. But just then the music begins and the strange arch, suddenly alive in golden rays, launches volleys of fireworks skyward. Beams of light, like the wand of the Jedi Luke Skywalker, sweep glimmering dust off the starry face of night. Now fireworks come from either side of the arch alternating awesome with sublime. Showered in sparks, the roof top is covered in witchy fingers, shrieking, grasping, squawking, and smoky red-violet fog rises like clouds to cover us and the crowds below.

I know the story behind the fireworks. The big guns on the French frigate La Cordeliere inflicted injuries on Mazatlán's defenders from more than a mile away. The first probe was repelled, but when the attack began again the big ship zeroed in on the defending positions while the French Marines in 14 landing craft raced toward land. Ten boats made shore and disembarked Marines to establish a beachhead. The fight was sharp and fierce. Commander Benítez, under Mazatlán's master of defense Colonel Gaspar Sánchez Ochoa, sent the French desperately fleeing back to their warship under heavy fire. Both sides took casualties. The frigate lingered out of range to decide if they would try again and decided not to.

My reverie is interrupted by ascending towers of fire that drop back and relaunch. When the side cannons fire *catchung!* starburst patterns shoot into the night leaving glistering mists swept clean by the great silent beams, like chapter headings—announcing and finishing. The symphony of light and sound plays with themes, echoes and solos. Each explosion is a brilliant unrepeatable moment to remember, not recordable by any devise. Someone below shouts "Mazatlán throws one hell of a party!" and I am humbled by the display, both triumphant and foreboding. I turn to look at Cynthia but she is on the far side of the roof in conversation with someone, only no one is there. I pay it no mind, choosing instead to remember the way the battle ended in 1864.

At 2:00pm on March 31, the La Cordeliere sailed out straight to the center of Olas Altas beach smack in front of the Belmar where Cynthia and I are enjoying the fireworks from another century. Turning broadside, the ship opened up with all of its cannons on Mazatlán itself, shooting as many as 400 shells into the city. México had won the battle but the war was just beginning.

"Cynthia wasn't that grand?" I call to her.

No answer. Later she explains that Abimiel was pointing out where he hid behind rocks while an Indian from a small town north of Sinaloa bravely manned his small cannon out in the open on the beach.

"Private Crispen Armenta shot cannon balls right on board the French frigate," she tells me.

But at this moment, right after the fireworks, I don't mind that Cynthia seems preoccupied and I turn back enjoying the feeling of being alone on that roof as the lights fizzle out and darkness falls all around me. Perhaps I am soaking up the silence like it is the eye of the hurricane. The quiet after the storm... or before it.

I feel winds around me—whirl winds like I had imagined the Sirocco Winds to be. Those winds that drive men mad. Is it the wildness of the night or had witchy fingers crept inside my head assaulting my feeble mind with a hurricane of feelings? I had often thought of the brain as a kind of transformer that takes in reality and lowers it to an acceptable voltage level, but it is short circuiting and I am getting zapped with emotion sweeping over me in overlapping waves edged in the froth that dissolves time and space and separation.

And then it happens. The ghosts. It is as if Luke Skywalker beams his light on and I see them all around me. Finally! And more than what I've bargained for, because by the fireworks of energy sparking between us I am able to know their thoughts. Or is it just a projection of what I researched about them that I know? Or is it what I want to happen? This must be what Cynthia has described to me. Short-circuiting reality, what is real is unreal.

From the periphery of my vision, a woman pale and thin as a sliver moon glides by, her white garment filmy as fog melting in the heat of her desperation, panic propelling her towards... Oh no! In front of her is only the jaw dropping plunge to the street. She stops. I feel her panic, it is paralyzing, her heart beats like a captive bird clutched in fingers of red violet. I smell it, the scent of love burning in perdition.

"No," I cry. "No, love is the flame!"

And then, though faint at first, I hear the patterned rhythm of dance. Unmistakable now, the soft guitar and the alluring voice of the man riding his *tornillo* horse, singing hope to the lady, calming her, pulling her back as he circles his dancing dapple grey round her. The mare arches her neck, her silver crest shines in front of certain death. And this man, who when hunted becomes the hunter, can only be the courageous Carrasco, the General called simply "Juan." And like emerald green overlapping waves, his songs are cooling, washing smooth the sharp edges of pain. Promising. He extends his arm and swings the woman up astride eternity.

Two little girls are running all around hiding in the shadows here and there. I hear them giggling, their voices high and tinkle light, but a ship's bell sounds. In silence, a sailor sets a wooden box in the circle of Skywalker's light. A coffin. I know him at once. He can only be Abimiel with the coffin he has carved for his Captain Malpica. He is polishing the bright brass on its lid revealing his Captain's name. Abi is grizzled but holds himself proud. Ever vigilant, he sets a spy glass to his eye, his gaze to the sea, his verbal observations directed to the coffin beside him.

Suddenly a marauder sends the little girls screaming. Agile as shadow play, a big dark man vaults forward over the maze of adjoining rooftops. He wears a red bandana for sweat and dust, his massive chest gleams wet in a wide open shirt over pantaloons baggy as those of a gypsy. Thick black hair, bound back, will not be contained, straying shaggy, curly and wild. He pulls off his sombrero and sends it spinning to the rooftop in a challenge, a signal to attack. One hand on his holstered gun, he brandishes his sword.

Now I see an adversary standing statue still, facing The Gypsy. Impossibly handsome, the stranger is all teeth and boldness and a safe distance away on a high roof. I hold my breath and hope he stays there but Captain Blood would never shy away from a fight. Flynn leaps in a move of elegance and grace unsheathing his sword as he flies across space.

The battle is on. I run to avoid them but they pay me no mind. They fight through and over me, jouncing and jumping and climbing walls, their swords thrusting to kill, blades clashing and crashing again and again. And finally beaten, his sword clattering onto the roof, The Gypsy pulls out his pistol. He fires Queen Juliana but too late, for Captain Blood Flynn has dispatched *El Gitano*. Flynn now stands alone covered in blood, his legs folding beneath him as he crumples to the roof top.

She comes from nowhere. The nurse dressed so strangely. Her coat floating behind her, a cross on her breast. She tenderly holds him. She speaks softly to him. She breathes life into this man bent on death.

Hell-bent, he's gorged on drugs and excesses, pouring all the riches of life into the emptiness of a bottomless pit. But in this grail moment, he looks at her in wonder. Her touch stops his bleeding, her arms embrace him and she holds him to herself. For the first time Errol Flynn feels the love of a mother for her child. He lays still and trusting while she works miracles of surgery carving self hatred from him, infusing self respect until he can love himself for the first time.

When she finishes she tells him he is good, and he believes her. She is more beautiful to him than any leading lady, than any woman he has ever known and she feels the goodness he sees in her, for they are like a mirror to each other. He springs to his feet, and they walk off together united not by matrimony or partnership but in the knowledge that they are whole and complete, integrated male and female full of each other, and that the wounds of their lives have opened them to receive this healing vision.

Stealthily behind Abi's back, the little girls have opened the coffin and now run shrieking away from the young officer who sits up and climbs out, dusting himself off, looking around. The name on the coffin announces him as Captain Hilario Malpica, of the gunship Tampico. Abimiel salutes and waits for orders. The Captain points starboard and immediately Abi goes to escort the man waiting in the wings. I see it is John Wayne. No one tells me, still I know what this is about. Captain Malpica will not come himself into this life and so must wait for Cynthia to be united with him in the next.

But he has chosen the best man here and now as her helpmate. A man who lived in the Belmar Hotel as she does now. Both of them American. Both of them with true grit. John Wayne is to America what Captain Malpica of Veracruz represents for México. The Duke is honorable beyond words. He will be capable, indeed masterful, resourceful and honest. He thinks like an American but loves México like a Mexican. Malpica knows Cynthia as his Maria Elena and he has invoked Wayne.

The Duke accepts this request, honoring the Mexican Captain, sad that America could not be more helpful to him when he was fighting aboard the Tampico. He says he will help Cynthia form a business of ghostly tours and appear now and then so people will believe. He salutes both Captain Malpica and Abimiel and walks off the roof toward his room in the Belmar, and the Captain climbs back into his coffin and shuts the lid on himself.

The girls, like mischievous little spirits, sneak back, throw open the lid again, and run. But this time fireworks burst forth all over the roof more beautiful than any that have fallen this evening, for they do not fizzle and fade but illuminate the entire scene dissipating the shadows. Love is like that. It bridges the gap of the broken pillar—the fear of the unknown. It is the only thing that lasts. It is the glue between the living and the dead, more powerful than our fears. I feel it now. Time and space do not confine it. Even now, as clearly as fireworks from the coffin can light the night, I know they also will work magic in the future. I think of Cynthia's ghostly tours! What an idea... But what about me?

Just then Simona appears. She simply walks all around the roof smiling out at the ocean and the crowds below like they are her family. Cynthia comes at once to her side and they seem like sisters. But Simona stops, extends her hand and beams a look across at me. A light I feel right through to my soul. I am blessed—so blessed by this vision—like she has given me something precious.

A night to never forget. And when the darkness settles and it is only Cynthia and me on the roof, I watch the twinkling light out on the ocean slide back around Deer Island, feeling grateful.

Wonder. That is the gift of my wounding. Life is like a play and we all have parts to act out best we can. "We love our wounds," Joaquín told me. When we are wounded, when in a moment of too much, we spin off energy. Phantom energy lingers to finish up even after we move on. We, the living, make our lives count because we have the power and the voice this time around. Those who have died are not only remembered when we tell their stories, they are imbued with power to move the play forward.

I look down. I feel something in my hand pulsing like the beating of my heart. A baton. A baton that before my eyes becomes my tools— a paint brush and a pen.

30

THE GRAVEYARD

FUNERALS AND WEDDINGS WERE JOAQUÍN'S EARLIEST MEMORIES. I pictured him as a little boy amid gardenia scented wreaths of flowers watching candlelight flicker across faces shadowed in grief or breathing in the smell of fresh dug earth. Probably playing in it, enjoying the dark moistness of living soil. Maybe at weddings he danced with satin and lace figures, whirling, twirling colors and joyful music. Certainly there would have been sweet foods set out to melt on the tongue and blessings to bolster souls. But I guessed Joaquín was bored with solemnity, shy amid the crowds and always curious, looking for answers to questions only ghosts could answer.

I am not surprised when Joaquín suggests we tour the graveyard. With all those funerals to attend it must have been like home to him, a favorite place where a child could hide out behind mysterious castle tombs to trace epitaphs engraved in granite and imagine the lives of the dead. Whatever his experience was, it made him what he calls himself today— a history detective.

"There can scarcely be a place more rich with little known details to sleuth out," he says, explaining his passion, his ongoing fascination with enigmas that went to the grave unsolved.

Joaquín had loaned me the book he had selected as his first read in English, *The Labyrinth of Solitude* by Octavio Paz. At once I knew that title could be applied to Graveyard #2, the Belmar Hotel, and Joaquín López Hernández.

The oldest graveyard left in Mazatlán, Joaquín's favorite and the one he would tour with us, was officially the #2, named after the soprano

Angela Peralta. In August of 1883 the Mexican Nightingale arrived by ship with her lover and 80 members of her performing company to present the opera Aida. Unfortunately, yellow fever was also stowed away aboard that vessel. The 38 year old singer of world acclaim was so impressed by the exuberant parade in her honor and having her carriage pulled by manpower to the hotel Iturbe that she appeared to briefly sing to crowds from her balcony before retiring, deathly sick. In and out of consciousness, she married on her deathbed. Seventy-six members of her troupe along with 2500 townspeople also succumbed to the yellow fever as the epidemic swept through Mazatlán. Her remains rested 54 years at this graveyard, and then were re-interred in México City.

There were many burial places in early Mazatlán. The burial site dubbed No. 1 was near the market but houses were built around and on top of it. Monuments were re-dated when they moved to graveyard #2 which was a short walk from the Civil Hospital located on top of an Indian burial ground facing the harbor. Graveyards were desperately needed to accommodate the legions who died from battles of liberation and revolution, reprisals, and epidemics of yellow fever, the flu and the plague. Mazatlán presently has five graveyards within the city.

Four pulmonias and several cars pick up the people on our tour early enough to wander through the entrance gates onto the brick paths among the various memorials of all sizes and shapes, noting the dates all the way back to the mid 1800s.

We are ready when Joaquín arrives precisely on time along with his daughters and a friend who carries portable power for a mike. He seems right at home in the graveyard, dressed

Joaquín Hernández speaking
at the graveyard

238

casually in new blue denim. Dark glasses and deeply tanned skin under a grey western hat contrasts with his brilliant smile. He is lean and crisply handsome and carries no notes. While the mic is getting set, he chats informally with those who have been taking pictures of mausoleums, angels and saints along the curving brick walkways.

"The Chinese have a very impressive mausoleum for their many citizens who died in the plague in 1903 and afterwards," Joaquín begins. "There are other mass graves and many styles of burial houses here since Mazatlán has welcomed people from every nation. Of course so many strangers affected the Mexican psyche. But speaking as a Mexican man, heritage is always within us. Even when we don't want to claim it, it shows itself in eye color, hair or even what we can do. As an example, consider slavery. Many slaves were brought here to work the mines. The Indians had slaves as did the Americans and Spaniards. So see, some of us have curly hair? Many of us just don't want to know. But I do. Bloodlines carry through."

Our crowd from Canada and America and many other places, some of whom have traveled all over the world, is gathered all around Joaquín to hear this Mexican historian speaking in English about honoring the dead. What is the average age of the people listening to him? Certainly we are not youngsters, perhaps some of us are thinking about mortality on this fine afternoon. It is a moment, as Wesley would say, to think on it.

I take notes and even though we had talked about some of the things he is explaining, I want it all down. I know that we had both been writing about the same things when I first met him. I was amazed at that. He would have organized his talk to hit what was important. I didn't want to miss his prioritizing.

When I have the opportunity, I ask about Mexican spirituality.

Joaquín starts out speaking about seeds.

"Seeds are dried and stored to plant again. Corn is like that. And from the seed springs the new plant. Energy is released from the container.

"About bones," he says, "There was a time when it was not legal to cremate because the bones would walk again like the song says: 'Them bones, them bones, gonna walk around.'

"In unsafe times, families felt safer in numbers. I know of a village, built along a river, where the dead relatives were buried beneath the floors of the homes so the family could stay together. For them, for real, history in the form of ancestors became their foundation for new life. When engineers came to install water pipes in that village they were horrified that every ditch they dug contained bones. In México, life is very near to the earth. Many homes have dirt floors. This is not the experience of many civilized and urbanized people.

"The best real estate available often was chosen to house the dead. Building on top of another sacred place was common in México. For example, just 90 minutes south of Mazatlán is Chametla, the most important archeological site in northwestern México. A church is built over one pyramid and the other is now a graveyard. Unfortunately, many young people have no idea of the history that is hidden beneath."

On the tour, we come soon to the grave of Captain Malpica. I linger there, remembering the story Abimiel told of mutiny and patriotism, and the love both the Federalists and the Constitutionalists had for this young man who took his own life rather than surrender. Joaquín notes that the graves of many seagoing heroes were all along the walk that paralleled the front of the graveyard. He gestures toward the harbor. Indeed at one time the shore was very near, close enough to hear the sea for those who had lived so much of their lives on it.

The way the graveyard is laid out is a kind of map to a rich and layered philosophy of life and death, which relates to the Belmar Hotel, also fronting on the ocean, also holding special significance to the people of Mazatlán. Already I think of the hotel as a graveyard of dreams caught in solid form, some of which is crumbling. Much of which has been bought and dispersed to other places. It is like the monuments that are vertical, rising straight up. Joaquín points out that for convenience, today's plaques are often flat to the ground. I make a mental note to think about that later.

Many of the grave markers have severe corruption. Joaquín gestures to a polished granite coffin-shaped memorial and the same shape made of concrete. The latter has deteriorated while the one made of stronger stuff is smoothly intact. I see the names of the old families that many of the streets of Mazatlán are named after. This graveyard is the Who's Who of Mazatlán. Size and grandeur indicate the fortune behind the name. Of course it cost money to buy a plot and be buried in a graveyard, and the words "for perpetuity" didn't mean very much once the precious lands that belonged to churches were confiscated by the government. They were sold and built over.

Angela Peralta #2 is in disarray. No one says this, but I see a lady pick up a piece of a gravestone and try to set it back where it belongs. Joaquín is speaking to our crowd now of vandalism.

"There is hope," he says. "A woman who lives nearby gathers up the scattered pieces of carved granite and wrought iron as she believes that one day people will restore the monuments."

I think of the heaps of furniture and broken pieces of the Belmar stored within the hotel and can see the connection. And Joaquín himself is like that. He has gathered bits and pieces of history so it will not be lost. It is so important to remember! To put the stories together and tell them to our young people. Give them back their heritage of heroes. Do they want to know?

So what is the idea behind a graveyard, and how does it relate to the hotel? I have read of a term and know the way of thinking. Memory is "spatialized." The graves claim a little bit of earth where memory can dwell, where one can retrieve the history we continue to write with our lives. Burial is about humanizing the ground. Here worlds can be built, memories retrieved to make sense of our present and project our future. It is a sad fact that some families in México have had to search for the remains of loved ones in order to bury them. They feel a responsibility to the dead to bring the dream to fruition.

Which brings me to another notion summed up in the word "necrocratic." We carry on the causes of the dead and often die trying to vindicate their humiliations. I think of reprisals such as the one the white guards placed at the grave of beloved Alphonso Tirado. *Eres Vengado,* "you are avenged." We often try to finish what our beloved departed couldn't do in their lifetimes. Again I think of the Belmar and this time of Simona's son who built the hotel. To honor their mother, her children paid to build a church in Monrovia, which like the Catholic Mazatlán Cathedral is dedicated to the Immaculate Conception.

While working six years in a pain clinic I experienced the memories stored within the patient's body. I am a believer. I now believe the Belmar holds energies of the people who built, staffed and stayed there. This hotel occupies a sacred place on a sacred beach in a sacred city consecrated in the blood of those who fought and died for their beliefs. It is thoroughly humanized. No wonder it has ghosts! I read somewhere that a graveyard is not necessarily the place to find ghosts. They haunt the living not the dead and seem to favor old hotels! But I struggle to stop the conversation in my head and listen to Joaquín who is speaking now about identity and how the Mexican people see themselves.

People look to ancestry to find identity and so does a nation. México traces right back to the Toltecs. Later the Aztecs fought the "flowery wars," battles with the sole purpose of taking captives for human sacrifice to their sun god, Huitzilopochtl. Believed favored above all others by their god, the Aztecs did not suffer fear of judgment by the Divine in the afterlife. Instead, the way a person died decided their fate in the next life.

The Aztecs believed themselves to be collaborators with the gods who were nourished with the divine fire called *teyolia* found only in the heart and blood of heroes. Those awaiting sacrifice received the highest esteem of their captors and were given royal treatment for they would carry messages asking for favors to the god. A dramatic ceremony was designed to extract the heart of a hero since his *teyolia* energized the sun god and sent the warrior traveling to the "sky of the sun" where those who died on the sacrificial stone or were brave warriors would ascend to the highest level of paradise called the "house of the sun." They would be rewarded by lively battles where they played war games and enjoyed a garden of the most beautiful flowers, the daily companions of the sun. After that they were transformed into magnificent birds that fed on the nectar of flowers. These privileged ones who the sun had chosen for his retinue lived a life of pure delight, resting in peace.

The more I study the history of México, the more I can spot the Aztec symbols in the customs and *corridos* that chronicled the life and death of heroes, including the symbol of the dove.

Of course, the dove is a symbol used in Christianity. It is the death dove, the soul ascending to heaven. It is the holy spirit descending upon the faithful waiting for inspiration. The image goes back to the mother goddess of the Mediterranean culture.

This graveyard is heavily invested in Christianity. I see the cross everywhere. I know that the Conquistadores were amazed to find that part of Aztec beliefs included an incarnate God named Quetzalcoatl who had died, was resurrected and had promised to return. Later, the Jesuits found so much similarity in the Toltec and Aztec Indian myths to Christianity that they easily built their Christian ideas upon these beliefs. They were converted. Or were they?

This mix has also yielded a curious set of beliefs and rituals around life and death peculiar to Hispanic culture. I think immediately of the two faces of the theatre: one the mask of elation and joy, the other side of melancholy and desperation, both dramatic. In the Day of the Dead celebration, the Mexican spirit of "fiesta" is made manifest and to the discerning eye it reveals something of México's identity.

Underneath the spectacle of bright colors of festivity the Cempasuchil flowers, known as marigolds evoking the sun whose petals guide the souls of the living and the dead, along with the humorous and endearing stories of the deceased, the pictures and foods placed to honor them, is an attempt to reverse death, to humanize it, to replace horror with laughter, to eat, drink and be merry and indeed consume its skulls made of sugar, chocolate and amaranth.

And all this takes place in the cemetery. Mexican's call it the *panteón*, which originally meant "where the gods dwell." Here the laws that operate outside are suspended because it is a sacred space. Indeed, on the night of the Day of the Dead there is no separation between the living and the dead. *Ofrenas* (offerings) are set up for the dead to share and have the first bite. Some families stay the night, sleeping right next to the graves of their loved ones. Rules suspended, it is a time to laugh at death. To simply throw its power out and eat the skulls, mock the idea. Only the family is important and the ghosts return on their Day directly to the family to see how they are doing with "finishing up."

Who cares anymore about this place? Why is it being vandalized? The great family monuments and those of the countries represented here are deteriorating. Why? Are they not worth saving? What do we build on when we let the foundations crumble with dishonor? When we lose the stories? Joaquín tells me this graveyard is almost deserted even on the Day of the Dead. The families have monuments in other bigger, newer graveyards. Cremation is permitted. Visitors are few and far between.

I am finally at the place of my own labyrinth. I see the old guard and the new. I understand that in China and Japan young people look to the future and many have little interest in the past. In Europe and North America we may be losing the idea of "sacred." In all the developed countries, there is also a complete separation from death—a getting as far away from it as possible—and yet this denial is of something that will claim every one of us.

People come to Mazatlán to marvel at families, see the beautiful children, feel the warmth of strangers, watch families gather on the Malecón, see people working, marvel at beliefs we have debunked, and enjoy simple pleasures like watching for the green flash of the sunset or carving a coconut. But it is changing as fast as it can to be just like where we have come from. Such a shame. Do we cling to the past or move forward? And where is forward? I think of the song "Dust in the Wind" that was inspired by a line of American Indian poetry. Do our lives count for anything? What lasts?

This is not a throw away society. To me, precious choices about our future are lost when we disregard the past. Standing in this graveyard, even in this broken state, I realize it is far more exciting than the austere, straight-lined, regulated burial places I have visited in the north of the United States.

Joaquín said that he grew up at funerals and weddings. So many of them. Our children today scarcely recognize the meaning of a casket lowered into the ground and dirt thrown over it. I remember the anger of a child who saw it for the first time. We try to protect them from the sight. Death is locked away and with that comes an indifference to life. With no limit, life can be wiled away. No shining guiding star. No meaning. Nada. Strangely enough, countries ranking very high on the easy living scale have high rates of suicide. What's missing in an affluent society?

The Belmar stands on precious property. Alongside it on Calle Constitución exists what once was the most powerful merchandising company in all of México, the nerve center for a fleet of cargo ships, a textile plant, several mining companies and the original Pacífico brewery. On the other side is the Street of Gold. What can be saved?

I think of Clyna who walked me through the Belmar showing me where she spent her youth. At the very end of the tour she sat down in what once was the Andaluz Patio and I thought she might cry. She had no way to tell me how beautiful it once was. The pictures, the fine furniture, the tiles, the glass, the glamor, the stars, all gone. She put her hands over her face for a moment and I said nothing, but I heard everything.

That night after a quiet ride home from the graveyard I ponder what I have done collecting these stories, listening to Joaquín and all my teachers here in México. Why do they bother to pull me along? So much work. So many hours I could have spent drinking wine, eating great food sunk in pleasure. Why struggle to gather up the bones, learn the secrets the ghosts can tell. Is it all meaningless, soon to be lost? But I have a song in my heart I cannot deny: "them bones, them bones gonna walk around." And in the Belmar, on the sixth floor, the chant of life wafts out onto the night air for those who are ready to hear.

The Hotel of Dreams

IT IS ONE THING TO READ ARTICLES AND BOOKS AND HEAR STORIES FROM people. Another thing to experience another reality. Reality? Is that the word? Because of too many coincidences to ignore, I have been questioning what I thought of as reality for years. What I experienced on the roof of the Belmar the night of the fireworks stretched my understanding to the breaking point.

I decide to talk to Cynthia again and maybe just walk through the building and let it speak to me. The building has a voice, I am sure of it now. I am beginning to believe that everything we see and touch has a voice. Maybe a vibration that is too high or low for a linear mind, but it's there.

I can see Simona smiling everywhere I look. Up half a flight from the patio, I walk the golden stairs that are almost worn through. How lovely are these steps. I look down at the part of the mural where the old woman pulls the rebellious child up the hill in the mural I always, always look at, and now I see it as México rising, the old ways pulling the hope for the future higher. She dares to dream. In every case, with every ghost I documented, the dream was bigger than one lifetime.

Why didn't I see it before? The Coat Nurse dreaming of healing and compassion, the Woman in White dreaming of beauty and romance, Abimiel of honor and freedom from foreign domination. The Gypsy, like a fierce guard dog, dreamt that he could use Queen Juliana to protect his master. His was a cause of reprisal and protection. Errol Flynn was the perennial bad boy hitting whatever restrained him, aiming at freedom, and most of his life he tried to attain freedom through pleasure. His was a slap at law, order, decency, morals, anything that told him how to live. As Janis Joplin sang in "Me and Bobby McGee," he learned that "freedom's just another word for nothing left to lose." And John Wayne? He wanted to be a flag of inspiration. He wanted to communicate something of the best of humanity and live it. Ahh, and Simona. She was the creator, the spirit of the women of Mazatlán. Splendid. They are all splendid.

By the time I reach Cynthia's room, I am eager to talk about the ghosts. She has had all the mind-blowing experiences while I dutifully researched and recorded but now that I have seen them too, I feel we share something precious and rare.

She greets me with a hug and sets coffee out for us. We decide to look out across her entrance at what once was the Belmar garden. The sun is high in the sky lacing all the leaves in light. It is coming on spring and I am happy warming myself with the coffee and our conversation, at first small talk, soon of some importance.

"Lori, yesterday when I walked out by the pool, John Wayne was sitting sunning himself. He wanted me to sit down with him. I know from Nicholas that others have had conversations with him there. I was thrilled to join him. I felt like Mattie in True Grit and he told me that was how he thought of me.

"And then he said I should tell *you* something."

"Me? You must be kidding. What are you supposed to tell me?"

"He said it was a quote he was famous for, and you would understand. 'Nobody should come to the movies unless he believes in heroes.'"

"Oh well, I love movies. What I love the most is when someone comes from behind and wins the race. Or maybe when everything goes wrong and just when it looks impossible, there is a miracle. Well, the best thing is if the miracle happens to the person and you see it in their eyes that they still have it inside to win at life. Heroes huh? Actually, Cynthia, growing up, you were my hero."

"I know. And I have spent my life living up to what you saw in me. Did you know that? I guess I should have thanked you. So many things left unsaid."

Silence.

"Why did you decide to write this book about the Belmar, Lori?

More silence. I am confounded by her questions. I had started to wonder at my motive too but the answer still alluded me.

"Well then, how did you learn the stories of all the characters you are writing about?"

Just as I was about to list those who had helped me, Cynthia did it for me but in a way that pressed at why I was doing this book.

"Why did Encarnación help you? And your partner, Bill? He has been a trooper hasn't he, doing all the things you ordinarily do while you write and research? And all of us that have showed up like Joaquín and Wesley, like Jorge and all the ghosts and even me? Not to mention your writer's group, listening and saying 'Yes. Go for it!' And Joe Price wanting to take photos for you and Hector who owns the hotel asking to meet you. Why? You mentioned Simona giving you that baton in that meltdown you described where you saw all the ghosts on the night of the fireworks. What are we all telling you, Lori?"

She's right. The idea just wouldn't let me go. It nagged at me every time I walked by this giant old hotel. All I can think of to say to Cynthia is the name of a movie I saw back in the 1990s, "The Field of Dreams." And so I say what I remember best from that movie: "If you build it, they will come."

Now it is Cynthia's turn to be silent, like maybe I have hit on something and she is going to let me follow it through, so I go on.

"Everyone wants me to tell these stories I've stumbled on. I've heard them from Mexican people like Jorge or Joaquín or Nicholas and I want to tell them. I want the unfinished business of these ghosts to come to light. They are all heroes and we need heroes today. We need the comeback kid, we need the one who cares enough, and we need the old hotels that have sheltered the hopes and dreams of a nation. Isn't that the Belmar though? Every handmade tile, every baluster made of ebony, every granite stair tread worn smooth. The historical center of this city is the beating heart of Mazatlán and like Mexicans honor their dead, their old people and their heroes, we need to tell the stories from the Belmar, the Hotel of Dreams."

Cynthia takes a sip of her coffee at that and smiles at me.

"Heroes," she says, "overcome terrible times and go on with a little help from their friends. It's easy to know my story, it's right here in the lines on my face. And every ghost I have seen is like a part of me. Maybe that is why I see them so clearly. Because I need to own that part of me that is so afraid, or is brave, dedicated, or even loves music and dancing.

"But we are talking about you now, Lori. The Field of Dreams? There was unfinished business that brought about the miracle in that story. Something significant that never got said or done. It's almost impossible to know how important things are while they're happening. Like in the story, the ghosts come back to help that corn farmer in Iowa finish something. And he plows up his corn field right when they are about to foreclose on his farm, but he keeps on, because everyone, himself included, has to finish. Hmm! Lori, what do you keep remembering from your past, that, like mine, is probably tied to some kind of painful experience?"

I know just what to say. No hesitation.

"I remember being a laughing stock from the country in a school of city kids, having only that I knew how to turn a tractor on a dime to be proud of, among all these young intellectuals who were mastering the Iliad and the Odyssey and the Old Testament. I know shame. And I know how my animals loved me when it seemed no one else did. I suppose that was the time I lost my face like you did. Mine was the face I put forward, my story of who I thought I was. I had to build it over and without the friends who knew me before, and I was afraid. Fear was always my main emotion. Then again when I came West alone and started over in midlife, I left everything familiar, everything I had built. But before I made my decision I remember thinking it would be easier to die. Joaquín said about the Mexican people, 'We love our wounds.' Those are the times when we are broken. Our know-it-all selves become humbled and open to learning. Once we decide to live, fear melts away and it all falls into place."

Since Cynthia didn't jump right in, her attentive listening seemed an invitation to continue. And continue I do. I am on a roll saying things I didn't know I knew. Connecting the dots.

"When I was a counselor, I kept a picture of a very tall birch tree. It hung on the wall in my office."

"What does a tall birch tree have to do with counseling?" Cynthia asks.

I go on with what I am sure of.

"The seed it grew from had fallen in a crevasse, a dark place in a canyon in a park my father built. Birch trees are not tall trees, but this tree had to grow tall to find the sun. So it is with kids that maybe have a hard start. From a broken place, they can grow bigger than they ever imagined, for they are open. It's like a forest fire in a pine forest."

"Really Lori, you are so full of stories, but I bite. What does that have to do with anything?"

"The heat of the forest fire melts the rosin shell around the seeds and the new tree can come out. Not that it has to be that way, but the kind of mind muscle it takes to survive a wound is available to those who follow their dreams and are open to listen. A person has to realize they can survive a failure. A failure is a small thing compared to the mind that looks on, and maybe the injured one has the courage to grow up toward the light in spite of a failure. Failures are just shadows in the way of the light. But, they separate those who try again from the victims who get scared and lose heart. And that brings me to México, the Mexican people, heroes, the Belmar Hotel, and the key I think unlocks the door to understanding—the ghosts."

"So, the ghosts hold the keys to the Belmar," Cynthia repeats thoughtfully. "Well, they will open doors for me. I think these stories you have put together in your book would be perfect for a Ghostly Tour of Mazatlán. The Duke says he was invoked by Captain Malpica, my lover from another lifetime, to help me start over and stay on right here in Mazatlán.

"You told me that the Belmar was built to entertain foreigners as well as the Mexican people. The Hotel stands today upon the foundations built by their dreams. And in Mazatlán's graveyards there are no borders."

"Oh Cynthia. You put it so well, but will people understand?"

"Of course they will. Why do you think people come to México anyway? Because they can live cheaply? Maybe. They may come to retire and eat *enchiladas* and hear the *banda* music. But very soon, it is because they fall in love again with the spirit of heroism that makes do, that fights on, that is close to the earth and values work, that brings people together, and they want to join in and build on the dreams they maybe forgot about. Lost sight of. That's when they need the stories.

"Here's a 'for instance' from my own life. John Wayne was my hero long before I came here. He played Breck Coleman in "The Big Trail" and his words have always stuck with me. They kept me going. In that story, the pioneers heading West got so discouraged that they wanted to give up. But Wayne said as only he could, *'What're you going to do? Lie down and die? Not in a thousand years. You're going on with me!'* Words like that. Stories like that! People need to hear them—hells bells— I needed his words then, and here in the Belmar I have found my hero again! Did you know that was how Finland kept strong enough to fight off Russia? They told their hero stories to each other in the only safe place they had—the sauna baths. Over and over, in poetry or music, they told their stories to keep the spirit alive."

"One more story, Cynthia, from me. It is the one that I have spent my life trying to figure out. They say understanding is the booby prize, but I would have settled for that before now."

Cynthia gives me a look like I might be crazier than she thought she was. She repeats the words "understanding is the booby prize?" as a question. And I know what she means. I never "got it" until this very moment.

"Understanding something is like getting your head around it. But it has to get to your heart. You have to be open enough for the spirit of the story to enter in and change you. The story that always, *always* confounded me was the search for the Holy Grail. Oh, it is a long story about how once a person drinks from the cup of spirit they thirst for it all their lives. I know it sounds religious, but it's way more than religious. I've tried to find it by thinking, but it can't be caught in words.

"Even this book I have been writing. Writing it is like being pulled by the old woman up the hill in the mural. The history of the Belmar on Olas Altas beach has been dragging me along, and I am that child wanting to find what I lost. Finding it my way. Knowing I am right. I have been trying, longing to capture up the spirit I once tasted when I was a little girl and then lost. Now I know it comes freely when you stop making it happen just for yourself, and let it go right through you."

Taking a deep breath, I look into my old friend's questioning eyes.

"You see," I explain, "early on, I got greedy. I saw you swinging higher and higher and seeing Lake Superior and I was too afraid to go that high. I was jealous. Why I even tried to have Glenn for myself. And then, a lifetime later, when you came here to the Belmar, you saw the ghosts, I didn't, and once again I was jealous. But every time I sat down to write or figure out the pictures for this book, it was as if I was swinging higher and higher too. And it wasn't about me anymore. It was just about opening up and letting the spirit work through the stories. I got high enough on those stories to see the other side. Ha. And share the view from the top of the hill—dragged there, it is true. On those nights and early mornings when I wrote, I met the ghosts over and over until they broke through my wanting to keep them, and well, I got taken for a ride. They are on the loose now. The best thing is, I am giving them away. Stories are meant to be told."

I reach for Cynthia's hand across the table and hold it tight.

"And one more thing, Cynthia, I got you back, my best friend who I have always loved! We are in this together. I never could dance like you did. Like you will, every time you tell a ghostly story. Oh, your words will shimmy and spin because you are a performer. And me? Courtesy of the ghosts of the Belmar, and the pickers of history, I am hoping we have something enduring to share. Joaquín said a lady is piling up the iron pieces left when the graveyard is vandalized, to use again. "Mexico is not a throw away society," he said. And the Hotel Belmar? It is the field of dreams, a labyrinth, and also the cup of spirits that finally brought us together."

NOTES

"Thar's gold in them thar hills." Take it from me who has been following the rich vein of Mazatlán history for the last two years mining stories. I could not have chosen a more exciting place to start digging than on *Playa del Olas Altas* (The Beach of High Waves) in Mazatlán. Maps? You bet. Carefully drawn, meticulously researched, I followed directions scribed by wordsmiths like Lisa Lankins, Sheila Madsen, Erik Strait, Maureen Dietrich and Diane Hofner Saphire all looking for sparkle just like me. But just when I thought I'd "broke my pick"—you know, gotten discouraged, I found the glory hole. By that I mean the locals came to the

After the cyclone of 1927

rescue of Johnny Newcomer—me. It seems historians like Joaquín López Hernández, a detective of history from Teacapán and Fernando Higueras whose website features pictures and videos of old Mazatlán had been collecting images and stories for years and they wanted to share their treasures. Memories. Here is an old photo sent to Peche Rice (Pechesario) by Manuel Gómez Rubio. It was copied from the Higuera website "Pechesaurio Dos" and shows Olas Altas and the Malecón after the cyclone of 1927. Notice the Statue of Liberty now relocated in San Francisquito, a town in the Municipality of Mazatlán. The lions at the foot of the statue are presently custodians of Mazatlán's municipal library in Hidalgo Square. And notice the Belmar standing proudly at the center of things!

Sue and Karma at the Graveyard

This historical novel represents considerable research, both oral and written. The ghosts have all been sited in the Belmar, and most of them are written about in published articles. I interviewed locals who grew up in the neighborhood trying to capture their impressions of the hotel next door. The plot is invented, but even Cynthia is real and a friend of mine who loaned me her story. Her name is changed to protect her, but the violence, the resulting injuries that plagued her, and her strong calculated stand against the perpetrator, are facts. I found pictures I could have without restriction, and digitally created images of the ghosts as I thought they would look. When possible, I fused in snapshots in "Public Domain"of the heroes. My aim was to entertain, to honor, and at the same time to tell the history of old Mazatlán and the Belmar Hotel in a way that English speaking people would enjoy enough to read and appreciate this place and their hosts. Mazatlecos are justly proud of their history.

A special"THANK YOU" to Bill Ray, my partner who worked around me and my computer for two years, driving him nuts, and to The Mazatlán Writers Group who kept reassuring me that ghosts have perspective and deserve to be heard. To my walking partner Kathi McCaw, I offer an apology for my constant whining. She patiently listened, advised on occasion, and took this picture of my dog Karma and me on one of our walks to my favorite place, the Graveyard. While I am at it, I may as well thank my Karma too for barking at cats in the middle of the night; the rude awakening served to send me "back to work."

I am using these notes to include a few tidbits that didn't really need to be in the manuscript, but I thought were too good to leave out of the book. A bonus!! And believe me, the more I learned, the more I realized what a fascinating history the Belmar Hotel has; so full of unsolved mysteries, unfinished business, passion, hopes, dreams and golden moments.

~ Chapter 1-3 ~

Miesse, Shiela.The fabulous Belmar Hotel. Posted in La Vida Buena. Mazatlán My City.(2012, May 1)Retrieved from http://www.mazatlanmycity.com/articles/69-the-fabulous-belmar-hotel.html

Ayala,Enrique Vega. Mazatlán Ayer y Hoy. (2008) Retrieved courtesy of the Mazatlán Archives.

~ Chapter 4-5 ~

Compilacion Enrique Vega Ayala, Ivan Hernández Ruiz, Agustín Lucero. Crónicas Originales Carnaval De Mazatlan 1898 a 1905, 1996, (De Enero) I translated this compilation and paraphrased the general idea. The document is available from the Archives of Mazatlán.

Collection: Rubio, Manuel Gómez. *Carnavales D Ayer. Carnavales_de_ Mazatlan.ppt.* From the photograph album of Manuel Gomez Rubio set to music directed by Enrique Patrón Rueda. Power Point Available from the Archives of Mazatlán.

~ Chapter 8 ~

Regarding the song Mr. Bojangles

Walker, Jerry Jeff. (1968) *Mr. Bojangles.* song recorded by Kristofer Åström, Chet Atkins, Hugues Aufray (French version, 1984), Harry Belafonte, Bermuda Triangle Band, David Bromberg, Garth Brooks, Dennis Brown, George Burns, JJ Cale, David Campbell, Bobby Cole, Edwyn Collins, Jim Croce, Jamie Cullum, King Curtis, Sammy Davis Jr., John Denver, Neil Diamond, Cornell Dupree, Bob Dylan, Arlo Guthrie, Tom T. Hall, John Holt, Whitney Houston, Queen Ifrica, Billy Joel, Dave Jarvis, Elton John, Frankie Laine, Lulu, Rod McKuen, Don McLean, MC Neat, Bebe Neuwirth, Harry Nilsson, Dolly Parton, Johnny Paycheck, Esther Phillips, Ray Quinn, Mike Schank, Helge Schneider, Nina Simone, Corben Simpson, Todd Snider, Cat Stevens, Jim Stafford, Jud Strunk,[5] Radka Toneff, Bradley Walsh, Robbie Williams Paul Winter, and others. Information retrieved from https://en.wikipedia.org/wiki/Mr._Bojangles_(song).

"Walker has said he was inspired to write the song after an encounter with a street performer in a New Orleans jail. While in jail for public intoxication in 1965, he met a homeless white man who called himself "Mr. Bojangles" to conceal his true identity from the police. He had been arrested as part of a police sweep of indigent people that was carried out following a high-profile murder. The two men and others in the cell chatted about all manner of things, but when Mr. Bojangles told a story about his dog, the mood in the room turned heavy. Someone else in the cell asked for something to lighten the mood, and Mr. Bojangles obliged with a tap dance."

Regarding the image Virgin de la Esperanza de Macarena de Sevilla

Retrieved from: http://www.traditioninaction.org/religious/a026rpMacarena.htm

La Macarena is much more than a statue for the people of Seville. "She knows all our problems," one man explained to a group of Americans. "We confide in her. She is Our Hope. That is her name."

"The image is also known for local folklore, most notably its discolored cheek allegedly caused by a wine bottle thrown by a drunken man at her face. After many attempts at restoration, pious legends claim the bruise is impossible to remove. The Virgin's popularity among the masses is often highlighted in the five rose-emerald brooches attached to her dress given by the famed bullfighter José Gómez Ortega, also known as Joselito and El Gallo, and the historical fact that the image has only worn an entire black vestment ensemble on a singular point in Spanish history; during el Gallo's death and funeral.

Virgin de La Macarena, Our Lady of Hope in mourning.

Virgin de la Esperanza de Macarena de Sevilla. Retrieved from https://en.wikipedia.org/wiki/Virgin_of_Hope_of_Macarena.

~ Chapter 10 ~

Mills, William B. (2017) *Treacherous Passage: Germany's Secret Plot against the United States in Mexico during World War I.* Lincoln, Nebraska. Potomac Books: An imprint of the University of Nebraska Press. pages 20-23.

The Melcher enterprise next door to the Belmar is described in detail. Melcher Sucesors was one of the most important companies in all of México and they stored their money, gold and silver in the Belmar vault. Abelardo Rodríguez established Mazatlán and the Belmar as an important banking center. So secure that it sheltered the riches of Spain during the revolution there.

~ Chapter 11 ~

Martinez, Saul D. (2014,May 20) *Abelardo L. Rodríguez, Mafia Ambassador.* Mafia Ambassadors, new docufiction on History Channel. Culture in the Crosshairs. Retrieved from http://www.lacronica.com/ EdicionEnlinea/Notas/Noticias/20052014/843234-

Vanderwood, Paul J. (2010) *Satan's Playground: Mobsters and Movie Stars at America's Greatest Gaming Resort.* Durham and London. Duke University Press.

112,119-20, 157;Agua Caliente and, 141, 148, 223, 246, 305-6; as governor of Baja California Norte, 120-22 247, 302, 362 n. 30;personal wealth of, 122-23, 328-29; as president of Mexico, 123, 231, 247-48, 304, 322.

~ Chapter 12 ~

Veracruz, named for the "true cross," was the linchpin of México, gateway to conquerors like Cortés, pirates, rulers, and slaves. Sea loving heroes worked, lived and fought in Veracruz, the city focused on commerce. México's Major Eastern Port. Here, music was composed that expressed the longing that fed the Mexican wars. It was here that Hilario Malpica was born and Veracruz lived in his heart.

Alvarez, Pedro Raúl Castro and Historian Mario Oscar Flores López. *Governors of Sinaloa.* Article published in the military magazine ARMAS Year 70 No.457. Pg. 50-56. Retrieved from: http://2006-2012.semar. gob.mx/unidad-de-historia-y-cultura-naval/articulos-revistas/1801-armas-457.html.

Klein, J.H. Jr. (1921) Annapolis: *The Career of the Mexican Gunboat Tampico.* United States Navel Institute Proceedings. pages 527-55.

Marinez and Contreras, *Héroes y Próceres del Ejercito, Fuerza Aerea y Armada de México,* p. 295

Mills, William B. (2017) *Treacherous Passage: Germany's Secret Plot against the United States in Mexico during World War I.* Lincoln, Nebraska. Potomac Books: An imprint of the University of Nebraska Press. The prologue: "The Morelos Will Be Ours" quote of Hilario Malpica. Description of the Ten Tragic Days during which President Madero and his Vice President José María Pino Suárez were killed and General Victoriano Huerta seized power. Pages 2-3 Prologue. Fight aboard the Tampico and the death of her Captain. pages 1-13.

Obregón, Francisco. *Biplano Sonora,* the airplane that made the first naval air bombardment in the history of world aviation. Posted May 4, 2017 in the personal blog of Hector Obregón. Story and pictures

The Biplane Sonora

retrieved from http://elhectorobregon.com/biplano-sonora-el-
aeroplano-que-hizo-el-primer-bombardeo-aeronaval-en-la-historia-
de-la-aviacion-mundial/

Fighting on Olas Altas beach under the Constitutionalist commander
General Juan Carrasco, the Rebels sent Federalists fleeing for their lives.
The escape was off a makeshift pier onto boats to the Gunship General
Guerrero. The fighting was fierce, 200 Rebel fighters were killed and
over 400 Federalists were killed, 500 wounded and 300 captured. Many
civilians were injured and killed. When Captain Guillermo Nelson captured Captain Reynoso and his 17 Federalist troops on Olas Altas beach,
it was all over. Executions killed those to the rank of General. *History
of Mazatlán.* Information Retrieved from https://mazatlantoday.net/
history_of_mazatlan_sinaloa_mexico.html

~ Chapter 13 ~

Leyendas de Mazatlán. (2015, October 25). Retrieved from https://
docediezmeraz.wordpress.com/2015/10/27/leyendas-de-mazatlan.

A blog written in Spanish that tells of the caves of Crestón, the first
graveyard, the ghosts of the Belmar, the Catrín of the Covarrubias, the
Coat Nurse and more.

~ Chapter 14 ~

Leyendas de Mazatlán. (2015, October 25). Retrieved from https://docediezmeraz.wordpress.com/2015/10/27/leyendas-de-mazatlan/

A blog written in Spanish that tells of the caves of Crestón, the first graveyard, the ghosts of the Belmar, the Catrín of the Covarrubias, the Coat Nurse and more.

Montoya, Herberto Sinagwa. *The Bubonic Plague in Mazatlán*: Cooperative program called the History of Mazatlán developed with DIF and Friends of Viejo Mazatlan. Prepared for delivery by Fernando Higuera using quotes from Don Miguel Valadés Lejarza, the port Historian. Retrieved from http://www.mazatlanmycity.com/es/feature-stories/19-into-mazatlan/1028-the-plague-in-mazatlan-1902.html

Valedés, Eduardo. (1875, August 24) *Romanita de la Peña is Born*. Special Memories of Mazatlán. Picture and article retrieved from https://www.noroeste.com.mx/especiales/memoriasdemazatlan/201508/24.html

Wilkins, Jas H. (1903, January 28) *The Bubonic Plague in Mazatlán*. Marin County Tocsin. California Digital Newspaper Collection. Volume 24 Number 45. Retrieved from https://cdnc.ucr.edu/cgi-bin/cdnc?a=d&d=MCT19030221.2.13

~ Chapter 15 ~

Goldstein, Lloyd. *General Juan Carrasco*.(2015,September 18) Posted in Mazatlán My City online Newspaper. Retrieved from http://www.mazatlanmycity.com/our-mazatlan-vintage-photographs/1674-general-juan-carrasco.html

I quote this paragraph from the above article:

Historian and writer of Sinaloa José Juan Carrasco C. Valdés described Juan Carrasco as follows: "Juan Carrasco was one of the most salient characterizations of rural Mexican Revolution. Rustic and an illiterate man; but generous and honest, he had a creative vocation. Intuitive by nature, he loved freedom. He believed in the social and political equality of men. He was excited for the progress. He had a lively intelligence and enterprising, and felt a real passion for command and government. He lacked, however, as the vast majority of rural people, the sense of anticipation.

Guzmán, Martín Luis, *General Juan Carrasco. Juan Carrasco Knight of Loyalty. The Death of the Knight of Loyalty. Juan Carrasco "The Human General". Carrasco Figura Non"* Compilation found within "Sinaloa, Culture and History."

Retrieved from http://sinaloajuancarrasco.galeon.com/index.html

Ayala, Enrique Vega. Official Chronicler of Mazatlán. General Juan Carrasco: Revolutionary mazatleco symbol. (13.01.2018) Culture Mazatlán.

Retrieved from http://www.carnavalmazatlan.net/publicacion.php?id=666

Regarding the picture at the end of the chapter:

Giacinti, Carlos McGregor. (1959) *Del Solar Sinaloense*. Talleres de la Editorial del Noreste de México. Culiacán.

Cover art depicting General Juan Carrasco is by Enrique Mendoza.

~ Chapter 18 ~

Bradbury Family Papers A Mexican-American Family's Story, 1876-1965

https://www.library.ucdavis.edu/.../bradbury-family-papers-mexican-american-familys...

This exhibit of the Bradbury Family Papers provides a view of activities in Mexico and California during the 19th and 20th centuries. Showcased are photographs and manuscripts, both personal and business-related, illustrating this Mexican-American family's history as well as elements of Mexico's colonial and revolutionary periods.

Lance, Jay. Simona M. Martinez Bradbury. Pictures and biography Retrieved from https://www.findagrave.com/memorial/126720990/simona-m.-bradbury

Rasmussen, Cecilia. *Bradbury's Architectural Gem.* 1999. (Dec. 19) LA Times, Dec. 19, 1999.

George Herbert Wyman, who like Frank Lloyd Wright had no academic training as an architect, at first turned down the offer, judging it unethical to accept. But while using a Ouija board with his wife, he received a message purportedly from his dead brother, Mark: "Take the Bradbury assignment. It will make you famous."

With that assist from the occult, Wyman used a radical new

The Bradbury Building

concept after reading "Looking Backward" by Edward Bellamy, a cult classic that imagined a 21st century world of cooperative housing and work spaces organized around crystal courts. That inspiration became the focal point of the building's breathtaking interior courtyard, which is bathed with sunlight that filters through a massive glass roof.

The ambitious and ornate five-story masterpiece boasted Italian marble, Mexican floor tiles, delicate water-powered bird cage elevators from Chicago, 288 radiators, 50 fireplaces, 215 washbasins and the largest plate-glass windows in Los Angeles.

But construction was not without its problems. Excavation uncovered a spring that threatened to undermine the foundation and raise costs substantially. Instead of capping the spring, steel reinforcements were installed to overcome the hazard, and the water was used to run the elevators and supply tenants with steam heat.

The open-cage elevators were ingenious. When water was pumped into a suspended cylinder, the elevator descended. When water was released, the elevator ascended with the aid of cast-iron counterweights. Decades later, the system would be upgraded and operated by means of a hydraulic jack and electric pump.

The delicate foliate grillwork was made in France and first displayed at Chicago's World's Fair before being installed in the building.

Bradbury never saw his building completed. He died unexpectedly in Oakland more than a year before it opened in January 1894 at a cost of $500,000, more than twice as much as expected.

~ Chapter 19 ~

Belem. *The Current Mexico according to Octavio Paz and Samuel Ramos (2016, Jan. 27)* Retrieved from https://elbilletenegro.wordpress.com/2016/01/27/el-mexico-actuao-segun-octavio-paz-y-samue-ramos/

According to Samuel Ramos, Mexicans have set for themselves goals that are impossible to accomplish, particularly because they have tried to imitate more developed nations, and this has imbued in them a feeling of inferiority that explains their individual and collective behavior. Ramos' book was very controversial, and sparked other similar studies about the Mexican character, like Octavio Paz's *El laberinto de la soledad* (1950).

Paz, Octavio. (1961) *The Labyrinth of Solitude.* New York. *The Other Mexico,* (1972) *Return to the Labyrinth of Solitude, Mexico and the United States, and The Philanthropic Ogre* (1985) New York. Grove Press, Inc.

"The other does not exist: this is rational faith, the incurable belief of human reason. Identity=reality, as if, in the end, everything must necessarily and absolutely be one and the same. But the other refuses to disappear; it subsists, it persists; it is the hard bone on which reason breaks its teeth. Abel Martin, with a poetic faith as human as rational faith, believed in the other, in the essential Heterogeneity of being," in what might be called the incurable otherness from which oneness must always suffer. —Antonio Machado

Gomez, Manuel. (2000) *Mazatlán, a European City.* Retrieved from http://www.mexconnect.com/articles/683-mazatlan-a-european-city

Ibarra, Ruben Romero. *Summary of Joaquín López Hernández chronicles of Angela Peralta in Mazatlán.* Article and pictures of the Angela Peralta Patheón No.2. http://mazatlaninteractivo.com.mx/a-134-anos-de-la-muerte-de-angela-peralta-en-mazatlan/

"On the other hand, and following the trace of the roots of Mexican music Joaquín makes the following reference: "Manuel M. Ponce, called the patriarch of Mexican music, together with Juventino Rosas studied with Verdi, romantic composer and Italian opera. Regarding this Italian influence, on one occasion Monsignor José Ruiz Medrano of Guadalajara, and who was also a music scholar, visited Manuel M Ponce making the following comment: -The Italian Opera influences Mexican music, and what Spain did not achieve in centuries, Angela Peralta with the Italian opera achieved it in a moment."

Mazatlán, México History. Historical Snippets. Retrieved from http://www.mazatlan.com.mx/city/story.htm

Pepperman. *The Spirit of John Wayne*. (2012, May 23.) Retrieved from https://www.tripadvisor.com/ShowUserReviews-g150792-d153634-r130469465-Hotel_Belmar-Mazatlan_Pacific_Coast.html#. This article references information from the bartender at the Belmar bar that told of John Wayne and also the little girl apparitions from the second floor.

~ Chapter 20 ~

Was the Governor's death an act of revenge?

The Ballroom where the governor was assassinated. Courtesy of Joaquín Hernández

La foto de Lucila Medrano, reina del Carnaval fatal del 44

Lucia Medrano in 1944

The Story Behind Los Osuna. Retrieved from http://www.wrsimports.com/assets/docs/LOSellSheetNP.pdf

https://es.wikipedia.org/wiki/Presidentes_municipales_de_Mazatlán

www.amigosdemazatlan.com.mx. Distinguished Mazatlecos: Alfonso

Tirado Osuna Homepage.

Poncho Tirado was a "commercial accountant and civil engineer born in the town of La Palma Sola on May 12, 1902. By 1933 he already owned different businesses in Mazatlán, a vinata in La Palma and the sugar mill of El Guayabo, thus representing the interests of the landowners in the agrarian struggles. Its administration was characterized by honesty and the achievement of good material improvements in the port. He did not receive a salary and awarded scholarships to the children of poor families. All his representation expenses were covered from his pocket, he was convinced that the municipal money should be destined to serve the community. He supplied abundant medicines for the less favored patients. He opposed Governor Manuel Páez when he approved the installation of a casino in the port, offering his resignation and that of his aldermen. He did not consent to the granting of extraordinary benefits to some municipal employees; he refused to pay with money from the town hall an expensive banquet offered to Plutarco Elías Calles, at the luxurious Hotel Belmar; He argued that the people's money was not for that; In exchange, he proposed to the deputy Ignacio Lizárraga to pay the bill between the two, which he did not accept. His political popularity transcended the municipality to the state. At the end of his period, he returned to his agro industrial labors. He died on June 10, 1838 at the Rosales de Culiacán hotel, murdered by the chief of the judicial police Alfonso Leyzaola, who was commissioned for such task by Governor Alfredo Delgado and deputy Rodolfo T. Loaiza, since Tirado was an important rival and political obstacle for the latter in the race to the governorship of the State."

~ Chapter 21 ~

"El Gitano," First Hitman from Sinaloa. 23.06.15/ 3:08 Archived in From the Frontier of the World, City Chronicles.

Read a full story with original information and integrated blogs *"News about the drug" El Gitano," first hitman of Sinaloa.* Posted: 15 Feb. 2014 02:04 PM PST http://carteldeenarcos. blogspot.mx/2014/02/historias-del-narco_15.html#1 "They say that the one who kills iron kills iron."

Luin, Giliath. (2010, Febrero 4) *Génesis del crimen y la barbarie.* Retrieved from https://lacamadepiedra.wordpress.com.

Sources listed for above blog:

SIPSE Group. Diego Enrique Osorno, " *El Gitano, the first hit man in Sinaloa* ".

Nicolás Vidales Soto, " *El hombre del paliacate* ".

José Luis Durán, " *Analysis of the Sinarquista Movement* ".

Online Links Héctor Aguilar Camín, " *Narco extraordinary stories* "

This blog is intended to address all those passages in the history of Mexico that have given us that personality and have forged our national identity, but without the desire for patriotic or symbolic exaltation, but in the most objective and impartial manner that can be adopted. The essential topics for the culture of *"the Mexican"* will be exposed. And for those who like to know the roots of this heterogeneous nation, issues that I believe, we have a duty to communicate for the benefit of people who have difficulties or impediments to access this information. The only forced duty that Mexicans have is to rescue our roots, however good or bad they may be, and to raise awareness among ourselves and those around us, to move forward with full knowledge of who our ancestors were, who we are and who our descendants will be.

Spota, Luis. (1944, June 13) *The First Sicario Sicario.* Published in the Excélser Newspaper, "There had not been another gunman like him, he had a brutal cold blood that became a legend in Sinaloa."

The Presidency of Lazro Cardenas 1934-40. Retrieved from
http://mexicanhistory.org/cardenas.htm

Was politics involved in the death of the Governor?

www.amigosdemazatlan.com.mx.
Distinguished Mazatlecos: Alfonso Tirado Osuna Homepage.

Commercial accountant and civil engineer born in the town of La Palma Sola on May 12, 1902. By 1933 he already owned different businesses in Mazatlán, a vinata in La Palma and the sugar mill of El Guayabo, thus representing the interests of the landowners in the agrarian struggles. Its administration was characterized by honesty and the achievement of good material improvements in the port. He did not receive a salary and awarded scholarships to the children of poor families. All his representation expenses were covered from his pocket, he was convinced that the municipal money should be destined to serve the community. He supplied abundant medicines for the less favored patients. He opposed Governor Manuel Páez when he approved the installation of a casino in the port, offering his resignation and that of his aldermen. He did not consent to the granting of extraordinary benefits to some municipal employees; he refused to pay with money from the town hall an expensive banquet offered to Plutarco Elías Calles, at the luxurious Hotel Belmar; He argued that the people's money was not for that; In exchange, he proposed to the deputy Ignacio Lizárraga to pay the bill between the two, which he did not accept. His political popularity transcended the municipality to the state. At the end of his period, he returned to his agroindustrial labors. He died on June 10, 1838 at the Rosales de Culiacán hotel, murdered by the chief of the judicial police Alfonso Leyzaola, who was commissioned for such task by Governor Alfredo Delgado and deputy Rodolfo T. Loaiza, since Tirado was an important rival and political obstacle for the latter in the race to the governorship of the State.

Accusation against General Pablo Macías Valenzuela of the ex-governor's death

Soto, César Ageilar. Acusación contra el general Pablo Macías Valenzuela de la muerte del exgobernador

coronel Rodolfo T. Loaiza Retrieved from http://historia.uasnet. mx/rev_clio/Revista_clio/Revista25/9_Acusacion.MuerteRodolfoT. Loaiza_CesarAguilar.pdf

"The Mexican." (2001) American romantic comedy-action-road film. Newmarket Films. Distributed by Dreamworks. Retrieved from https:// en.wikipedia.org/wiki/The_Mexican.

Starring Julia Roberts and Brad Pitts, the film is the story of finding and smuggling an antique gun under a curse, once used as a suicide weapon in a jilted love-triangle.

~ Chapter 22 ~

Juan Carrasco. *Manifest to the Mexican People*, 1922, June 24. Hacienda del Potrero, Sinaloa. Retrieved from http://www.biblioteca.tv/artman2/ publish/1922_223/Manifiesto_al_Pueblo_mexicano_de_Juan_ Carrasco_des_1531.shtml.

Paper ignoring General Alvaro Obregón in his capacity as President of the Republic.

~ Chapter 23 ~

Goldstein, Lloyd. (2016,June 21)*The Old Cantinas and Bars In Mazatlán*. Mazatlan My City. Retrieved from http://www.mazatlanmycity.com/es/our-mazatlan-vintage-photographs/1779-the-old-cantinas-a-bars-in-mazatlan.html

Schulman, Bob. *John Wayne. Mexico At Last*. Retrieved from http:// mexicoatlast.blogspot.mx/2011/03/belmar-hotel.html. Site has pictures of the John Wayne Room (48), writing about Tim O'Brien who decorated the room, Alicia Anorbe at front desk and the many famous people who had checked into the Belmar including Errol Flynn. Excellent pictures of the Belmar.

~ Chapter 25 ~

Roberts, Randy and Olson, James S. (1995) *John Wayne: American*: New York. The Free Press A Division of Simon and Schuster Inc. 738 pages.

Schulman, Bob. *Hanging Out in Mazatlan With John Wayne*. La Oferta. Retrieved From www.gomazatlan.com

Joaquín shares a letter, a Christmas card written in 1959 sent by Roberto Gorostiza the manager of the Belmar for 12 years at the height of the Belmar popularity. Ann and Robert and all three children were friends of John Wayne and also Joaquín Hernández. Robert gave many details about the Belmar used in the book. The hurricane that brought the Disney group to the Hotel happened during Robert Gorostiza's management.

There is so much more to know about John Wayne. His mother Molly, a deeply unhappy, penny pinching, jealous and increasingly angry woman, hated the meager circumstance she called their home. She was the complete opposite of his father Clyde, who was easy going, generous, optimistic, friendly and attractive to women. They were at war—one that John Wayne avoided, tip-toing around the house, best he could, big as he was, until at least 95% of his waking moments were spent at work, school, at the YMCA, playing sports, and doing the work of the Boy Scouts. He worked hard from the time he was a child, the family sometimes relying on his paper route money to make ends meet. And it only got worse when he was saddled with shepherding his much younger brother around at every social gathering he might finally get to attend. Because his father was a mason, young Marion could belong to DeMoly which emphasized the seven jewels in the crown of youth: filial love, reverence for sacred things, courtesy, comradeship, fidelity, cleanliness and patriotism. These lessons formed the code John Wayne lived by much of his life. They explain why he was like that.

Deep down, John Wayne was driven to succeed by what the Poet Maria Rilke observed: "children dance to the unlived lives of their parents." The unfulfilled dreams of his mother were the dance card of his life. Though he reached unheard of heights of popularity, bought her everything a woman could desire, sent her on glorious vacations, and showered a fortune upon her, he could never please

John Wayne

her, and she was heard to exclaim "I don't give a damn about him." She saw to it that her second child would have the name the Duke was christened with. Robert was Molly's father's name and she took it from Duke, who she thought was too much like his father, and gave it to her next child, a boy. John Wayne was from that time named Marion Mitchell Morrison. Marion sounded like a girl's name and he got in fights over it, until the family dog took to following him everywhere, and classmates and friends called the boy "Duke," after the Airdale. John Wayne liked that.

The Duke was talented beyond belief. He had a fine memory. He was a straight A student, bright, a champion at debate, a voracious reader and a stand out football player. His success as a student and athlete earned him a scholarship to the University of Southern California.

Portraits of John Wayne still adorn the walls of truck stops, gas stations, sports bars, tool sheds, saloons, garages, gun shops, hunting camps, auto parts stores, wherever men gather. The Duke never served in the Armed Forces of the United States and that was painful for him. His wife and the four studios he worked for as well as the President of the United States thought he best served as a hero in war movies, and a working class common man. Papers of deferment were repeatedly filed by "others" and finally, it was too late to join. But world leaders, even of countries the United States battled in War, wanted to meet him. In September of 1959, Eisenhower promised Nikita Khrushchev a first class tour and told John Wayne he was the main attraction—so show up. Although he was deep into difficulties filming the Alamo at the time, they met at a Hollywood banquet. John Wayne was a Goldwater Republican and outspoken anti communist and here was the world's most powerful communist, all smiles and brotherhood in whispered cordiality. Soon, arm and arm, they retired to the bar where they had a cold war experimenting over which was better, Russian Vodka, or Mexican tequila. That Christmas the Duke received a crate stamped with Russian letters CCCP (USSR) and shipping instructions all in Russian. "Hell open it, it's too damn big for a bomb," said Wayne. Inside was a note: "Duke. Merry Christmas. Nikita." That same Christmas there came to the Kremlin a couple of cases of "Sauza Commemorativo" tequila signed, "Nikita. Thanks. Duke."

In Duke's World War II films, he had killed hundreds of Japanese warriors, but Emperor Hirohito of Japan, when a guest of President Gerald Ford wanted to see Disneyland and John Wayne. Why? Because the Duke was like a samurai. His movies held to a showdown between good and evil. Over time his face took on a chiseled Mount Rushmore quality. He was like that.

One more thing. Nancy Reagan admired John Wayne as "the most gentle, tender person I ever knew." She never forgot that he called her daily to reassure her when her husband faced vicious criticism when he was the governor of California. His kindness was legendary. So to put it all together, John Wayne fits perfectly into the drama of the Belmar Hotel. He was the hero of the working class, embodied the bravery of the matador, admired the beauty and grace of Latino women, worked and played alongside the greatest celebrities of Hollywood, sailed and fished the Sea of Cortez with Mazatlán's best and bravest. Like Errol Flynn, who also never pleased his mother, John Wayne worked all his life to embody manhood, to please and protect. In his dying days, he returned to Mazatlán to share Christmas with the hotel manager, his wife and children. And perhaps, to visit again with Our Lady of Hope. Her tears were meant for such a man as John Wayne.

~ Chapter 26 ~

Valdés, Eduardo.*The Cyclone that brought Disney to Mazatlán*. (2016, August 6.) Retrieved from http://mazatleco.com/ciclon-trajo-walt-disney/

Letter from Manager-Christmas Card courtesy of Joaquín López Hernández. See Chapter 25.

~ Chapter 27 ~

Scandals of Classic Hollywood: *In Like Errol Flynn*(2013, Feb. 13)The Hairpin.

Retrieved From https://medium.com/the-hairpin/scandals-of-classic-hollywood-in-like-errol-flynn-ae0f32c6c99

Flynn, Errol (1978) *My Wicked Wicked Ways*. (2002) Cooper Square Press Edition, an unabridged edition with an introduction by Jeffrey Meyers, of the first publication in 1959, New York by G.P. Putnam's Sons, a member of Penguin-Putnam Inc. 438 pages.

Niven, David. (1975) *Bring on the Empty Horses*. Great Britain: Hamish Hamilton Limited. Errol. Pages109-132.

Errol Flynn high on the
mast of his schooner Zaca

No wonder that Errol Flynn's Room in the Belmar was impossible to rent. He could scarcely contain the war within himself. He was terrified by high places yet forced himself to climb the high mast of his ketch, the Sirroco. Flynn's playfulness and wit and boldness were legendary. He was addicted to passion and adrenalin and lived the life of a high roller on a dime. Like John Wayne, his rejection by his mother drove him. And both these men loved the Belmar and Mazatlán. On page 112, David Niven said Flynn was a great athlete with evident physical beauty and boundless charm. "Errol stood, legs apart, arms folded defiantly and crowing lustily atop the Hollywood dung heap, but he suffered (said Niven)from a deep inferiority complex: he also bit his nails."

~ Chapter 28 ~

Mazatlán is blockaded by the French Warship La Cordeliére and the French Navy prowls the waters off the port. A divided Mazatlán struggles to survive the French blackade. Mar-Nov 1864.Retrieved From https:// mazatlantoday.net/history_of_mazatlan_sinaloa_mexico.html

Disney buys Lucas film for 4Billion. Retrieved from

https://www.usatoday.com/story/money/business/2012/10/30/disney-star-wars-lucasfilm/1669

Luke Skywalker. Retrieved from https://en.wikipedia.org/wiki/ Luke_Skywalker

Mills, William B. (2017) *Treacherous Passage: Germany's Secret Plot against the United States in Mexico during World War I.* Lincoln, Nebraska. Potomac Books: An imprint of the University of Nebraska Press.

~ Chapter 30 ~

Sánchez, Carlos Alverto. *Death and the colonial difference*: An Analysis of a Mexican Idea. The Journal of Philosophy of Life Vol.3, No.3 (September 2013): pages 168-169

Paz, Octavio. *The Labyrinth of Solitude.* Translated by Lysander Kemp. Grove Press, Inc. 1985.

p. 57. "The Mexicans indifference to death is fostered by his indifference toward life. He views not only death but also life as nontranscendent. Our songs, proverbs, fiestas and popular beliefs show very clearly that the reason death cannot frighten us is that life has "cured us of fear." It is natural, even desirable to die, and the sooner the better. We kill because our own life or another's is of no value. Life and death are inseparable. And when the former lacks meaning, the later becomes equally meaningless. Mexican death is the mirror of Mexican life. And the Mexican shuts himself away and ignores both of them."

page 58. "The Mexican (in contrast with the way the word 'death' burns the lips of the North American) "is familiar with death, jokes about it, caresses it, sleeps with it, celebrates it; it is one of his favorite toys and his most steadfast love."

p. 62. "Ultimately, what the Mexican idea of death retrains that modernity's does not is a connection to the past. While death for the modern European signifies flight from existence, death for the "modern" Mexican signifies a return to its origins. Thus, Paz writes, "Death as nostalgia, rather than as the fruition or end of life, is death as

Burial site of Angela Peralta who
rested here for 54 years

origin."

The Panteon No. 2

Ibarra, Ruben Romero. *Summary of Joaquín López Hernández chronicles of Angela Peralta in Mazatlán.* Article and pictures of the Angela Peralta Patheon No. 2. http://mazatlaninteractivo.com.mx/a-134-anos-de-la-muerte-de-angela-peralta-en-mazatlan

Her full name: María de los Ángeles Manuela Tranquilina Cirila Efrena Peralta and Castera. "It has been 134 years since she died." The Teacapán Chronicler Joaquín López Hernández in a remarkable and colossal citizen effort narrated passages of the life of the artist and her artistic influences. The historian laments that "there are no real leaders in Mazatlán leading the rescue of this site listed as historical."

~ Chapter 31 ~

McGee, Richard D. *John Wayne: Actor, Artist, Hero.* (1990) Jefferson, North Carolina. McFarland and Company Publishers. p. 145

"The boundaries which divide life from death are at best shadowy and vague. Who shall say where one ends and where the other begins?"

~ Poe, Edgar Allan (1844), "The Premature Burial"
The Philadelphia Dollar Newspaper

Made in the USA
San Bernardino, CA
11 December 2018